SOCIAL ENGLAND

ILLUSTRATED EDITION—Vol. V. Section II

FROM THE VICTORY OF WILLIAM PITT IN 1784 TO THE BATTLE OF WATERLOO

A TABLE D'HÔTE IN PARIS.

By Thomas Rowlandson.

SOCIAL ENGLAND

A Record of the Progress of the People

IN *RELIGION, LAWS, LEARNING, ARTS, INDUSTRY, COMMERCE, SCIENCE, LITERATURE AND MANNERS, FROM THE EARLIEST TIMES TO THE PRESENT DAY*

EDITED BY

H. D. TRAILL, D.C.L.

SOMETIME FELLOW OF ST. JOHN'S COLLEGE, OXFORD

AND

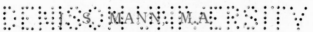

J. S. MANN, M.A.

SOMETIME FELLOW OF TRINITY COLLEGE, OXFORD

VOLUME V. SECTION II

NEW YORK: G. P. PUTNAM'S SONS

LONDON: CASSELL AND COMPANY, LIMITED

1909

CONTENTS.

CHAPTER XIX.

REVOLUTION AND REACTION. 1784-1802.

CHAPTER XX.

ENGLAND'S STRUGGLE FOR EXISTENCE. 1802-1815.

CONTENTS.

LIST OF PLATES.

(Brief Notes on some of these will be found with those on the remaining Illustrations.)

———•◦•———

NOTES TO ILLUSTRATIONS.

VOLUME V. SECTION II.

———◆◇◆———

First published in 1810. The guests take wine with one another, touching glasses after the French fashion, and much by-play is going on, while the hotel dog, a Savoyard woman with a hurdy-gurdy, and a girl with a triangle, add to the disorder caused by the waiters' mistakes. This is, of course, caricatured; but such dinners seem to have been usually rather noisy. Among the wine bottles on the floor are Frontignac, claret (a mistake of the artist, for the French term is "Bordeaux"), Burgundy, and "Vin du Pais" (*sic : i.e. vin ordinaire*). In an earlier drawing by Rowlandson of the same subject, the kitchen is shown, with repulsive details, and the provisions include cats and frogs. Rowlandson, who had French relatives, travelled and lived much in France between 1772 and about 1781.

Lord North, Burke, and Fox assailing Warren Hastings.

In Wilberforce's Diary for 1787, he says (*Life* I., 150): "When I had acquired so much information [about the slave trade] I began to talk the matter over with Pitt and Grenville. Pitt recommended me to undertake its conduct as a subject suited to my character and talents. At length, I well remember, after a conversation with Mr. Pitt in the open air at the root of an old tree at Holwood, just above the steep descent into the Vale of Keston, I resolved to give notice on a fit occasion in the House of Commons of my intention to bring the subject forward." Holwood Park was purchased by William Pitt in 1785, and a large part of Keston Common was thrown into it. Unfortunately his improvements involved the destruction of a great part of a very perfect Roman camp.

background on the left, Price that in spectacles in the centre. Fox as Cromwell's ghost is preparing to repeal the Test and Corporation Acts ; the figure asking for consideration for " poor players " is Sheridan. Fox took a first step towards the repeal of the Acts by introducing a resolution on March 2, 1790, but it was opposed by Pitt and Burke, and negatived by 294 votes to 105. The libel on John Newton is very gross. He had been charged with inconsistency for attending dissenting chapels and for disregarding differences outside the Evangelical creed common to Churchmen and Nonconformists, and had published an " Apologia " in reply, defending Church Establishment, in 1789.

    Bentham was a remarkably precocious child ; he began Latin at the age of four, and French at six, and after five years at Westminster School was admitted an undergraduate of Queen's College, Oxford, before he was 13, and graduated as Bachelor of Arts before he was 16.

    From a collection of caricatures by Kay, of Edinburgh, a selftaught artist who began life as a barber, and depicted most of the notabilities of Edinburgh, seizing and slightly exaggerating their chief characteristics with remarkable acuteness.

    Physician, botanist, and poet ; the grandfather of Charles Darwin, who was the youngest son of Erasmus's third son, Robert Waring Darwin and Susannah, daughter of Josiah Wedgwood.

    The College of Physicians at this time used to examine all physicians not educated at the English universities (chiefly Scottish graduates, *cf*. text, p. 569), and license them ; about 1767 the College passed a bye-law excluding such licentiates from its Fellowship if they had ever practised surgery, and the licentiates broke into the College and assaulted the Fellows at dinner, September 23, 1767. The dispute was decided, by legal proceedings, in favour of the Fellows. The illustration, which is from a print of 1768, entitled " The March of the Medical Militants to the Siege of Warwick Lane Castle," shows the old College, with the assailants in front.

    Both Dr. John Hunter and his less famous brother William were dependent very largely, like other anatomists of the time, on the "resurrection men," and John was specially popular with them in his youth. John delivered a course of lectures in 1773, described by his unfriendly biographer Foot as "a skirmishing course," dealing with points in surgery, physiology, and comparative anatomy, and probably needed human subjects to illustrate them ; but I am unable to discover further particulars about this scandal.

the hook from which a weight of 18 lb. was suspended. The separate condenser is the vertical pipe at the side, which is closed at the top, but originally joined the cylinder, and is secured below into a metal box, from the top of which there is a vertical tube which was the barrel of the air-pump. From the top of the separate condenser a small tube projects, closed by a shifting valve, opening outwards. The condenser and air-pump were enclosed in a cistern of cold water, the air-pump, of course, being fitted with a piston. The model has been rendered unworkable, possibly by Watt himself, through fear that the results might be appropriated before he could take out a patent. Steam was admitted into the cylinder by a cock through a hole in the top, now soldered over, and, filling the cylinder, it blew through into the upper part of the condenser and out through the escape valve. When the air was thus displaced the steam-cock was shut off, and the piston of the air-pump pulled up. The barrel of the air-pump was then empty and cold, the steam from the cylinder rushed in and was condensed, and the piston lifted the 18 lb. weight, which enabled Watt to measure the condenser pressure.

JONATHAN HULLS'S STEAM TUGBOAT 627

The machine is driven by a cylinder, in which, a vacuum being created by the condensation of steam (as in Newcomen's engine), the pressure of the atmosphere pushes down a piston. To this piston is attached a rope at M, passing round the circumference of the central wheel D. This is on the same axis as two other wheels ; from the remoter one, D b, a rope, F b, passes to the wheel H b, which is on the same axis as the paddles at the stern. When the piston descends the wheels D, D b, D a, move forwards, and with them the paddles ; meanwhile the wheel D a pulls up the weight b by the rope passing round the wheel H a. When steam is again admitted under the piston and sends it up, the rope F a is automatically slackened, the weight b falls and drags round the wheel H a, so that the paddles still move forward, though the motion of the piston which pulled them half round is reversed. They are prevented from running backwards at the change of stroke by catches L L on their axes. Hulls, in short, got his paddles half-way round by the direct action of the downward stroke of the piston, and completed their revolution by the agency of the weight also raised by this stroke. The whole power of the upward stroke was thrown away, and there must have been some danger of the rope M fouling the wheel D. This clumsy device is of extreme interest as exhibiting the difficulties removed by the invention of the crank, the sun and planet gearing, and other devices for converting reciprocating into circular motion.

PUMPING ENGINE OF 1777, BY JAMES WATT 628

The oldest steam engine extant ; constructed by Boulton and Watt for the Birmingham Canal Navigations in 1777, and regularly at work at Smethwick till 1898, when it was removed and re-erected at Ocker Hill, Tipton, to be preserved as an illustration of the effect of good management on good machinery.

MODEL OF AN INVERTED STEAM PUMPING ENGINE 629

This arrangement was proposed by Watt in 1765–6, but abandoned in favour of the Newcomen beam type. It was afterwards taken up by William Bull and his son, but they infringed Watt's patents and were checked in 1795. The exhaust pipe is provided with a jet and used as a condenser, being cleared by the vertical air-pump, but the jet is only on during the exhaust stroke.

MODEL OF COMBINED FORGE AND TILT HAMMERS 630

Both "driven by one heavy cam on an engine shaft, the forge hammer being lifted by the belly and the tilt hammer by the tail ; there is provision for a spring beam over the forge hammer," to increase the force of the blow. The curved segment at the end of the beam takes a chain from the piston rod, which indicates that the engine was single acting, and used steam of very low pressure, the work being done by condensing the steam under the piston. (*Catalogue ut sup.*) The forge hammer is seen in the foreground, the tilt hammer is behind.

MODEL OF SUN AND PLANET GEARING 633

James Pickard (*see* footnote, p. 632) patented the application of the crank and connecting rod in 1780. Watt, after making models of various alternative arrangements, adopted this device. The cogwheel driven from the beam revolves round its neighbour, and thus converts reciprocating into rotary motion.

RICHARD CRAWSHAY (artist unknown) 635

MODELS OF CABINET STEAM ENGINE 637

The form of slide valve employed (" the long D "), probably invented by Murdock, is seen in the section on the left.

MODEL OF ROLLING AND SLITTING MILL, BY JAMES WATT . . 639

The rolls are driven by the connecting rods from the beams of the engine, which is fitted with sun and planet motion.

RADCLIFFE'S IMPROVED HAND-LOOM ; CARTWRIGHT'S POWER LOOM 640, 641

The problems Cartwright had to solve were very complicated. The hand-loom weaver has to open the shed (*i.e.* lift the warp threads to let the shuttle pass) to throw the shuttle, to beat the warp together, and to wind up the cloth regularly as it is woven. Besides doing all this, the power loom must stop automatically if the thread should break or the shuttle stick, and other more complicated contingencies must also be provided for. Cartwright, however, anticipated *à priori* almost every contingency in plain weaving, and many of the details of his patents have been developed and made commercially profitable since his day. Radcliffe tried to improve the hand-loom, and subsequently in 1802 brought down the cloth beam from the usual position at c to the warp at c^1, adding a ratchet wheel take-up motion as shown in the dotted lines. (A. Barlow, *History of Weaving*, 235–245.)

WEAVING BY POWER-LOOMS : CALICO PRINTING 643

The calico is passed between a central cylinder (often covered with felt or some similar substance) and one or more smaller rollers arranged round it. Each of these latter is engraved with a pattern and furnished with a different colour by a supply roller, which revolves against its circumference and also in a colour box. A steel blade, fitting closely to the surface of the engraved roller, scrapes off all the colour except that which fills the engraved portions. These machines are of about 1830.

PITT CRUSHING THE SMUGGLER 647

From a satirical print of 1784, entitled " Catlap for Ever, or the Smugglers' Downfall." Besides the measures mentioned in the text, Pitt required the East India Company, which imported all the tea which was not smuggled, to hold four sales every year, under certain restrictions as to price. (Macpherson, *Annals of Commerce*, IV., p. 50.) Sam House, who is seen in the print, was a noted politician who kept a public house near Berwick Street, Soho, a strong supporter of Wilkes and an ardent canvasser for Fox in the famous Westminster election of 1785. A biographical sketch shows him to have been an eccentric character, rough, brutal, and foul-mouthed, but with a certain geniality and good feeling. He had the good taste to avoid those parts of the constituency specially canvassed by the beautiful Duchess of Devonshire, for fear that their names should be coupled, to her discredit, in a newspaper paragraph, and when, on an accidental meeting with her, an attempt was made to effect an introduction, he escaped, declaring with oaths that he saw no Duchess, and that an attempt was being made to hoax him. He caught a chill during the election, and died on April 23, 1785. Fox visited him on his deathbed.

Sheridan and Fox hanging, Pitt and Dundas looking on.

The third of a guinea was of gold ; the sixpence and shilling were the only silver coins (other than counter-struck dollars and token coins) issued between 1760 and 1816, and of them only seventy or eighty thousand pounds' worth were struck. Messrs. Dorrien and Magens, in 1798, requested the Mint to coin silver supplied by them (as they were legally entitled to do) into shillings, in order to meet the deficiency of small change, but the Government forbade the issue by Order in Council, and directed the coins to be melted down. (Grueber, *Handbook of English Coins in the British Museum*, p. 149.)

Depicting that life of insolvent debtors which is so well known to us at a later period from the works of Dickens.

Tom Paine, Sheridan, and Whitbread as conspirators.

Paine had been a staymaker.

In the debate on the introduction of Lord Grenville's Alien Bill, 1792—occasioned by the influx of French refugees, and designed to enable the Government to expel foreigners—Burke threw down a dagger and stated that three thousand had been ordered at Birmingham. He declared that they were intended not for legitimate warfare, but for murder. "This is what you are to gain by an alliance with France ; wherever their principles are introduced, their practices must follow." Sheridan, however, exclaimed, "You have thrown down the knife, where is the fork ? " and the House was less impressed than Burke had desired. The dagger had been actually sent to a Birmingham manufacturer as a pattern, but the circumstances seemed so suspicious that the order was not executed, and the pattern was sent to the Secretary of State, from whose office Burke borrowed it for exhibition in the House. Dundas is in the extreme rear, then Pitt, then Fox, then Sheridan, and finally Michael Angelo Taylor, who began his Parliamentary life as a supporter of Pitt, but eventually became a Whig, and ended it as "Father of the House."

The story told by the print is sufficiently obvious, but the print is accompanied by a reference to an account of the occurrence in the *Morning Advertiser* of August 6, 1800, no copy of which exists in the British Museum.

during invasion or insurrection. In some cases their services were specifically limited to London, or even to their own district or parish. Three of the nine troops (of 65 men each) of the London and Westminster Volunteers were dismounted riflemen. The Surrey Yeomanry are stated to have ranked with the best regulars in discipline. The volunteers shown in the next illustration constituted small bodies, each of about 80 men.

Only a few of the whole number of motions can be shown. The cartridge is bitten, a little powder is shaken into the pan, to be ignited by a spark from the gun-flint; the cartridge is then rammed home, and finally the gun is raised two inches from the ground, flung upwards with the left hand, and caught firmly in the right by the butt, so as to be brought to the shoulder.

Captured from the 8th French Light Infantry in a charge on General Laval's division by the 87th Royal Irish Fusiliers and three companies of Guards. It seems to have become the property of Major (afterwards Viscount) Gough.

From a print, by W. M. Craig, of Nelson's Funeral Procession.

The Cross of the Legion of Honour on the spectator's right was taken from the breast of a French captain at Vittoria. The medal on the left belonged to Lieut. Hay; the five clasps commemorate his services at Fuentes D'Onoro, Vittoria, San Sebastian, Nivelle, and Nive. The horn cups were used by him during the campaigns of 1810–1814. The sword-knot is that of an ensign killed at Albuera. The officer's pouch and belt were worn by Lieut. Augustine F. Evans, 60th Regt.

"Representing that period of the action after the British light infantry had charged with the bayonet and put to rout the left wing of the French army."

The British expedition besieged and bombarded Flushing from the sea and from Forts Ramekens and De Nolle. The sick, who suffered chiefly from malarial fever, were taken to Kondekerke and put in barracks, where many died: several gravestones still exist. Middelburg and Kondekerke are visible from the forts. The illustration of the siege is taken from a contemporary English print, that of Middelburg from a drawing of the period, both in the Middelburg Museum.

On one wall hangs a plan of Minorca; the scene depicted on the other doubtless refers to the retreat of the British troops through the streets of Buenos Ayres. Byng was condemned and shot on March 14, 1756–7 (*cf.* p. 277), for failing to relieve Minorca. The drawing is entitled "The Ghost of Byng."

The invention was suggested by the loss of H.M. brig *Snipe* off Yarmouth in 1807, when upwards of sixty persons perished after attempts at their rescue had been made for several hours, it being impossible to get a rope to the ship. The rope was connected with the shot by plaited hide, which neither broke nor took fire at the discharge. The mortar was fired by a "priming tube" filled with gunpowder, and ignited by firing a pistol charged with powder at it—a sort of anticipation of the percussion caps and friction tubes of more modern times. George William Manby was barrackmaster of Great Yarmouth.

Launched at Chatham, May 7, 1765 ; length, 226 ft. ; extreme beam, 52 ft. ; tonnage, 2,162. Her original armament was 104 guns, 12-, 24-, and 32-pounders. She was, of course, employed in the French wars from 1778 onwards, and was flagship at Toulon 1793 and St. Vincent 1797. After the battle of Trafalgar she formed part of the Baltic fleet, and was paid off in 1812. She was made flagship for Portsmouth Harbour in 1825, and served that purpose till 1903, when, however, she was struck and seriously injured by an obsolete ironclad, the *Neptune*, which was being towed away to be broken up.

The model is known to be that of the *Prince Regent*, launched at Chatham in 1823 ; the earliest, however, of the four ships of this class built in England during about the first quarter of the nine-teenth century was built in 1808. The rigging shows fidded royal masts, snaked fore and mainstays, and sprit and sprit topsail yards in position. The square forecastle was abandoned eventually, as more penetrable by grape than the rounded bow. The ship carried 120 guns, the largest being 32-pounders and the smallest 12-pounders. Her complement was 875 men, her tonnage 2,602, and her length on gundeck 205 ft. ; her extreme breadth 58 ft. (Information kindly furnished by the authorities of the Victoria and Albert Museum.)

Dean of Christ Church, Oxford, from 1783 to 1809.

This group of forty-eight portraits represents the distinguished men of science who were alive in 1807–1808 assembled in the library of the Royal Institution. The idea was that of William Walker, an engraver : the portraits were taken from other portraits, and the grouping was designed by Sir John Gilbert. Among those represented are Sir Joseph Banks, Boulton, Bramah, Brunel (father of the designer of the *Great Eastern*), Cartwright, Crompton, Dalton, Davy, Sir W. Herschel, Jenner, Maskelyne, Maudslay, Millar and Symington (inventors of paddle steamers), Trevithick, Watt, Wollaston, and Young.

Painted in 1807 for Sir George Beaumont, Bart.

Morland died in 1804, but this picture, said to be painted from the White Lion Inn at Paddington, was exhibited at the Royal Academy in 1791, and is considered to be his masterpiece.

murder of a tame hawk (of which he is innocent), and condemned to death. The father, however, finding out what is going on, saves the dog from the gibbet, and scolds the children both for their cruelty and for their disrespect to his friend, Keeper's owner, but *does not punish them*, and forgives the chief culprit on his writing an epitaph upon the hawk. For the example shown in the background, *cf.* the scene in Mrs. Sherwood's *Fairchild Family*, the popular Sunday-book in Evangelical households during a large part of the nineteenth century, where the children, having quarrelled, are taken to see the corpse of a man hanging in chains who had murdered his brother in a fit of passion. When the book on "Keeper" was recast in 1826, the hanging episode was altogether omitted—a circumstance which may illustrate the growth of humanitarianism.

"Wolfe was buried in his father's grave at Greenwich at the request of his mother; but the grief excited by his premature death in the moment of victory is manifested by the unusual proportions of the monument containing" [on the bas-reliefs] "the most elaborate delineation of the circumstances of his death." Only Horace Walpole's interposition prevented its displacing the tomb of Aymer de Valence; but room was found for it by destroying the screen of the Chapel of St. John the Evangelist, and dislodging the monument of Abbot Esteney. It "marks the critical moment of the culmination and decline of the classical costume and undraped figures of the early part of the eighteenth century" (Stanley, *Memorials of Westminster Abbey*, p. 237). The bronze bas-reliefs are by Capitsoldi. The delineation of the Canadian scenes is stated to be exact to the minutest detail.

Painted in 1795 for Joseph Cottle, of Bristol.

Coleridge lived here from 1797 to 1800.

To Dove Cottage, once the "Dove and Olive Bough," Wordsworth came with his sister Dorothy in December, 1799. He brought his bride hither in May, 1802, and lived here till May, 1808, writing the second volume of the Lyrical Ballads, parts of the *Prelude* and *Excursion*, the *Ode on the Intimations of Immortality*, the *White Doe of Rylstone*, and other poems meanwhile. Here also he was visited by Coleridge, Southey, Charles Lamb, Sir Walter Scott, and Sir Humphry Davy, De Quincey, and other eminent men. De Quincey occupied the cottage afterwards. (Rawnsley, *Literary Associations of the English Lakes*, ii., 145.)

CHAPTER XIX.

REVOLUTION AND REACTION. 1784–1802.

THE victory of Pitt at the election of 1784 seemed, at first **ARTHUR HASSALL.** sight, the decisive event in the great struggle between George **Political** III. and the Whigs which had continued since the opening **History.** of the reign. There was a general feeling in the country that the House of Commons was becoming as tyrannical as the Stuart Monarchy, and the triumph of George III. was thought by some to prognosticate the ruin of the Whig party.

The king undoubtedly regarded Pitt as the minister of his choice, and one who would carry out the royal views. In reality, however, the defeat of the Whigs in 1784 was effected by the people, who had full confidence in Pitt. That statesman entirely appreciated the necessity of a close alliance between the king and the mass of his subjects, and by dint of consummate tact he obtained such an influence over George III. that the constitution was in no wise impaired by the apparent triumph of the royal power. During Pitt's tenure of office the ministerial **Pitt's** authority was consolidated, Cabinet Government developed **Work.** naturally, and the attempt of Thurlow to revive the pernicious departmental system, which allowed the existence of independent views on the part of ministers, resulted in his retirement from office in 1792.

Till 1792 Pitt devoted himself to carrying out reforms **Pitt's** in all branches of the administration. He turned his attention **India Bill** first to the affairs of India, and in 1784 passed his India Bill, creating a Board of Control, consisting of six members and forming a department of the Government. Though the responsibility for all political affairs was left to the Board, everything pertaining to commerce remained in the hands of the Company. Dundas (p. 685) became the first President of the Board of Control, which governed India till 1858. In

230

1788 the trial of Warren Hastings began, and continued till
1792. He was accused of tyranny, malversation, and cruelty,
but was acquitted on every point. His trial, however, marks the
growing interest taken in Indian affairs, and the Governor-

Photo : Walker & Cockerell.
WILLIAM PITT, BY JOHN HOPPNER, R.A.
(*National Portrait Gallery.*)

Generalship of Cornwallis (1786–93) saw the beginning of definite
attempts to improve the lot of the peasants in Bengal.

In April, 1785, Pitt introduced a Parliamentary Reform Bill,
proposing the disfranchisement of many boroughs and the increase of the county constituencies. Burke and Portland, with
North and most of his followers, opposed the Bill; while Fox,

**Parlia-
mentary
Reform.**

who approved of the principle of parliamentary reform, disliked **Financial Reform.** the details of the measure.   Leave to introduce the Bill was refused by 248 to 174, and during the rest of his life Pitt never supported the efforts of the parliamentary reformers.   Nevertheless, he established an audit of the Government accounts, checked jobbery to the utmost of his ability, and from the period of his ascendency may be dated the cessation of direct parlia-

THE POLITICAL BANDITTI ASSAILING THE SAVIOUR OF INDIA.
(From a satirical print of 1786.)

mentary   corruption.   His abandonment of reform of Parliament did not check in the slightest degree his efforts to cure financial maladministration.   He had an extraordinary aptitude for mastering the intricacies of the national finance, which he found in a deplorable condition.   A large unfunded debt existed, smuggling had increased to an enormous extent (p. 472), and the deficiency of the year 1784 was not less than three millions.   During the early years of his tenure of office Pitt boldly attacked these abuses, and succeeded in placing the finances on a sound basis.   By his "Hovering Act" he checked smuggling; in 1786 he adopted the excise scheme which

Walpole had failed to carry in 1733, and in various ways he lessened the numberless frauds on the revenue. In 1787 he consolidated the different branches of customs and excise. Like Shelburne, he had imbibed Adam Smith's views about free trade, and though through the short-sighted opposition of the English merchants, supported by Fox and Burke, he was unable in 1785 to carry a measure for equalising the duties of England and Ireland, he succeeded in 1786 in concluding a commercial treaty with France which was the most valuable result of his legislative activity. He next adopted measures to reduce the National Debt, which amounted to £250,000,000. He determined to apply a sum of £1,000,000 a year to the redemption of the debt, and till 1807 the system of a sinking fund was steadily pursued (p. 646). By that time it was realised that, though useful in a period of peace, Pitt's scheme had failed during the war against France, when the nation was forced to borrow large sums at high interest and to apply part of them to pay off a debt which bore a low interest. At the time of the Peace of Amiens, in 1802, the National Debt had reached the sum of £574,000,000.

The Slave Trade. Till the outbreak of the French Revolution and the insurrection in St. Domingo, Pitt urged the abolition of the slave trade. In 1788 he supported a Bill for the better regulation of slave ships, and in 1789 he joined Fox, Burke, and Wilberforce in carrying resolutions condemning the slave trade. Mr. Lecky[1] thinks that his speech in 1792 on the abolition of the traffic " was perhaps the greatest he ever delivered." After 1792, however, Pitt's attitude toward the question changed, and he refused to destroy the slave trade in the French and Dutch colonies conquered by England; English ships were employed, and in consequence the English slave trade more than doubled during Pitt's administration. During the early stages of the French war, the abolitionist movement ceased to rouse any general interest, and it was not till 1804 that Wilberforce renewed the struggle.

The Regency Bill. In 1788 the illness of the king threatened to overthrow Pitt. The appointment of the Prince of Wales as Regent with unlimited powers would certainly have been followed by the accession of the Whigs to office. Fox declared that during the incapacity of the king the control of the government of the

[1] " History of England in the Eighteenth Century," V., p. 65.

country devolved upon the Prince of Wales by right; Pitt, on the other hand, asserted that the prince had no more right to the Regency than any other subject. In the House of Lords, however, the Duke of York, on behalf of the Prince of Wales, announced that

"His Royal Highness understood too well the sacred principles which seated the House of Brunswick on the throne of Great Britain even to

THE WILBERFORCE OAK, HOLWOOD PARK, KESTON, KENT.

assume or exercise any power, be his claim what it might, that was not derived from the will of the people expressed by their representatives and their lordships in Parliament assembled."

Eventually Pitt brought in a Bill making the Prince Regent with modified powers. But early in 1789, before the Bill was passed, George III. recovered, and till the end of his reign enjoyed great popularity.

Between the king's recovery and the beginning of the great French war, Pitt continued his progressive policy. In 1791, the Quebec Government Act divided Canada into two provinces, and Mitford's Bill removing some of the disabilities of the Roman Catholics was passed (p. 551), and was followed in 1792 by Fox's

Pitt's Work, 1784-1792

Libel Act. Pitt's administration coincided with the most active period of that great industrial revolution which has transformed English society, and effected a considerable change in the distribution of wealth. It was also coincident with a gradual elevation of the standard of religion and morals, the result of the movement inaugurated by Wesley (p. 317). In all directions were to be found life and vigour, and Pitt, basing his power upon the support of the constituencies, formed a new Tory party, which, till the outbreak of the excesses of the French revolution, attempted to carry out an advanced liberal policy.

The French Revolution.

The first effects of the French revolution were not, on the whole, prejudicial to liberal legislation. Though the attempts of Beaufoy and Fox to repeal the Test and Corporation Acts failed, and though Pitt, in 1790, refused to support Flood's motion for parliamentary reform on the ground that it was inopportune, it remains true that it was not till 1792 that the panic caused by the French excesses began to interfere seriously with the beneficial legislation which characterised the earlier years of the ministry. Pitt had indeed welcomed the Revolution, hoping that a constitutional Government would be established in France, and saw no reason for alarm. The rapid and disorderly development of the movement, however, arrested the growth of sympathy for the French nation; and Burke, in his " Reflections on the French Revolution," published in November, 1790, exercised a powerful influence upon public opinion, and contributed to the growth of a strong war party in England.

Reaction Set up.

The deposition of Louis XVI., on August 10th, 1792, followed by the September massacres, the conquest of Belgium, the opening of the Scheldt, the Decrees of November 19 and December 15, the threatened invasion of Holland, and the execution of the French king, roused great indignation in England, and led to the declaration of war, on February 1st, 1793. With this came a severe crisis (p. 648).

All schemes of reform were at once suspended ; a Bill for the abolition of the slave trade was postponed by the House of Lords, Fox's motion for the removal of certain disabilities of the Dissenters was defeated, and Tom Paine was convicted for seditious writing. Fox's Libel Act remains the only progressive measure passed in 1792. In 1793 the reaction set in apace. A motion, proposed by Mr. Grey, for parliamentary reform was

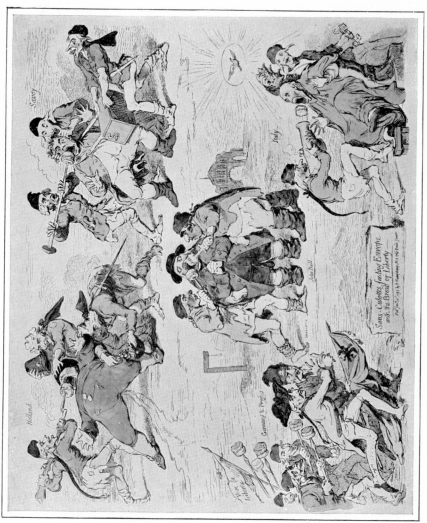

SANS-CULOTTES FEEDING EUROPE WITH THE BREAD OF LIBERTY, 1792.

(From a satirical print by Gillray.)

rejected by 294 to 105, while an Alien Act for the supervision, and, if necessary, for the removal, of aliens was passed, and was followed by the Traitorous Correspondence Act. In 1794 the Habeas Corpus Act was suspended. Political offences were dealt with in a harsh manner. In 1793, Muir, a Scotch advocate, was transported for having urged parliamentary reform, and Palmer, a clergyman, suffered the same fate for circulating an address (p. 686). In 1794, Horne Tooke, Hardy, and Thelwall, who were tried in England for treason, were acquitted; and from that time the attempts to interfere with personal liberty on frivolous grounds ceased.

HORNE TOOKE.

(*Fitzwilliam Museum, Cambridge. By permission of H. A. Chapman, Esq.*)

The French Revolution had thus produced a revulsion of feeling in the country, and the reaction against a progressive policy continued till about 1822. In 1794 the famous secession of the Duke of Portland, Burke, and many of the old Whigs took place. All liberal legislation ceased, Pitt no longer brought in wise and enlightened measures, but became associated with repressive laws; the Whig party suffered complete shipwreck. Only a minority of its members remained under Fox and Grey, in opposition to Pitt, who, though he had entered the war with France with reluctance, carried it on with vigour, while continuing a repressive policy at home. In 1795 the Treasonable Practices Bill and Seditious Meetings Bill were carried at a time when a reactionary feeling was making itself felt in the country. Pitt himself was anxious for peace, and in 1796 entered into negotiations with the Directory, which soon broke down. Affairs in England had, indeed, become critical. In 1797 a

monetary crisis occurred (p. 652), through a deficiency of gold The Financial Strain.
and silver, caused by the heavy payments to the Allies. To
save the finances from falling into confusion, the Government
authorised the Bank of England to suspend cash payments, and
it was not till 1816 that the Act, which was meant to be a
temporary measure, was repealed. In 1798 an income tax of ten
per cent. on incomes over £200 was imposed, and the same year

ROYAL ANTI-SACCHARITES, 1792.
(*From a caricature by Gillray.*)

Fox and his followers, regarding Pitt's policy as dangerous to
liberty, seceded from Parliament. In 1800 the series of repressive measures was completed by the passing of the Corresponding
Societies Bill, by which, in the words of Erskine May, " the
popular constitution of England was suspended." It was in July
of the same year that the Union of Great Britain and Ireland
was effected, an event which led to the fall of Pitt.

In 1782 Ireland had secured legislative independence from
the Rockingham ministry, and till 1800 was ruled by Grattan's
Parliament (p. 692). The insurrection of 1798 convinced Pitt of
the necessity of a legislative union between England and Ireland,

Fall of Pitt. and in 1800 the Act of Union was passed. Pitt's attempt to remove the Catholic disabilities had been less successful (p. 695). George III. was strongly opposed to Catholic emancipation. The Irish Catholics, on the understanding that Pitt would bring in remedial measures, had not opposed the Act of Union. The Prime Minister's regard for George III., whose health was again causing anxiety, prevented any attempt to carry his supplementary measures through Parliament; and, finding himself in a dilemma, he resigned his office in March, 1800. He was **Addington Succeeds.** succeeded by Addington, who formed a ministry which included Lord Chancellor Eldon, the Duke of Portland Lord President of the Council, and Lord Hawkesbury (afterwards Lord Liverpool) Foreign Secretary. During Addington's ministry the first period of the great French war came to an end. Both France and England were desirous of peace, and the Peace of Amiens was signed on March 25th, 1802.

England and Europe, 1784-1802. After the close of the American War England remained till 1788 isolated in Europe. Engrossed in his schemes of reform, Pitt was content for some years to subordinate the European interests of England to financial and administrative considerations. In 1784, in spite of Vergennes's attempt to secure the co-operation of England, no steps were taken to prevent or protest against the Russian seizure of the Crimea in time of peace; and in 1785 France supported the Dutch in their opposition to Joseph II.'s aggressions, mediated the Treaty of Fontainebleau on November 8th between the emperor and the Republic, and made a close military and commercial alliance with Holland. A very serious blow had been dealt at the influence of England in Europe, one of her oldest allies had been detached from the English connection, and the supremacy of France in the United Provinces seemed fraught with danger to the balance of power.

Crisis in Holland. In Holland the lower orders, following the tradition of centuries, supported William V., the Stadtholder, and the English connection, while the wealthy citizens formed the "patriot" party, which advocated a French alliance, relied on the wealth and resources of Holland, and aimed at abolishing the hereditary stadtholdership, or, at any rate, of depriving the Prince of Orange of all real weight in the State. The task of opposing these schemes, of maintaining the English interests, and of resisting the French party, devolved on Sir James Harris, the English minister at the Hague. In September, 1786, the "patriot" party deprived William V. of his command of the army, and the situation became critical. Frederick the Great had refused to aid the Stadtholder, who had married his niece, and had advised him to make no opposition to France; while Pitt was disinclined to pledge the honour of England to support the Orange party, and was averse to risking the chance of going to war.

On August 17th, 1786, Frederick the Great died, and his successor being of an adventurous disposition and not unwilling to enter into an alliance with England, Harris wrote to Pitt, pressing hard for active intervention in Holland to prevent the entire subjection of the United Provinces to France. In February, 1787, Vergennes died, and his incompetent successor, Montmorin, found it impossible to continue his predecessor's energetic foreign policy. In May Pitt agreed to advance £20,000 to the Stadtholder. On June 28th the Princess of Orange was insulted by some free corps near Gouda, and on September 19th a Prussian army entered Holland. The Stadtholder was restored to his former position, Montmorin agreed to disarm and not to interfere in the affairs of the United Provinces, while Pitt, who had determined to oppose by force of arms any aggression on the part of the French, signed treaties with Holland and Prussia in April, 1788, and made an alliance with Frederick William II. in June. In this manner was consolidated the Triple Alliance of 1788, which, having for its object the maintenance of the peace in Europe, exercised during the next four years a great influence on Continental affairs. The French policy had been defeated, English influence had been restored in Holland, the hereditary stadtholdership was guaranteed to the House of Orange, and Sir James Harris was created Lord Malmesbury as a reward for his services.

The Triple Alliance, 1788.

Before the completion of the Triple Alliance Turkey had, in August, 1787, declared war upon Russia, and in February, 1788, Joseph II. came to the aid of the Tsarina and attacked the Porte. The Russians met with signal successes, defeating the Turkish fleet and capturing Ochákov in December, 1788; but the Austrians suffered reverses, and Joseph II., before the end of the year, returned to Vienna ill and discouraged. Till the outbreak of the Turkish war, friendship with Russia had

England, Russia, and Turkey.

been one of the traditions of the English Foreign Office. The attempt, however, of the two Imperial Powers to partition the dominions of the Porte roused the alarm of Pitt, and since his ministry, England has shown a lively interest in the relations of Russia and Turkey.

Sweden and Europe.   In the summer of 1788 Gustavus III. of Sweden, taking advantage of the Eastern war, invaded Finland, and threatened St. Petersburg with an attack. This unexpected invasion of Russia furnished a valuable diversion in favour of the Turks, and alarm was felt in the Russian capital. But the Russian fleet, after an engagement, shut up the Swedish ships in the harbour of Sveaborg, while a mutiny of the officers in Finland paralysed the operations of Gustavus III., who further found himself exposed to an attack by Denmark. In September, 1788, a Danish army had invaded Sweden, and the independence of that country was seriously threatened. The members of the Triple Alliance at once took action to prevent the Baltic from becoming a Russian lake. The Danes, at the threat of English and Prussian intervention, signed an armistice with Sweden in October, 1788. The political balance in the Baltic was restored; Russian interests had suffered a serious blow; the independence of Sweden was assured; and these results were not a little due to the skill and energy of Hugh Elliot, the English minister at Copenhagen. Russia was furious at the conduct of England, refused the mediation of the Allies, attempted to form a Quadruple Alliance with Austria, France, and Spain, and continued the war with Turkey and Sweden. The next great task of

Peace between Austria and Turkey.   England and her allies was to bring about the pacification of Europe by means of a separate peace between the Emperor and the Porte. Though the operations of Austria against Turkey were, in 1789, successful, grave discontent existed in the Austrian Netherlands, in Hungary, and in Bohemia; and in January, 1790, the Austrian garrison having been completely driven out, an Act of Union of the Belgian United Provinces was drawn up. On the subject of mediation between Austria and Turkey that unanimity which had existed among the Allies with regard to the Danish Invasion of Sweden was wanting. The King of Prussia wished to take advantage of the difficulties in which Austria found herself to acquire Danzig and Thorn, and to recognise and support the independence of the Austrian

Netherlands. This policy the English Government found itself unable to countenance. It had no wish to render all future connection with Russia impossible; it was convinced that the result of the adoption of the views of Frederick William would be a still closer alliance between Austria and Russia. Though Pitt was prepared to co-operate with Prussia and Holland in preventing the dependence of the Austrian Netherlands upon

TAMING of the SHREW: *Katharine & Petruchio; — The Modern Quixotte, or, what you will.*

PITT AVERTING THE PARTITION OF TURKEY.
(*From a satirical print of* 1791.)

France, he was opposed to any recognition of Belgian independence, and hoped that a reconciliation between the emperor and his revolted provinces would eventually be accomplished. At the beginning of 1790 the aggressive policy of Prussia threatened Europe with a general war, and it seemed that England would be compelled either to support the designs of Frederick William or to break up the Triple Alliance. On February 18th, 1790, Joseph II. died, and his death saved Europe from an extension of the war. Prussia had in January made a treaty with Turkey, and in March she concluded an alliance with Poland. The conciliatory, though firm, attitude of the Emperor Leopold, however, gradually dissipated these dangers to the peace of Europe, and he was supported in his policy by England and Holland, the Governments of which continued to labour for the pacification of the Continent. Frederick William, discovering that the Poles refused to consent to the cession of Danzig and Thorn, and that England would not support his warlike policy, became more inclined to peaceful views. In August, 1790, he made with Leopold the Treaty of Reichenbach, the emperor agreeing to make peace with the Turks. A year later, on August 4th, 1791, the Peace of Sistova was signed between Turkey and Austria, and Russia was left to continue the war alone. Leopold was enabled to turn his attention to the Netherlands, and early in 1791 his power was completely re-established.

England and Russia. With Russia England was less successful. Early in 1790 Catherine had demanded the mediation of England, but Pitt refused to support the Russian claims, and hoped, by means of the Triple Alliance, to set up a barrier against the ambition of the Russian and Bourbon Powers. He opposed the occupation of Ochákov by Russia, and adopted in 1791 a strong anti-Russian policy (p. 536). The country refused to support this policy, and Pitt receded from his position. The Duke of Leeds, who had strongly advocated a warlike policy, retired, and Lord Grenville took his place at the Foreign Office. The triumph of Russia was complete, and on January 9th, 1792, anxious to take advantage of the outbreak of the French Revolution in order to further partition Poland, Catherine made the Treaty of Jassy.

The Affair of Nootka Sound. During these years Pitt had with difficulty avoided a war against the combined forces of France and Spain over the affair of Nootka Sound. A trading settlement had been made by some English merchants at Nootka Sound, on the coast of what is now called Vancouver Island (p. 532), and in April, 1789, the Spaniards seized an English ship, the *Iphigenia*, put her officers and crew in irons, hauled down the British flag, and destroyed the settlement. Later in the year other English vessels were also seized and detained. The news of these outrages reached England in February, 1790, and Pitt at once made extensive preparations. On May 5th a message from the king, announcing the prospect of war, was read to both Houses of Parliament, an envoy was sent to Madrid to demand full reparation, and Holland and Prussia declared themselves ready to support Great Britain. Spain on her part looked to Russia, and especially to France, for assistance. France and Spain were connected by the family compact of 1761, and Spain had during the American War come to the aid of France. It seemed at first unlikely that Louis XVI. could refuse to accede to the Spanish demands. A war in 1790 on the part of France and Spain against England would have changed the whole course of the French Revolution. Mirabeau, who was the most important member of the National Assembly, declared himself against England and in favour of war. If peace was to be preserved, and Pitt was always in favour of peace, some means must be

AN OUTRAGE AT NOOTKA SOUND, AUGUST, 1790.
(From a contemporary print.)

brought to bear upon Mirabeau and Lafayette. Pitt thereupon sent Hugh Elliot, who had just returned from his successful embassy at Copenhagen, to Paris, and his influence with Mirabeau effected a complete change in the latter's attitude. Mirabeau declared in favour of peace. Lafayette, who had been influenced by Miles, another English agent, made no opposition. At the end of October, 1790, all danger of war between France and England was over; and Florida Blanca, the Spanish minister, finding that no help could be looked for from France, made with England the Treaty of the Escurial, in which Spain yielded all the disputed points (October 28, 1790). Pitt had won a great triumph. He had destroyed the family compact he had preserved peace, and France remained isolated. Thus

the Triple Alliance had been almost uniformly successful, and
England, with her resources unexhausted, was able in 1793 to
enter with vigour into the great war with France.

**England
and
France,
1795-1802.**
Till the close of 1792 Pitt persevered in his efforts to preserve
peace. He had from the outbreak of the French Revolution
declared distinctly that he intended to maintain a policy of
neutrality, and his Budget of the spring of 1792 was framed
upon a peace footing. But the progress of the Revolution
made it impossible for him to hold aloof from hostilities. The
French, after defeating the Prussians at Valmy, in September,
had adopted aggressive tactics. Nice and Savoy were seized.
Belgium, after the battle of Jemmappes, was occupied, the
Scheldt was declared open, and Holland was threatened with
invasion. The decrees of November 19th and December 15th
showed the temper of the Girondists, while the determination
of Dumouriez to invade Holland rendered it necessary for Pitt
to take measures to carry out the terms of the Treaties of 1788.
After Louis XVI.'s death, on January 21st, 1793, it became
impossible to preserve peace between the two countries. War
was declared on February 8th, England, Prussia, Austria, Spain
and Holland attempting to conquer France, and Pitt's efforts
were devoted to keeping together the coalition. The conquest
of Holland in 1794, and the desertion of Prussia and Spain in
1795, rendered Pitt's task increasingly difficult, and upon the
establishment of the Directory he opened negotiations for peace.
In 1796 he again attempted to bring about a general pacification, and Lord Malmesbury was sent to Paris. The French,
however, refused to entertain his proposals, but in 1797, at
Lisle, negotiations were again opened, with the same result.

In 1798-9 Pitt formed the Second Coalition, which, at first
successful, ended in the retirement of Russia and the overthrow of Austria. In 1801 the resignation of Pitt (p. 506) left
his successor, Addington, to continue the war. The defeat
of the French by Abercrombie, in the battle of Alexandria
on March 21st, was followed by the overthrow of the Danish
fleet in the battle of Copenhagen on April 2nd. The Armed
Neutrality (p. 650), reorganised in 1800 by the Tsar Paul,
received a severe blow, the accession of Alexander I. converted Russia into an ally of England, and Addington was
recalled to make the peace of Amiens. Though not a

JOHN BULL'S PROGRESS.

(From a satirical print of 1793 by Gillray.)

great war minister, Pitt had enjoyed the confidence of the country. During the war England had held her own at sea and in the colonies, and his retirement on the question of Catholic emancipation was honourable both to himself and George III.

G. Le M.
GRETTON.
The Army.
Rise of
Our
Indian
Empire,
1742-1761.

THE declaration of war between England and France in 1742 had found the trading companies of three European states with a footing in India. At Bombay the English had a factory, as the trading settlements were then termed. Close to Calcutta, the Dutch, the English and the French were planted on the Hooghly. On the east coast, the English at Madras struggled against the rivalry of the French at Pondicherry, where Dupleix, the Governor of the settlement, took every opportunity of injuring his British neighbours. Dupleix was a man of boundless ambition and remarkable talents. He perceived that in the vast peninsula there was no unity, nothing but a loosely connected and seething mass of disorganised despotisms, differing in race and creed; and he realised that a daring European nation might rule over the whole of India provided that the principle *Divide et impera* became the keynote of their policy. He had long meditated the establishment of a French military empire in Southern India, and, as a first step, the expulsion of the English from Madras. The war gave Dupleix a chance; he captured Madras and held it until the peace of Aix-la-Chapelle, when France exchanged it with England for Louisbourg, in Cape Breton Isle. This peace was but a truce; badly kept in America, in India it was virtually ignored, for the European Companies carried on their quarrel by selling their services to the rival princes whose struggles for the possession of the Deccan and the Carnatic devastated Southern India.

Clive.

At first the French and their allies were successful; but in 1751 Clive began to stem the tide of their victories. Three names stand out conspicuously in our military annals in the eighteenth century—Marlborough, Wolfe, and Clive. Marlborough and Wolfe were bred to arms, and learned their trade as subordinates before they rose to positions of command. Not so with Clive: he was not educated as a soldier,

and at twenty-seven he was a mere clerk in the factory at
Madras, when, under pressure of the French troubles, more
officers were needed, and he was appointed captain in the
service of the East India Company. Almost before the ink on
his commission was dry, Clive had leapt into independent com-

Photo : Walker & Cockerell.

ROBERT, LORD CLIVE, K.B.; PORTION OF PICTURE BY
NATHANIEL DANCE, R.A.

(National Portrait Gallery.)

mand, and had surprised the city of Arcot, an important point **Defence of**
in the enemy's dominions. The French and their allies ad- **Arcot.**
vanced against Clive, drove him into the citadel, and proceeded
to besiege it. The fortress was more than a mile in circumference ; the walls were in many places ruinous, the ramparts
too narrow for guns to be mounted on them, the parapets
weak and low. The only flanking fire along the walls was
from half-ruined towers, and in none of these could more
than a single cannon be mounted. The ditch was virtually

useless, for where it was not dry and filled up with rubbish, it was easily fordable. To hold this apparently undefendable fort Clive had a garrison of 200 Europeans and 300 sepoys, native soldiers trained by the English at Madras. Outside its crumbling walls were 2,000 sepoys, disciplined and led by French officers; 5,000 irregular infantry, 3,000 cavalry, and, more dangerous than all the rest, 150 picked French troops. After forty-eight days of siege the enemy attempted to storm, but, thanks to Clive's admirable arrangements and the good fire-discipline of his handful of men, the masses of infantry who swarmed up the breach were met by steady and perfectly controlled volleys. The heads of the column were swept away again and again, and their discomfiture was completed by showers of hand-grenades which the garrison flung among them. The attack failed : next day the siege was raised, and Clive was free to turn to Trichinopoly, which the French were then besieging. After obtaining reinforcements Clive marched southwards, to find a Franco-Indian army across his path at Kaveripak. After desperate fighting Clive defeated them with the loss of their artillery, and thus rendered possible the relief of Trichinopoly and the capture of the whole French army. But the guns he seized and the prisoners he made constituted but a small portion of the advantage which Clive won for his country on this hard-fought field. Before the siege of Arcot the natives of India believed that Englishmen could not fight; and even after Clive's defence it was considered that his conduct was the exception which proved the rule. But after the battle of Kaveripak the quick Oriental mind realised that not only could the English fight, but that they could beat the French. The prestige which Clive thus acquired greatly helped him, a few years later, to wrest Bengal from the bloodstained hands of Surajah Dowlah.

Plassey.   Towards the end of 1756 Clive was summoned to Madras to save the Company's factory at Calcutta from impending ruin. Surajah Dowlah, the Nawab of Bengal, an Oriental despot of the worst type, had seized the Company's property ; he had done to death 122 English men and women in the Black Hole of Calcutta ; and the survivors of the little colony were in terror of their lives. Clive landed with a few hundred troops, worsted the Nawab in several skirmishes, and wrung

from him compensation for these outrages.   A nominal peace
was made, but the longer Clive studied the character of the
ruler of Bengal the more he became convinced that there
would be no safety for the English while Surajah Dowlah
remained in power.   He therefore determined to depose him,
and to replace him by a creature of his own—a puppet,
through whom the Company should control Bengal.   A suitable tool was found in Mir Jafir, one of Surajah Dowlah's

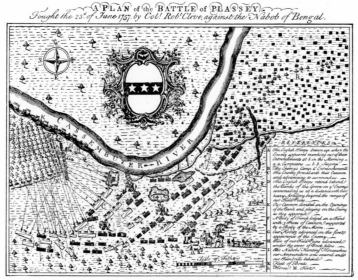

PLAN OF THE BATTLE OF PLASSEY.
("*Memorials of the Revolution in Bengal,*" 1760.)

generals.   To obtain the throne this traitor agreed to betray
his master, and to desert with all his troops at the battle
then impending between the Nawab and the English.   Surajah
Dowlah's army, though numerically very formidable, was unwieldy, and, as far as his 35,000 infantry were concerned,
poorly trained and disciplined; but his cavalry, 18,000 strong,
were resolute, well-drilled men, all recruited from the fighting races of Northern India.   His artillery consisted of a
small field battery, manned by French soldiers, and fifty-three
large cannon, in charge of native gunners.   Each of these guns
was mounted on a huge wheeled platform, so heavy that the

combined efforts of forty yoke of oxen tugging in front and
an elephant pushing behind were required to move it. To meet
these masses of fighting men Clive had only 950 European
infantry, fifty sailors and half a dozen midshipmen to work
his eight light guns, 200 half-castes, and 2,100 sepoys. When
the two armies met on the field of Plassey, Clive for several
hours stood on the defensive; then, after repulsing a charge
of the Nawab's cavalry, he ordered an advance. Surajah
Dowlah fled; his generals hurriedly retreated, and the only
troops who opposed Clive's forward movement were the French
gunners, who fought with all the gallantry of their nation.
Mir Jafir, who had waited until the last moment to declare
himself, now joined his patron, Clive; and with the desertion
of his large body of troops the battle ended. The victory of
Plassey rendered the East India Company masters in fact,
though not in name, of the three rich provinces of Bengal,
Orissa, and Behar; for though Clive installed Mir Jafir upon
the throne with all the customary solemnities, the new Nawab
soon realised that his tenure of office was absolutely dependent
upon the goodwill of his English allies.

Hyder Ali.   While Clive was securing for the Company the position of
paramount power on the Ganges, his lieutenant had won for
England high consideration among the rulers of Southern
India. By the series of victories over the French which cul-
minated in Lally's surrender of Pondicherry in 1761, England
acquired much territory and more prestige. Our assistance
was eagerly sought by the native princes in their endless
wars; and thus we ultimately became embroiled with Hyder
Ali, the sultan of Mysore, a celebrated adventurer who raised
himself from the position of a private soldier to that of the
most powerful sovereign in Southern India. When, in 1780,
the French were again at war with us, they allied themselves
with Hyder Ali, and furnished him with officers who accompanied him in his terrible raid on the Carnatic, when at the
head of 80,000 men he devastated the low-lying plains around
Madras.

In 1783 we made an inglorious peace with Tippoo, who,
on the death of his father Hyder Ali, had succeeded to the
throne of Mysore; and we brought to an equally inglorious
termination the first of our series of wars with the great

Mahratta Confederacy. For a few years there was compara- The
tive quiet; but as soon as war again broke out between England French
and France, French intriguers resumed their activity at the and
native courts. England feared a French invasion of India, India.
and in 1798–9 such an invasion by no means seemed impossible. In the north-west the troops of Scindia, one of
the great Mahratta chiefs, were officered by French adven-

HYDER ALI KHAN.
(Drawn by J. Leister in 1776.)

turers. In the Deccan the Nizam of Hyderabad was guarded
by a regiment officered by Frenchmen. At Mysore, Tippoo
(*le citoyen Tippoo*, as the Parisians called him), to please
his French retainers, allowed them to plant a tree of liberty
in his capital, and to ornament their uniforms with buttons
engraved with the Phrygian cap. Through the Governor of
the Mauritius he entered into an alliance with the Republic,
and corresponded with Napoleon in Egypt. Bonaparte, who
was longing to play the part of a modern Alexander, wrote
to him from Cairo:—" You have been already informed of

my arrival on the shores of the Red Sea with an innumer-
able and invincible army, full of the desire of releasing you
from the iron yoke of the English." On discovering Tippoo's
alliance with the French, the English promptly invaded
his dominions with 30,000 men. They were accompanied
by a large body of troops provided by the Nizam of Hyderabad, whose Frenchmen we had sent back to France, and
who had now returned to his old allegiance to the Company.
Wellington, then the young colonel of the 33rd, who was
placed in command of this contingent, gives an interesting
account of the order of march of the combined army. The
Nizam's troops and the British force marched in two columns
parallel to each other "almost in form of a square or oblong,
of which the front and rear were formed of cavalry, and
about two or three miles in extent; the right and left (owing
to the immense space taken up in the column by field pieces,
drawn by bullocks) about six or seven miles. In this square
went everything belonging to the army."[1] Wellington goes
on to say that 60,000 bullocks were employed in the British
service; the grain for the Nizam's troops was carried by 25,000
oxen. When the whole army was in motion it covered about
eighteen square miles.

A weary march brought this unwieldy army to the gates
of Seringapatam; and after a siege, in which Wellington
greatly distinguished himself, this stronghold of Mysore was
carried by storm on May 4th, 1799.

The Mahrattas Overcome. Tippoo perished in the breach, and by his death relieved the
English at Madras of a dangerous neighbour. Two years later
the ever-recurring Mahratta trouble came to a head. The
restless and warlike Mahratta tribes were a standing danger to
their neighbours, the native states whom by treaty we had
bound ourselves to protect; and, had they been united, they
would even have threatened our power in Bombay, in Central
India, and on the Ganges; but, happily for the ultimate peace
of India, quarrels arose between two of their great chiefs—
Scindia, whose territories were in the North-west, and the
Peshwa, who ruled at Poona, near Bombay. The Peshwa
obtained our assistance, and Scindia, his rival, prepared for war.
Two expeditions were sent against him, both of which were

[1] Wellington's Supplementary Despatches, i. 204

brilliantly successful. Lake won the battles of Aligahr and
Laswari, captured Delhi and Agra, and scattered Scindia's
French troops to the winds. Wellington was equally successful
at the battles of Argaum and Assaye. At Assaye he fought   Assaye.
against enormous odds, and gained his victory by the same calm
good sense and rapid intuition which he afterwards exhibited on
the battlefields of Europe. On the morning of September 23rd,
1803, Wellington, as he
reconnoitred the enemy,
found them posted along
the bank of the River
Katna, near its junction
with the Jewah; 30,000
of the far-famed Mahratta
cavalry were drawn up in
glittering squadrons on
the plain; 10,000 picked
infantry, trained and officered by Frenchmen, a
swarm of irregular in-
fantry armed with match-
locks, and a park of 128
guns, also in charge of
French adventurers, rested
on the village of Assaye
on the left of the line.
After a flanking move-
ment by the English,

TIPPOO SAHIB.
(From a drawing by Mauraisse.)

followed by a corresponding change of front by the enemy,
the fight began. Wellington decided to attack the enemy
on their right, and, therefore, ordered the troops on the
British right to advance slowly and with frequent halts. But
the orders were not obeyed, and the infantry and artillery on
our right hurried forward, only to be met by so well-directed
a fire from the Mahratta guns that they staggered under it.
The native general, with the eye of a true soldier, ordered his
cavalry to charge the shaken infantry; but Wellington was too
quick for him. He hurled four regiments of cavalry at the
Mahratta horsemen; the English dragoons, supported on either
flank by their Madrassee comrades, charged at speed across the

plain, fell upon the enemy before they had fairly got under
way, and drove them headlong back.   While, under cover of
this cavalry fight, the British troops recovered their solidity,
Wellington was steadily winning on the left and centre of his
line ; the Mahrattas, fighting hard, fell back across the river, and
there formed up in threatening masses.   Our cavalry dashed
across the stream, dispersed the enemy's infantry, and then
turned back to meet a fresh and unexpected danger.   Numbers
of the Mahrattas, pretending to be dead, had allowed our men
to pass over them.   Now they had manned the abandoned guns,
and played upon us as we advanced beyond them.   After effectually quieting these impostors, Wellington's cavalry once more
met their peers.   The Mahratta squadrons again advanced, but our
men so fiercely charged them that Scindia's far-famed horse fled
for twelve miles before them, without once drawing rein.
Ninety-two guns fell into our hands, and the victory, though
costly, was decisive.   Wellington went into action with about
4,500 men, of whom only one cavalry regiment and two infantry
regiments were English regulars.   He was also nominally supported by 5,000 cavalry from the Peshwa's army, whose fidelity
was more than doubtful, and who took no part in the engagement.   His losses were 428 killed, and more than 1,100 wounded,
figures which conclusively prove that a new era in our Indian
wars had commenced, and that in the future we should en-
counter foemen worthy of our steel.

The
Conquest
of India.

To trace year by year, or even decade by decade, the marvellous growth of British power in India would be here impossible.   Suffice it to say that when Clive exchanged the pen
for the sword, the East India Company occupied three or four
small trading stations in Hindustan, where, by the grace of the
native princes, they were permitted to live and sell their goods.
Half a century later, at the end of the second Mahratta war in
1805, the English were paramount along the Ganges Valley from
Delhi to Calcutta ; while on the east coast their territory
extended from the Hooghly to Cape Comorin, and comprised
nearly the whole of Southern India.   The troops by whose
valour this mighty expansion was effected were always vastly
inferior in numbers to the native armies whom they fought.
Nor were our soldiers all Europeans.   On the contrary, the proportion of Englishmen to natives in the Company's service was

always small. Thus, in 1773, 9,000 white men and 45,000 sepoys **Native Troops.**
wore the British uniform in India; and at the close of the
second Mahratta war there were 25,000 English soldiers to
130,000 natives   But the British in India greatly surpassed
their enemies in courage, in mobility, and in discipline; our
sepoys were drilled and trained on exactly the same system as

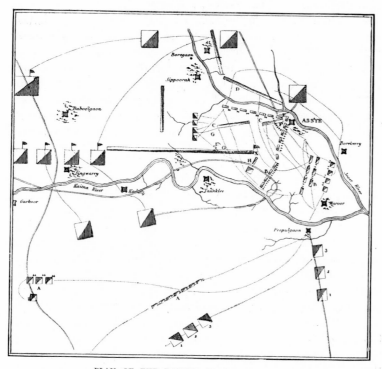

PLAN OF THE BATTLE OF ASSAYE, 1803.

(*W. T. Thorne, " Memoir of the War in India under Lake and Wellesley,"* 1803–6.)

A A, successive positions of British, as they moved up to the ford of Peepulgaon;
1, 2, 3, Peshwa's Mysore cavalry, keeping off Mahratta cavalry (not shown) from
harassing British; B B, the two armies formed up for battle after the flanking
movement designed to attack the enemy on its *original* left, x; E, Mahratta
horse at left of second line of enemy (which was at right angles to the position
of the first line) preparing to charge British right; c c, British, having broken
first line, forcing Mahrattas across the Juah; D, Mahrattas formed up across the
river; G G and H, scene of conflict between British cavalry and Mahrattas who
had recovered the abandoned guns. The large squares half-shaded and the line
ending at x are the earlier Mahratta positions.

their white comrades, and when well led by good English officers,
always proved themselves ready to follow wherever the British
troops would lead. The tactics by which our generals won their

Tactics. battles in India against overwhelming odds were to threaten the front, while making as strong an attack as possible against the enemy's weaker flank. His vast numbers of infantry, too poorly drilled to be able to change front to meet the sudden danger, fell into confusion; our frontal attack, suddenly and vigorously pressed home, produced a panic; the line broke, the enemy fled in all directions, and the victory was ours. Both in India and in England our drill was modelled on that devised by Frederick the Great for the Prussian army. It is curious to notice how little the " close order " drill of a battalion has varied in *essentials* during the last hundred years. No doubt the movements then were numerous, and so complicated that General Dundas, an English military writer of the eighteenth century, devotes a huge quarto volume to elucidating them. Now they are very few in number and perfectly easy to understand; but the same principles underlie them both—the rapid transference of men from column into line, and back again into column.

Reform in Military Management. Before alluding to the vicissitudes of the British arms in Europe it is desirable to mention an important reform which was effected in 1783 in the management of the army. In Chapter XV. (IV., p. 512) reference was made to the extraordinary financial relationship existing in the Stuart period between the Crown and the officers of each regiment, by which the latter in effect contracted, in return for a lump sum paid to them annually, to raise and to pay, to equip and to maintain, a specified number of soldiers fit for active service. If there were a profit on the transaction for the year, a dividend was declared among the officers who commanded companies; if, on the other hand, the outgoings had been heavy and recruits expensive to procure, the deficit was met by a call, which had to be made good out of the captains' private means. This system, a survival of medieval times (II., p. 448), lasted more than a century; and it was not until Burke's Act was passed that the War Office, by assuming direct control over the recruiting and financial arrangements of the army, removed from the British officer's path the temptations to peculation which had previously confronted him at every moment of his career.

In 1793 our last and greatest struggle with the French commenced, as has been the case in most of our wars, with a disaster. The Duke of York, a royal prince, whose stupidity as a man was only equalled by his ignorance as a general, was sent with a contingent of 20,000 British and 10,000 Hanoverian troops to reinforce our Allies in the Low Countries. His English troops were bad, for since the close of the American war the army had sunk into a wretched condition, " lax in its discipline, entirely without system, and very weak in numbers. Every colonel of a regiment managed it according to his notions or neglected it altogether. There was no uniformity of drill or movement ; professional pride was rare ; professional knowledge still more so. . . . Every department was more or less inefficient. The regimental officers, as well as their men, were hard drinkers, and the latter, under a loose discipline, were addicted to maraud- ing and acts of licentious violence." [1] As in their *morale*, so in their *physique*, these soldiers left much to be desired, for many of the recruits who landed at Antwerp in 1793 were either too old or too young for active service ; while whole regiments were unable to march to the front on account of physical infirmities. It is not surprising that these indifferent troops, commanded by such a general as the Duke of York, failed to distinguish them- selves. Although they fought bravely on many occasions, they could not withstand the savage energy of the French. In 1794 Pichegru, after defeating the Allies at Fleurus, turned upon the Duke of York, chased him through Holland, in all the horror of the worst winter known for a century, and finally hunted into Bremen the wretched remnant of this miserable expedition. The loss in the actions in which our troops took part was not heavy ; but our sanitary and hospital arrangements were so bad that, in 1794, a return of " killed or dead in service " gave the startling figure of 18,596 lost in the campaign of 1793. Through- out this expedition, indeed, disorganisation reigned supreme, and forethought, system, and arrangement were alike con- spicuous by their absence. The commissariat was so inefficient that frequently no rations were served out to the soldiers for forty-eight hours together ; and the men's shoes were not replaced as they wore out, though the troops were marching through deep snow and across frozen rivers. The staff officers were utterly ignorant of their duty ; and no man in the army, from the Commander-in-Chief downwards, seemed to take the

[1] Bunbury, "Narrative of Campaign in North Holland" (London, 1849), pp. iii., iv.

slightest account of time. Wellington, who served in this disastrous campaign, and who profited much by its painful lessons, used in after years to say that it was a marvel to him how any of the English escaped. " If we happened to be at dinner and the wine was going round, it was considered wrong to interrupt us. I have seen a packet handed in from the Austrian headquarters, and thrown aside with the remark, ' That will keep till to-morrow morning.' "

Distant Conquests. During the next four years no British army landed on the Continent ; but combined naval and military operations in Africa and in Asia gave occupation to our soldiery. The virtual absorption of Holland by the French Republic had enlisted the Dutch on the side of our foes ; and we accordingly wrested from Holland two all-important strategic points on the way to India, Ceylon and the Cape of Good Hope. There were also minor expeditions against the islands in the West Indies, in which we were usually successful, though at a heavy cost. The climate, not the enemy, was chiefly responsible for the loss of the services of more than 40,000 soldiers, who, in 1795–6, were discharged, invalided " on account of wounds or infirmity."

An Un-popular Service. These distant expeditions and the disgrace of the Duke of York's *fiasco* did not tend to popularise the army ; men would not join the ranks ; and when, in 1799, another expedition to Holland was planned, militiamen had to be bribed with heavy bounties to enlist into the regular service. It is difficult to realise that the country again allowed the king to foist his incompetent soldier-son into a command on active service ; but so it was. The Duke of York commanded the mixed force of English and Russians who landed in Holland. He lost about 10,000 men in five engagements, was badly beaten, and obliged to retreat to the shores of the North Sea, where he expected to find a fleet of transports. No transports appeared, however, so he surrendered to the French, and his hapless followers only escaped detention in French fortresses by being exchanged for a corresponding number of Frenchmen, then prisoners of war in England.

Undaunted by their Dutch experiences, in 1800 the English Ministry organised another expedition, the command of which was given, not to the Duke of York, but to Sir Ralph Abercrombie, a professional soldier of repute. His destination was

Egypt, where the French army, though abandoned by Napoleon, still maintained its position, and threatened our power in the East. His orders were if possible to work in co-operation with Baird's expeditionary force from India, to obtain assistance from the Turks, and to drive the French out of the valley of the Nile. On the voyage our troops suffered considerably. The transports were so leaky that the men were constantly wet through; so ill supplied that the soldiers had no hammocks and slept on the bare decks with no bedding but their blankets. After touching at Malta, the island fortress which we had just taken from the French, Abercrombie was detained for six weeks at Cyprus waiting for cavalry remounts promised by the Turks. This time was usefully employed in constantly training the troops to embark and disembark with rapidity; so that when, on March 7th, 1801, our fleet of nearly 200 sail anchored in Aboukir Bay, every soldier thoroughly understood his duty. When the signal to land was given, the men swarmed down the sides of the ships, and without confusion took their allotted place in the boats. On a second signal, these troop-boats, formed up in three long lines of fifty each, made for the shore, in silence broken only by the regular dip of hundreds of oars in the water. When they came within range of the French who lined the yellow sandhills on the coast, a tremendous fire of grape and musketry was opened upon them. Several boats were sunk outright, and the troops, crowded together at the bottom of the boats, with their muskets between their knees, suffered severely. But there was no thought of pausing; the bluejackets pulled harder than ever, the soldiers cheered lustily, and as soon as the water was shallow enough, sprang overboard and waded to the shore. Rapidly forming up, they rushed the sandhills and drove away the French at the point of the bayonet. Thus the landing of the first division of the English force was triumphantly effected, but at a heavy loss; the French fire cost 650 gallant men their lives.[1] As soon as the remainder of Abercrombie's troops were landed, he followed the French towards Alexandria, although he was without any news of Baird, who, as a matter of fact, was still beating against head winds in the Red Sea.

England in Egypt.

[1] An excellent account will be found in the prize essay of Major Elmslie, R.A. (*Journal of the United Service Institution*, May, 1895).

**Battle of
Alex-
andria.**

On the 21st of March took place the battle of Alexandria, an engagement insignificant in point of numbers, for there were but 12,000 combatants on each side, but of very great moral effect, as it proved to the world that there were still troops in Europe who could beat the French in fair and open fight. Abercrombie was encamped on a sandy isthmus, a mile wide, which separated Lake Naadah from the Mediterranean. Opposite to him, entrenched on a line of heights in front of Alexandria, lay the French, determined that before the Turks began to menace their flank in Syria, or Baird arrived from India to threaten them in rear, the English should be driven headlong to their ships. It was still black night when our troops, in accordance with Abercrombie's rule, roused themselves from sleep and stood to their arms ready for action. Suddenly a rattle of musketry at the front showed that the precaution was well taken and that the enemy were advancing upon the outposts. On the left the French contented themselves with a distant cannonade; in the centre the steady aspect of the Guards prevented them from coming to close quarters; the danger of their attack was on the right of our line. It is difficult to imagine anything more confused and at the same time more picturesque than this battle, begun in the darkness of the night and continued in the mist of the morning. Columns of French suddenly appeared among our troops, and were driven back by steady, well-directed volleys; guided by the flashes, the enemy hurried up reinforcements in the gloom, which actually passed unnoticed between the two wings of an English regiment. When our men discovered that they were thus divided, they wheeled inwards and attacked the enemy with the bayonet. There were fierce charges and counter-charges, and guns and colours were lost and won before the French column disappeared into the darkness from which they had surprised our men. During this combat the 28th Regiment (the Gloucestershire) were immortalising themselves hard by. While the regiment, in two ranks, were hotly engaged with the enemy in front, a watchful officer suddenly heard behind him a French word of command, and recognised the glazed hats of the Republicans closing upon the rear. Without a moment's hesitation the English colonel ordered the rear rank to "turn about," and thus, standing back to back, the "thin red line" thrust the French

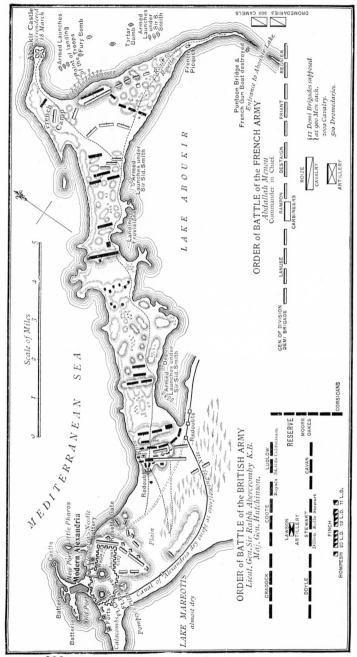

THE ABOUKIR CAMPAIGN, 1801.

(After a contemporary plan.)

resolutely from them.   Then twelve hundred French cavalry
swept wildly through our camp ; they nearly broke the 42nd
(Black Watch) by falling on their flank in the dim light, but the
Highlanders formed groups and repelled them with the bayonet.
At length the French retreated, leaving 2,000 men upon the
field.   Our loss was 1,500, and the brave General Abercrombie
received his death wound in the battle.   Hutchinson succeeded
him, and in the course of a few months had made prisoners of
24,000 French troops, the whole garrison of Egypt, who, in
accordance with the terms of their capitulation, were transported
back to France.   The Indian contingent under Baird arrived
just in time to take part in the concluding operations of the
campaign.   Their voyage from Bombay to the Gulf of Suez
had lasted six months, and immediately after landing they had
performed the feat of marching, in nine days, a hundred and
forty miles across the desert, from the Red Sea to the Nile, in a
temperature of 115° in the shade.

Peace of Amiens.   The Peace of Amiens, in 1802, put an end to hostilities: we
abandoned our conquests, excepting the islands of Ceylon and
Trinidad, and we agreed to restore Malta to the Knights if the
Great Powers would guarantee them its possession.   With the
childlike belief in the durability of peace which has always
distinguished this country, our ministry proceeded to disarm.
They disembodied the militia, which had been nine years under
arms, and they disbanded the numerous fencible regiments
of infantry and cavalry which had been raised during the war.
A few months after the Peace of Amiens was signed the regular
army in England was reduced to about 40,000 men ; and thus,
when the war broke out again in 1803, the whole process of
re-establishing our land forces had to be hurriedly undertaken
at infinite expense and great loss of efficiency.

W. LAIRD CLOWES. The Navy. Maritime Enterprise.   THE naval voyages undertaken during this period for the
purposes of exploration, or of the extension of the empire, were of
considerable importance.   In 1785, a body of merchants, called
the King George's Sound Company, chartered two vessels to open
up a trade from the north-west coast of North America to China,
and gave the command of them to Henry Portlock and George
Dixon, who had been companions of Cook on some of his

voyages. And in 1787, Commodore Arthur Philip, in the *Sirius* (20), Captain John Hunter, accompanied by the *Supply,* and nine transports, having on board a great number of convicts of both sexes, left Spithead for New South Wales, in order to establish a penal colony at Botany Bay. The expedition was escorted one hundred leagues to the westward by the *Hyæna* (20), Captain Michael de Courcy. Philip arrived on January 14th, 1788, and when the convicts had been landed he assumed the governorship. Soon afterwards the French expedition, under **England and Australia.** La Peyrouse, which had left France in 1785, touched at the place; and during its stay many of the convicts made deter-mined attempts to escape with it. There were numerous other difficulties, but in time Philip van-quished them all; and when he returned to England in 1793, the young colony, which has since grown to such im-portant proportions, and has become so different a place from what was originally intended, was firmly established. An-

ARTHUR PHILIP.
(After F. Wheatly.)

other venture of 1787 was the formation of the Sierra Leone Company; but it requires mention here only because the scheme owed its origin to Lieutenant John Matthews, who had made a voyage to the coast in 1785.

It is doubly surprising that the fate of the *Bounty* mutineers (p. 543) remained so long in doubt, when it is recollected that during part of the interval the Pacific was being explored by one of the most energetic and successful of maritime discoverers, Captain George Vancouver, who, in the *Discovery* (10), accom-panied by the *Chatham* (4), armed tender, under Lieutenant William Robert Broughton, left the Thames on January 26th, 1791, and quitted the Channel early in the following April. His **Vancouver's Expedition.**

instructions were to proceed to, and survey, the Sandwich
Islands; to go thence to Nootka Sound (p. 510), and to take
over from the Spaniards the settlement there; to survey the
coast of what is now Vancouver Island; and to return home by
way of the Sandwich Islands, Cape Horn, and the western coast
of South America. Having gone out by the Cape of Good Hope,
he struck the south-west point of Australia, coasted eastwards,
sighted Van Diemen's Land, surveyed part of the south shore of

BOTANY BAY IN 1788.
(Arthur Philip, " Voyage to Botany Bay.")

New Zealand, and spent nearly a month at Otaheite. Thence
the vessels went to the Sandwich Islands, and so to Vancouver,
then known generally as Nootka, the shores of which were
thoroughly explored and surveyed. In Nootka Sound, after
some time, the expedition was joined by the *Dædalus*, store-ship,
which had been sent out from England under Lieutenant Richard
Hergest, who made several valuable discoveries, but was killed
at Oahu ere he reached the American coast. The Spaniards
proved unwilling to surrender Nootka, and there was consequently much delay, which Vancouver utilised by making
further surveys up and down the Pacific shores of the continent.
In October, 1793, Lieutenant Broughton was sent home with
despatches, and the command of the *Chatham* was entrusted to

Lieutenant Peter Puget, whose name was thus associated with the great inlet in what is now the State of Washington. Explorations and surveys were continued along the west coast of America and in the northern Pacific; and on February 25th, 1794, Hawaii was formally taken over by Vancouver in the name of King George III. Later, the shores of what is now British Columbia were also taken possession of; and when, on the 20th October, 1795, the *Discovery* arrived in the Thames, she had been absent

THE *DISCOVERY* ON THE ROCKS IN QUEEN CHARLOTTE'S SOUND.
(*George Vancouver, "Voyage of the 'Discovery' on the North Pacific Ocean," 1798.*)

four years, eight months, and twenty-nine days. A few months earlier, Broughton, then a commander, had commissioned, and departed in, the *Providence* for another voyage. He went out to Nootka by much the same route as had been taken by Vancouver, and upon his arrival found that the Spaniards had evacuated the place. Thence he crossed the northern Pacific to Japan and China. Although he lost his ship, he continued his explorations and surveys in a purchased schooner of 80 tons, and, after having done very valuable service, returned to England in February, 1799.

During the peace the subject of promotion from post to flag-rank on several occasions occupied the attention of the country and of Parliament. In 1787, Sir Matthew White Ridley took up

Naval Pro-
motion.
in the House of Commons the case of Captain David Brodie,
who, though a captain of nearly forty years' standing, and much
senior to many officers who had been given their flags, had been
repeatedly passed over. This came to nothing, but in the
following year, in the House of Lords, the general subject of promotion to the flag was brought forward by Lord Rawdon. By
an order in Council, dated 1718, the Admiralty had been
directed to proceed in the promotion of officers to admiral's
rank, according to the seniority of the captains on the list, regard
being only had to their service qualifications for the rank to
which promotion was sought. Another order of 1747 had
directed the Admiralty to superannuate such captains of long
and meritorious service as might be disabled from serving as
admirals, owing to age or infirmity. But in the promotion of
September, 1787, when sixteen captains were promoted to flag
rank, upwards of forty captains were passed over. Some of these
had refused the offer of superannuation, because they not only
deemed that their past services entitled them to better treatment, but also believed themselves to be perfectly fit for future
service; and the partial nature of the promotions, perhaps
naturally, created a good deal of disgust, disappointment, and
apprehension, since no officer could thenceforth feel sure of
securing the rewards which he felt that he had earned. Such was
Lord Rawdon's contention. His motion was finally negatived
without a division; but that fact did not prevent the same
question from being immediately afterwards brought forward in
the Commons, where three separate debates on the same subject
took place at short intervals. Although it appeared that no pro-
ducible rule had been employed in making selections for flags,
and that, while some officers who were infirm had been promoted, others who were equally meritorious and not infirm at all
had been passed over, the Administration was in each case
victorious, in deference, no doubt, to the general sense that there
might be more danger in promotion by seniority tempered only
by physical health, than in promotion by seniority tempered by
selection, even if, in the latter event, no reasons for the ministers'
action were vouchsafed. The senior captain promoted in 1787
had held post-rank for thirty years, and the junior had held it
for twenty-six years; and had not some such course as was
taken been adopted, not only would the flag list have had an

increasing tendency to consist almost exclusively of men on the verge of dotage, but also certain officers who subsequently rendered the most valuable services in war-time would have been kept on the captains' list for so long a period that they would not have been eligible for the commands in which they gained

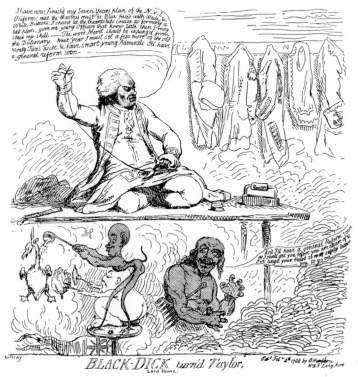

BLACK DICK TURNED TAILOR.
(*From a satirical print of* 1788 *by Gillray.*)

their greatest fame. The selection of the sixteen captains chosen for promotion in 1787 by Lord Howe, who was then First Lord of the Admiralty, is best justified by the fact that the list contains the names of William Hotham, afterwards Lord Hotham; Sir John Jervis, afterwards Earl St. Vincent; and Adam Duncan, afterwards Viscount Duncan. If a similar method had not been pursued then, and for some time subsequently, it would have been impossible for Nelson to obtain his flag, as he did, after less than eighteen years' service as captain, and, in all probability,

the fleet at the time of Trafalgar would have been under the
orders of an officer of between seventy and seventy-five, instead
of under those of a man of forty-seven. The action of the
Admiralty, therefore, though it certainly pressed hardly on
individuals, was undoubtedly for the good of the country.

Bounties to Seamen. In the meantime seamen were encouraged. In 1788 a proclamation was issued, recalling all British seamen from foreign
service, and prohibiting them from entering into foreign service
without a licence; and in 1791, at the time of the Russian scare
(p. 510), the following bounties were offered :—To an able seaman, £3; to an ordinary seaman, £2; and to an able-bodied
landsman, £1. At the beginning of the war in 1793, in addition
to the royal bounty, the City of London offered £2 to every able,
and £1 to every ordinary, seaman; and in the following year
the same public-spirited body held out to every able seaman
10 guineas; to every ordinary seaman, 8 guineas; to every
landsman, 6 guineas; and to boys, 1 and 2 guineas, according to
height. In 1795 the bounties rose still higher, in some places
exceeding £30 a head; yet the supply was so unequal to the
demand that in that year an Act had to be passed for the raising
of a certain number of men from every county, the proportion
varying from 23 in Rutland to 1,071 in Yorkshire; and a few
weeks later another Act ordered an embargo on all British
shipping until a further quota of men, levied upon the several
ports, should be raised. In this case the assessment varied from
three for the Scilly Islands and Prestonpans to 1,711 for Liverpool and 5,704 for London. In 1795, also, an Act was passed to
enable warrant and petty officers and seamen to allot part of
their pay for the maintenance of their wives and families, and
to enable seamen's letters to pass to and fro at a uniform charge
of one penny. Another Act permitted officers, on appointment
from half-pay, to apply for a certain amount of pay in advance.
And in 1796 the pay of lieutenants was increased. But the
demands of the service, especially for men to man the fleet,
continued to outrun the supply, and in 1798 it was found
necessary to suspend all protection from the operations of
the press-gang for one month in the case of the coal trade, and
for five months in other cases. Amid such circumstances it is
astonishing that the sea-borne trade of the country was not
crushed out of existence. Still more astonishing is it that in

A SNUG CABIN, BY THOMAS ROWLANDSON.

40

spite of the press, and of the enormous number of captures made by the enemy, the trade, after the war had fairly begun, developed amazingly.

But it is not astonishing that, when the ships were largely manned by a process of kidnapping, and when the scum of the population went, together with some of the better elements, into the Navy, there was a vast amount of discontent—a discontent that was not diminished by the tyranny of a certain class of officers.

Unsuitable Officers.

Then, as in all ages, there were officers and officers; but the conclusion of the American war left us with, perhaps, a larger proportion than at any other period of officers who were more or less unsuitable for the position. One case may be cited as an illustration of the kind of man who, at that time, might and did become a post-captain. John Perkins, known throughout the Navy of the end of the eighteenth century as "Jack Punch," was a lieutenant of 1782, a commander of 1797, and a captain of 1800; and he died in Jamaica in 1812. His bravery and dash cannot be challenged, and his success, particularly while in command of the *Drake*, *Arab*, and *Tartar*, was extraordinary; but he was surely one of the strangest characters who ever held a British post-commission. According to an officer who served with him on the Leeward Station, the general belief was that he was a mulatto, born out of wedlock in the Island of St. Domingo. His father was probably some British captain, who, as the readiest way of providing for the young incumbrance, placed him on his own, or a friend's, quarter-deck. Be this as it may, Perkins had so little education that he could neither write nor read, though, for service purposes, he had learnt the mechanical art of signing his name. He seems never to have been appointed to a ship serving elsewhere than in the West Indies; and whenever he was on half-pay he lived at Kingston, Jamaica, where his establishment, so far as his relations with the other sex were concerned, scandalised a not very exacting generation. There cannot have been many officers like Perkins; yet an age which admitted him, and which permitted Lord Rodney to promote his son John from the rank of midshipman to that of post-captain in one month and four days, at a time when the boy was only fifteen years and five months old, must, it is evident, have been an age when almost any abuse was possible.

To this cause may be referred many of the alarming and

**The
Mutinies.**

disgraceful mutinies which were characteristic of the period.
That of the crew of the *Bounty* (p. 543) is attributable quite as
much to the severity of Bligh as to the attractions of Otaheite.
In 1797 a serious mutiny in the fleet at Spithead was followed
by an even more dangerous one in the fleets at the Nore and in
the North Sea.   In these lamentable cases the alleged grievances
were, in the first instance, insufficient pay and pensions, insufficient provisions, lack of care for the sick, and embezzlement of the
comforts supplied for seamen's use, insufficient leave on shore,
and stoppage of pay of wounded men ; and, in each of the
directions indicated, concessions were made by the Admiralty.
But when the disaffection spread to the Nore, additional
demands were made to the effect that officers who had been
turned out of any ship by the mutineers should not be again
employed in the same ship without the consent of the ship's
company ; that indemnification should be made to any man
who had run, and that he should not be liable to arrest as a
deserter ; and that the Articles of War should be altered in
several particulars.   To most of the fresh demands the Admiralty
returned a refusal ; and as Richard Parker, the leader of the mutineers, persisted, the situation became most threatening, for a very
large number of ships were implicated.   Happily, the Admiralty
showed a firmness to which it had before been a stranger ; and
after a period of terrible anxiety, the country learnt that the
mutiny had collapsed.   Here, tyranny was not pleaded as an
exciting cause, though in certain ships, and in several minor
mutinies of about the same time, it was undoubtedly a factor.
But in the case of the terrible mutiny of the crew of the
Hermione, in September of the same year, tyranny, and tyranny
alone, was responsible.   The frigate, under Captain Hugh Pigot,
a brave man, yet a consummate bully, was cruising off the west
end of Puerto Rico, when, exasperated by the last of a series of
brutalities, the crew rose and murdered the captain.   Such an
act of vengeance can, of course, in no instance be justified, but
in this case it was rendered even more abominable by the
excesses with which it was accompanied.   Not only Pigot ; but
also nine other officers, including a midshipman, a mere boy,
were massacred ; and the villainy was completed by the handing
over of the frigate to the enemies of the country.   The nearly
simultaneous mutiny in the *Tremendous* at the Cape of Good

Hope was also professedly brought about by the cruelty of the captain, who, however, when, at his own request, tried for it, was honourably acquitted. The same thing was probably also at the bottom of the mutiny of the *Danaë*, in 1800, and of other similar outbreaks.

At the moment of the commencement of the war with France, in February, 1793, the active personal establishment of the Royal Navy was as follows :—Admiral of the Fleet, 1 ; admirals, 16 ; vice-admirals, 25 ; rear-admirals, 22 ; post-captains, 431 ; commanders, 163 ; lieutenants, 1,429, and masters, 297 ; and the total number of seamen and marines, including officers of all ranks, was 45,000. In October, 1801, at the time of the cessation of hostilities preparatory to the signature of the Treaty of Amiens, the establishment consisted of—Admiral of the Fleet, 1 ; admirals, 45 ; vice-admirals, 39 ; rear-admirals, 59 ; post-captains, 516 ; commanders, 391 ; lieutenants, 2,135 ; and masters, 517, making, with seamen and marines of all ranks, a total of 135,000. In the same period the supplies voted for

Strength of the Navy.

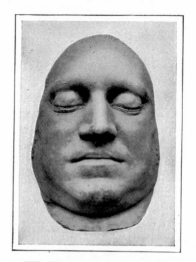

THE DEATH MASK OF RICHARD PARKER.

(*By permission of C. Davies Sherborn, Esq.*)

naval purposes grew in proportion. In 1793 the total was but £4,003,984 ; in 1801 it was £16,577,037. It will be seen that the increase in *matériel* was commensurate :—

Class.	1793. No.	1793. Tons.	1801. No	1801. Tons.
First rates	7	15,859	13	30,384
Second rates	24	46,892	21	41,719
Third rates	119	186,448	151	249,434
Fourth rates	25	27,004	28	31,390
Fifth rates	93	74,729	150	140,920
Sixth rates	41	22,923	44	24,062
Sloops	49	14,732	116	39,316
Bombs	2	609	14	4,687
Fireships	6	2,547	3	1,091
Total	366	391,743	540	563,003

These lists do not include all the small craft, yachts, transports, etc. Including everything, the Navy of 1793 embraced 411 vessels of 402,555 tons; and the Navy of 1801, 781 vessels of 650,976 tons. The increment was largely due to hostile vessels captured and purchased into the Navy. During the course of the war Great Britain took from her various foes 570 ships of war, of one sort or another, mounting 15,934 guns; and lost to her enemies only 59 ships of war, mounting but 1,272 guns; so that there remained in favour of this country a difference of 511 ships of war and 14,662 guns. In addition, she captured 903 foreign privateers, some of which also were bought into the Navy.

Tactics.   Improvement in naval tactics was a natural evolution, the result of experience. In the seventeenth century, and the beginning of the eighteenth, a sea battle was generally fought as if by tacit agreement between the two commanders-in-chief, on set principles, the central and ruling idea ever present to the mind of each admiral being that he must, with his fleet in column of line ahead, place himself as nearly as possible on a course parallel with that of his opponent, and so engage, ship to ship and broadside to broadside. He was taught, as well by service traditions as by the printed regulations, that he must at all hazards keep his fleet in its columnar formation, and not suffer it to quit that formation upon any pretence whatsoever. Yet, from time to time, bold spirits attempted innovations, even at the risk of their professional position. What may be called the personal, as distinct from the official, method of conducting an action received several illustrations—to which, perhaps, sufficient attention has not been paid by naval writers—during the Dutch wars of the Commonwealth and the reign of Charles II.; and admirals became gradually less and less hidebound by written rules, until progress was temporarily checked by the finding of the court-martial in the case of Mathews, after the unfortunate battle of 1744 (p. 277). Mathews had ventured to quit the line; but as some of his captains, with the fear of the regulations before their eyes, if not, indeed, from less worthy motives, had not followed him, failure had resulted, and Mathews was broken. Deterred by the fate of Mathews, Byng went to the other extreme, and was punished still more severely for the fiasco of 1756. But these trials, though so lamentable, and, it may be, so unjust in their results, had the effect of clearing the air. Hawke had been with Mathews, and had been the one captain who had properly backed him up. The trial

ADMIRAL LORD HAWKE, BY FRANCIS COTES, R.A.
(By permission of the Right Hon. Lord Hawke.)

did not affect the strong character of Hawke as it had affected the weaker character of Byng. It did not render Hawke timorous about incurring responsibility. Nor did it daunt Rodney, who, though he had not fought in the battle off Toulon, had been one of Mathews's *protégés*. These officers, and especially the former, seriously studied naval tactics, not as if the beginning and ending of them were contained in the Fighting Instructions, but as if tactics were still an infant science. Independently they came to the conclusion that there might be better systems of attack than those contained in the Instructions ; and, independently, they decided that, when themselves leading a fleet, they must pay more attention to conditions of time, position, and opportunity than to any formal or traditional directions. Each carried out this decision. Hawke, at Quiberon Bay, flung convention to the winds, and won a startling victory. Whether the breaking of the enemy's line, at the battle of the Saintes, was the deliberate work of Rodney is exceedingly doubtful; but Rodney did some unconventional work on other occasions, and, in the battle of the Saintes, the breaking of the line by Rodney's fleet undoubtedly set, as it were, the final seal of success upon the previously still contested theory that a commander-in-chief must command rather by means of his personal ability and initiative than by any rule of thumb. From that time the ancient methods of fighting were almost neglected. Byng, and even Mathews, would have stood aghast at the spectacle afforded at the Nile, Copenhagen, or Trafalgar. The progress, nay, the revolution, effected in half a century was due mainly to the force of character and self-reliance of a few of the men to whom England was so fortunate as to entrust her naval destinies at the most trying periods of her later career ; but it was due also, in some measure, to work done, not at sea but on shore, and not only in England, but also on the Continent. The treatises of Paul Hoste, of Bigot de Merogues, and of Clerk of Eldin, were assuredly not without influence upon the development of practical naval tactics, and so upon the triumphs of the British flag.

The course of the War of 1793–1802 cannot be followed in detail here. It only needs saying that, as Mahan points out, quoting Henri Martin, " The Montagnards and the Jacobins were resolved, like the Girondists, to propagate afar, by arms, the principles of the Revolution, and hoped by hurling defiance at all kings to put France in the impossibility of recoiling or stopping herself." When the French people had fairly launched themselves upon this mad policy, they could not be checked save by armed physical opposition. The desired result "had been effected and maintained chiefly by the Sea Power of Great Britain, the prime agent and moving spirit—directly through her Navy, indirectly through the subsidies drawn from her commerce; and the latter had nearly doubled while carrying on this arduous and extensive war. In 1801 the aggressive tendencies of the French nation, as a whole, were exhausted. So far as they still survived, they were now embodied in and dependent upon a single man, in which shape they were at once more distinctly to be recognised and more odious. They were also less dangerous; because the power of one man, however eminent for genius, is far less for good or evil than the impulse of a great people."

By the side of Cook's achievements all subsequent ventures of English explorers between 1780 and 1815 are insignificant. The chief of these was associated with a romantic history. In December, 1787, one of Cook's old companions, Lieutenant William Bligh, was sent out to introduce the bread-fruit tree from Tahiti into the West Indies. Before doubling the Horn violent westerly gales led him to turn, cross the South Atlantic, and make Tahiti from the west. He loaded his ship with bread-fruit trees and sailed again on the 4th of April, 1789. But on the 27th the whole crew mutinied (p. 543), except eighteen men; these, with the captain, were cast adrift in the launch with 150 pounds of bread, 28 gallons of water, a little rum, wine and pork, some cocoanuts, four cutlasses, a quadrant and compass. "He'll find his way home," shouted some of the mutineers, "if you give him pencil and paper; he'll have a vessel built in a month." Bligh made his way in this open boat, 23 feet long, without a chart, a distance of 3,618 miles, from Tahiti to Timor, discovering a part of the New Hebrides on the way that had not been noticed either by Cook or Bougainville. The voyage entailed terrible sufferings, but the men were saved by being able to stop on the thirtieth day on the north coast of New Holland. On the forty-first day, 14th June, 1789, they reached the Dutch settlements. Bligh returned to England in a schooner from Timor, March 14th, 1790, and his narrative of the voyage excited immense interest and some indignation. After a time the frigate *Pandora* was sent out to Tahiti to punish the mutineers. But only ten were found;[1] the rest had escaped to Pitcairn's Island, lately

CHARLES RAYMOND BEAZLEY.

Exploration: The "Bounty."

---

[1] These were brought home, and three of them were executed in England.

discovered by Carteret, with their Tahitian wives and some
other islanders (1790). Here they remained unknown, except
for an American visit in 1808, till in 1814 an English frigate
touched at the island, and found John Adams, the originator
of the Pitcairn settlement, alone surviving from the crew, but

RELICS OF THE *BOUNTY* MUTINY.
(Royal United Service Institution Museum, Whitehall.)

with a colony of forty-seven people under his rule, of mixed
English and Tahitian blood.

An Arctic Voyage.   The greater part of English exploration in this period was
undertaken in the southern quarters of the globe. There was
comparatively little effort to extend our discoveries in the
northern parts of Asia or America. A further attempt was,
indeed, made at Arctic exploration (p. 29) by "the Spitzbergen
route" in 1773; but the two ships, *Racehorse* and *Carcass*,
despatched on this mission, under command of Captain
Phipps (p. 283), found it impossible to penetrate the Polar

pack to the north of the Spitzbergen group, and returned to
England after an absence of three months. But the British
conquest of Canada, like that of Central India, prepared the
way for the minute survey of vast continental tracts but vaguely
known before.

At the end of the
eighteenth century a
fresh start was made,
and with this three
great names are asso-
ciated. James Bruce,
by his travels in
Algeria, Nubia, and
Abyssinia (1765–72),
and his discovery of
the source of the Blue
Nile at Geesh (1770),
was the pioneer of latter
day exploration in the
interior of the dark
continent. Mungo
Park, again, by his two
journeys in Western
Africa (1795-97 and
1805-6), and his ex-
ploration of much of

MUNGO PARK.
(From a drawing by H. Edridge.)

the course of the Upper Niger, started English enterprise **Africa and**
upon a line of discovery which, since the days of Andrew **Australia.**
Battell, in the reign of Elizabeth, had been too much neglected
by our countrymen. Once more Matthew Flinders, a surveyor
of the first quality, followed up Cook's work on the Australian
coasts, in 1795–1800 and in 1801–3, with such effect that his
plans still form the basis of the Admiralty charts for a great
deal of the northern, eastern, and southern coasts of the great
island, and for nearly the whole shore-line of its little atten-
dant "jewel," Van Diemen's Land.

Among these discoverers Park gave not only his time
and energy, but his life for the cause that claimed him.
To increase our knowledge of the highly dangerous, unhealthy, and important region to be opened up he had first

233

journeyed from Pisania on the Gambia to Sego on the Niger, descending the river to Silla, and returning to the coast by a more southerly route through the Mandingo country; but on his second journey he fell a victim to hostile natives near Boussa, and thus fulfilled his promise to Lord Camden that

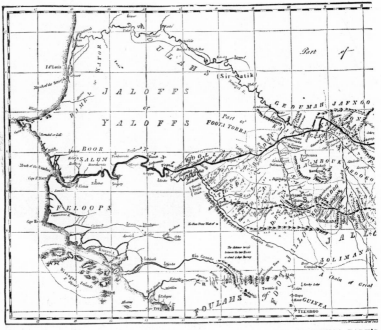

MAP OF MUNGO PARK'S
(From his "Travels in the In-

if he could not follow the course of the mighty stream he was exploring to the sea, he would "at least die on the Niger."

CHARLES
RAYMOND
BEAZLEY.
The Estab
lished
Church,
1715–1815.

THE history of the Church of England in the eighteenth century is proverbially dull. As a church, it never seemed more ashamed of itself; as an estate of the realm, it ceased to hold its representative assembly: as a religious force it saw itself distanced by Nonconforming agencies; as an establishment, it became steadily more inadequate.

It could not be denied that during the century that followed the Restoration the Church of England had the main direction of English religion, yet, in 1751, the greatest of her clergy, Bishop Butler of Durham, bemoaned a " general decay of religion in the nation which is now observed by

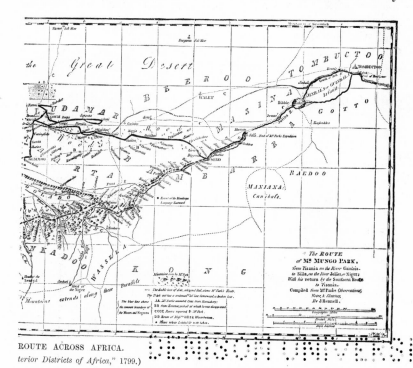

ROUTE ACROSS AFRICA.
terior Districts of Africa," 1799.)

every one." The influence of Christianity, he declares, is more and more "wearing out of the minds of men." Dis- **Growth of** sent, which, in 1700, did not number more than one-twentieth **Dissent.** of the English people, was supposed, by 1800, to include fully one-fifth, and the churchmanship of the remaining four-fifths was almost less than nominal. For religious movement and interest we must go, as everyone knows, to agencies repre- sented by the Wesleyans or the Evangelicals, which issued in separation from the Church, or at the least, in a practical rejection of her distinctive teaching.

First of all the political or external history of the Church

**Church
and State.**

in the eighteenth century must be taken, apart from the internal or social, or from that highly developed branch of modern theology, the controversial.   Never before or since, perhaps, has the separation been more clearly defined between the outward and the inward life of the Church of England, between its Whiggery in high places and its intense Toryism in the mass, between the dignity and wealth of its prelates and the degradation of its lower clergy.

**The
Jacobite
Clergy.**

On the accession of the Hanoverian dynasty a number of clergy had declined the oaths, and so separated themselves from the Establishment (IV., pp. 699, 731).   A much larger number, headed by Atterbury, Bishop of Rochester, accepted the new Government, but only as a parliamentary settlement, which they might induce Parliament itself to abrogate.   These "Jacobite" clergy continued to offer, till 1722, an opposition which called itself constitutional, and seemed at any rate within the bounds of Tory churchmanship.   Thus they opposed the "Act for strengthening the Protestant interest," of December, 1718, which proposed the repeal of the Act against Occasional Conformity, of the Schism Act, and of some parts of the Test and Corporation Acts ; and they resisted with still greater energy the Quakers' Affirmation Bill, brought into the Lords in January, 1722, and allowing an indulgence, as Atterbury outrageously said, "to a set of people who were hardly Christians."   But, in 1722, the "Jacobite" leader fell under the shadow of treason.   Since August, 1717, he had been in constant correspondence with the exiled family ; this was suspected by, if not thoroughly known to, Walpole ; and, as Atterbury would not be bribed with a pension of £5,000 a year and the reversion of Winchester, he was arrested August 22nd, 1722, on a charge of three treasonable letters to the Earl of Mar, James's Secretary of State.   The Government proceeded against him in Parliament by a Bill of Pains and Penalties ; he was condemned to be deprived of his two benefices, the See of Rochester and the Deanery of Westminster, and to be banished for life.[1]   From this time Jacobitism of the clerical type died out rapidly, and when the Young Pretender entered England in 1745 he got scarcely

---

[1] He died in Paris, still in the communion of the English Church, in March, 1732.

any of the encouragement he looked for from the Church. Meantime, after the silencing of Convocation in 1717 as the result of the "Bangorian" Controversy, the selection of men for the government of the clergy under the State was carefully regulated by the political sovereign, as it had been regulated under the Tudors.

FRANCIS ATTERBURY, D.D., BISHOP OF ROCHESTER.
(*By permission of the Dean and Governing Body, Christ Church, Oxford.*)

Convocation had been prorogued in the summer of 1717, not to meet again till 1852, because it had dared to censure the theology of a friend of the Government. Bishop Hoadly of Bangor, in his "Preservative against the Principles of the Nonjurors," and in his sermon, preached before King George I., March 17th, 1717, had denied the existence of any visible Church; the Lower House of Convocation on May 10th of the same year unanimously condemned his utterances as subversive of all government in the Church; but before the bishops could declare themselves, the clerical Parliament was

Convocation Closed.

prorogued, and kept in a state of suspended animation for 135 years. All inconvenient independence being thus taken

The Whigs and the Church. away from the spiritualty, the Whig administration was able to keep a sufficient hold over the Church by making Whiggery a *sine quâ non* for high church office. Thus, in 1737, on the death of Archbishop Wake, Gibson of London, who had for years been the ecclesiastical adviser of Walpole, and was admittedly the most learned and statesmanlike of the prelates, but who had opposed the Ministers' Quaker Relief Bill and procured its rejection by the Lords, was passed over for Potter of Oxford. Ten years later Herring of York succeeded Potter in the primacy, simply on the strength of unblemished loyalty to political and religious Whiggism; and the same were the credentials of Gibson's successor, Sherlock of Salisbury, in the See of London, and of most of the bishops appointed during the eighteenth century.

Relief to Nonconformists. It might have been expected from this long continuance of liberalising prelates that something would have been done to modify the Prayer Book and reconcile the Dissenters. But the great principle of the English Government in dealing with Church matters, from Walpole to Wellington, was to let well alone, provided the Church itself showed no unpleasant signs of activity, and to this, for instance, was due the defeat of the Anti-Subscription movement. To the same instinct, aided by the vigorous opposition of the prelates, was owing the loss of the Dissenters' Relief Bill, brought before Parliament in 1773. However, in 1778, the Roman Catholics were relieved from some of the most severe of the provisions of the penal laws, and, in 1779, the Dissenters' Relief Bill was re-introduced and carried. But the toleration shown to " Papists " led immediately to the Gordon Riots of 1780; and the attempts, in 1787, 1789 and 1790, to procure the repeal of the Test and Corporation Acts were not successful. The outbreak of the French Revolution delayed any further progress in this direction for nearly forty years (p. 504), except as regards the Roman Catholics; who, suffering as they now did in France, gained a deal of sympathy in England, and were again relieved in 1791, being exempted from the penal statutes still unrepealed, on condition of taking an oath of allegiance (p. 501).

But, significantly enough, the main feature of Church history

in the eighteenth century is controversy. The prominent and *Theo-*
successful churchman of this age is the keen pamphleteer, and *logical*
it seemed more important to argue about the most abstract *Polemics.*
theological and metaphysical subtleties than to attend to any

BENJAMIN HOADLY, BISHOP OF BANGOR, BY WILLIAM HOGARTH.
(*St. Catharine's College, Cambridge.*)

part of the practical life of the Church. The result of this
polemical mania was in the highest degree disastrous to religion,
which now seemed to be losing its force and attraction just
in proportion to its disputatiousness.

The first of these controversies was the Bangorian, which *The*
has been already noticed as the direct cause of the suspension *Bangorian*
of Convocation. But there was another interest about this: *Contro-*
for it brought into notice one of the most gifted religious writers *versy.*
who have ever found a home in the Church of England—

William Law, the author of the " Serious Call," whose " Letters to the Bishop of Bangor " (Hoadly) were, perhaps, the ablest essays of the century in religious controversy.

A "Broad" School.

The Latitudinarian attack did not cease with the end of Hoadly's original campaign, but it gradually divided itself into two branches ; one party advised liberal theologians to disregard the difficulties of subscription to Church doctrines, and to stay in and " leaven the mass " ; the other urged the removal of the doctrinal tests.   Dr. Samuel Clarke, the moralist (IV., p. 777) rector of St. James's, Westminster, is often considered as the founder of the former school, so unconsciously satirised by an Eastern prince, who learnt from it to escape the difficulties of his own religion.   (" I take them like my Christian friends take theirs.   I say I believe in Buddha, but I don't.")   Clarke's " Reformed Prayer Book and Collection of Psalms and Hymns," published in 1718, practically furnished the Arian churchmen with a suitable liturgy for use in a Trinitarian Church ; and the editor explained away any scruples that might be felt by the assurance that " every person may reasonably agree to forms imposed by Protestant communities whenever he can, in any sense at all, reconcile them with Scripture."   Naturally, this position was hard pressed both from the side of the Dissenters and from that of the orthodox churchmen, by the author of the " Address to the Conforming Clergy " as well as by Daniel Waterland.   The latter's " Case of Arian Subscription Considered " (1721) opened a wordy warfare, which, at last, led to most of the leaders of the " complaisant Arians " resigning their preferments, and joining in the second great attempt of the Broad School in this age, the Anti-Subscription movement.   One of the earliest steps in this direction, after the accession of the House of Hanover, was a volume of essays published in 1749 under the title of " Free and Candid Disquisitions Relating to the Church of England," and attacks on these were vigorously met by one who now became the leader of the Anti-Subscription party, though he had no hand in the Disquisitions—Francis Blackburne, Archdeacon of Cleveland.   It seems remarkable that no permanent result followed these efforts, for the views of their promoters were in favour in the highest quarters. It was Archbishop Hutton of York who presented Blackburne

RELIGIOUS AND POLITICAL DISSENTERS IN 1790.

(From a contemporary satirical print.)

to his Archdeaconry; and Herring, who was translated from the northern to the southern primacy in 1747, was warm in his approval of such works as Clarke's "Prayer Book" and Hoadly's "Plain Account of the Lord's Supper" (1733). In 1750 Bishop Clayton of Clogher, in his "Essay on Spirit," pressed for the omission of the Athanasian Creed and a general review of the Prayer Book, and the whole principle of subscription to formularies was unsparingly attacked by Blackburne in his Letter to the Archbishop of Canterbury (1754) as the cause of the bad morality of the nation and the inefficiency of the clergy. In his main work, the "Confessional," published in 1766, Blackburne follows up the same line, denies that any general assent to Church doctrine as a whole can be accepted as honest, and proceeds to denounce all confessions of faith as terms of qualification for office.

On the accession of Archbishop Cornwallis, in 1768, the Anti-Subscriptionists presented "Proposals for Relief in the Matter of Subscription" (1771) and brought these before the House of Commons, February 6th, 1772. Scarcely more than 200 persons had signed it, but such important people as Bishop Law, Dr. Paley, and Dr. Watson were in sympathy with its principle, though too cautious to commit themselves. The Commons rejected the proposals (or rather the motion to consider them) by 217 against 71, and Burke contemptuously described the petitioners as men who "want to receive the emoluments appropriated for teaching one set of doctrines while they are teaching another."

A second memorial to the same effect presented to Archbishop Cornwallis in 1772 likewise failed to produce any effect, and, as the Evangelical and Methodist revival was now beginning to be very deeply felt, the interest in the Anti-Subscription movement slackened, for the Revivalists regarded this whole development as an attack upon the essential Christian beliefs under the guise of Liberality.

The Deists.

The Deistical controversy proper belongs more, perhaps, to the eighteenth century philosophy than to religion. But, in a great measure, it was an attack upon the formal creed of the Church, and as such we must notice Anthony Collins's "Discourse on the Grounds of the Christian Religion" (1724), Woolston's "Discourses on the Miracles of Christ" (1727) (answered by Sherlock's "Trial of the Witnesses of the Resurrection"), and Tindal's "Christianity as Old as the Creation," devoted to proving that a religion of nature is all that man requires (IV., p. 777).

It was especially to answer these criticisms that Joseph Butler, while Rector of Stanhope, composed his "Analogy of Religion," published in 1736, and that Berkeley wrote his "Dialogues of Alciphron, or the Minute Philosopher" (p. 58). But with Hume (p. 322) the ground of the controversy passed beyond Deism to more fundamental scepticism. His tenth Essay (on Miracles) was met at the time by John Leland, in his "View of Deistical Writers," issued in the very year that saw the publication of Lord Bolingbroke's posthumous works (1754), which rejected "every opinion that would embarrass a Sceptic arguing with a Christian." Of the philosophical side of this controversy, now concerned with those first principles which underlie the fundamental disposition of the human mind for or against supernatural beliefs, some account will be found elsewhere (pp. 322, 560).

The "Hutchinsonians," Jones of Nayland (the original founder of the "British Critic"), and George Horne, Bishop of Norwich, with their sympathisers, were perhaps the most important defenders of religious principle in this philosophical struggle, as Hume had been the most prominent, Gibbon the most subtle, Priestley[1] (p. 326) the most moderate, and Tom Paine the most outrageous among the Rationalistic champions.

The social history of the Church during this time is especially interesting from the abundant material that remains to prove the almost incredible subservience and degradation of many of the lower clergy at this time. But it can only be summarised here. *(margin: Condition of the Clergy.)*

Among the usages that pressed most heavily upon the clergy was their dependence on lay patrons as enforced by "bonds of resignation," whose true meaning was declared by Archbishop Secker to be only to "enslave the incumbent to the will and pleasure of his patron."[2] But whatever the grievances of incumbents, those of the assistant clergy were

---

[1] In his "History of the Corruption of Christianity" (1782) and "History of the Early Opinions Concerning Jesus Christ" (1786).

[2] These bonds, however, were disallowed by the House of Lords in 1782.

much worse. Before the French Revolution their income was
settled by the bishops at some figure which could not exceed
£50. The wealthy curate only began with the Act 36th of
George III., which fixed the maximum at £75, and legislation
for the Church at this time meant, as Sydney Smith declared,

ECCLESIASTICAL PROMOTION.
(From a satirical print.)

Pluralities. legislation for the bishops. The pluralities and non-residence
of the higher clergy were as great a scandal as the pauperising
and social degradation of the lower. While a deanery or
canonry was regularly annexed to certain sees, and in other
cases added to reward a new bishop for his self-denial in
resigning a comfortable living (as was the case even in the
distinguished instances of Atterbury, Butler, and Henry Phil-
potts), the country parsons were, as a rule, scarcely above the

social state pictured by Fielding for his Parson Adams, and by
Goldsmith for his Vicar of Wakefield. The ordinary wife for
the poorer country parson was a servant or an innkeeper's
daughter. Still more servile was the state of the domestic
chaplains. For their position was literally that of a servant,
and not of the head servant either, in power or perquisites
(IV., pp. 492, 650, 739), where, for instance, the butler had a very
solid advantage. Local customs often survived into the last
century to prove this singular condition of things. In Cum-
berland it was long the fashion for the parish priest to take
his knife and fork and go the round of the farmers of
his district, boarding with each for a week as part of his
stipend.

Most luckless of all were the half-starved clergy who could
get no appointment; and Oldham's bitter satire complains
that there were plenty of these in the earlier part of the
century :—

> "You'll hardly meet
> More porters now than parsons in the street
> And half the number of the sacred herd
> Is fain to stroll and wander unpreferred."

The lowest point of the religious life of the century was
reached in the later years of Walpole's ministry. From this
time began the great revival of the Wesleys, of Whitefield,
and of the Methodists and the Evangelicals.

The Wesleyan movement has been dealt with elsewhere
(p. 317). Its chief effect upon the Church of England was
twofold—a shock and a revival, the loss of many of her most
earnest people, the gain of the new life given to her by the
Evangelicals of the later part of the century, whose leaders—
Wilberforce, Simeon, Toplady, Venn, Newton, Cowper and the
Milners—were rather followers of Whitefield and the Calvinistic
Methodists than of Wesley himself. It was they, as has been
said, who began to make the fox-hunting parson and the
absentee rector at last impossible. "In the nation at large"
they brought about "a new moral enthusiasm which, rigid
and pedantic as it often seemed, was healthy in its social
tone, and whose power was seen" in the lessening of the
"profligacy which had disgraced the upper classes, and the
foulness which had infested literature, ever since the Restora-

*Wesleyans
and Evan-
gelicals.*

tion." A yet nobler result of the same movement was the revival of the spirit of mercy and kindness, and the new attempts "to remedy the ignorance, the physical suffering, and the social degradation" of the outcast and the poor. "The Sunday schools established by Raikes of Gloucester at the close of the century were the beginnings of popular education. By writings and by her own personal example, Hannah More drew the sympathy of England to the poverty and crime of the agricultural labourer. A passionate impulse of human sympathy with the wronged and afflicted" was the special glory of religion at the end of the eighteenth century, and it has a right to claim the honour of training and inspiring those uncanonized yet true saints—Wilberforce, Clarkson, and John Howard.

ROBERT RAIKES.
(*After Drummond.*)

Lastly, in the persons of such men as Bishop Wilson, of Sodor and Man; Bishop Jebb, of Limerick; and Alexander Knox, the High Church movement of the nineteenth century had its forerunners, a link between the fervent but irregular Sacramentalism of John Wesley and the Oxford Tractarians of 1833–45.

Early Church Schools.

Similarly, in the foundation of the National Society for the Education of the Poor in 1811 we have the first definite step towards the present system of Church schools. But at the close of this period (1815) the Church as an institution was scarcely ever upheld on higher ground than that of Bishop Porteous in his last charge—"An ancient and venerable *establishment*, constructed by some of the wisest, most pious, and most eminent men of any period." The more active and aggressive thought among the Churchmen of this time now usually took the form of a Calvinism so rigid and

so morbid, so complacent and often so bitter as to show a Calvinism.
curious contrast to the practical excellence of life which it
largely succeeded in producing. Thus Simeon, towards the end
of his life, declared himself so corrupt that he could only wonder
at being still kept out of hell. Henry Venn congratulates his
son on the opposition of the Huntingtonians, for " their hatred

CHARLES SIMEON, 1808.
(King's College, Cambridge.)

is much to be preferred to their praise." Toplady, in 1772,
addresses his spiritual father, a man twice his age, with all
the violence of a "bold young man," as the victim of his
attack coolly described him.   "Time, sir," he writes to John
Wesley, "has already whitened your locks, and the hour must
shortly come which will transmit you to the tribunal of that
God on whose sovereignty the greater part of your life has
been one continued assault." Still more scurrilous were his
rhymes on the supposed intention of Wesley to raise a persecution against the Calvinists. This plot, as fabulous as the
" Popish " of Charles II.'s day, is told in the form of a fable :—

" There's a fox who resideth hard by,
  The most perfect and holy and sly
That ever turned coat, or did pilfer or lie.

" As this reverend Reynard one day
  Sat thinking what game best to play,
Satan came by, a brief visit to pay.

" ' Oh, your servant, my friend,' quoth the priest;
  ' Though you carry the mark of the beast,
I never shook paws with a welcomer guest.'

" ' Many thanks, holy man,' cried the fiend;
  ' It's because you're my very good friend
That I came by, with you a few minutes to spend.' "

By the side of these Evangelical controversies, the old
technical High Church disputes lost their interest, and for a
time it even appeared probable that the Church in the colonies
would be altogether left to shift without " Bishoply government,"
as useless and possibly dangerous. The Nonjurors tried to revive
the use of King Edward VI.'s First Prayer Book, but the appeal
to " Catholic antiquity " fell unheeded ; the " regular " Nonjurors
became extinct[1] in 1779, and the last of the " irregular bishops "
died in Ireland in 1805.

The Church in America. On the other hand, through the consecration of Samuel
Seabury by the Scotch Episcopate as Bishop of Connecticut
on November 14th, 1784, the American Church was organic-
ally linked with the mother Church of England, as some of
the Latitudinarians had feared, and as few Churchmen at the
time thought necessary. It seems to have been looked on as
a piece of pedantic ecclesiasticism by most, but it perhaps was
the first clear sign of the modern reaction within the Church
from apology to confidence, from a defence of its institutions
as not absolutely bad to a proclaiming of their superiority
over all " independent " forms of Christianity.

THOMAS WHIT-TAKER. Philo-sophy and Science. HUME's sceptical conclusions were not long in stirring up
reaction against the Cartesian and Lockian principles that
had led to them. The chief exponent of this reaction was
Thomas Reid (1710–96), the founder of what is known as the

[1] After a lively flirtation with the Russian Church in 1720–22, like that of
Archbishop Wake with the Gallicans in 1618.

Scottish school of philosophy. Reid's reply to Hume, the "Inquiry into the Human Mind on the Principles of Common Sense," appeared in 1764; his "Essays on the Intellectual Powers of Man," in 1785; "Essays on the Active Powers of Man," 1788. By the French "spiritualist" school of Cousin and Jouffroy, Reid's appeal to "common sense" was taken up as the

The Scottish School: Reid.

Photo: Walker & Cockerell.

REV. WILLIAM PALEY, D.D., BY (OR AFTER) GEORGE ROMNEY.
(*National Portrait Gallery.*)

watchword of their own reaction against the development in France of Locke's principles. Credit is now usually allowed to Reid for seeing the true historical genesis of Berkeley's idealism and of Hume's scepticism. His own philosophical doctrine has been called by disciples "natural realism." He holds that in perception we have direct knowledge of objects. Sensations serve only as signs to perception. The mind originally possesses certain judgments, of which we become conscious by intuition. It is these that Reid calls "principles of common sense." Their existence is to be established by internal observation; hence the

importance of psychology in Reid's view. On the study of
psychology, it is admitted by some who do not think very highly
of his general philosophy, Reid had a favourable influence.

Paley's Ethics. Among the ethical writers of the period, William Paley
(1743–1805), in his "Principles of Moral and Political
Philosophy" (1785), gave the clearest possible expression to
the doctrine known as "theological utilitarianism." For this
doctrine, the end of the individual man is his own happiness.
The means of attaining happiness is to obey the command of
God, reward being attached to obedience, punishment to disobedience. To know by the light of reason whether an action
is in accordance with the will of God, we have to find out
whether it is conducive to general happiness—for this is what
man is commanded to promote. In his "Natural Theology, or
Evidence of the Existence and Attributes of the Deity Collected
from the Appearances of Nature" (1802), Paley sets forth what
is known as the design-argument for theism, taking his stand
especially upon human anatomy.

Bentham's Ethics. The ethical doctrine of Jeremy Bentham (1748–1832) was
utilitarianism without theology. Bentham's greatness was most
of all in the theory of legislation. So far as the political ideas
are concerned within which his legislative theory is circum-
scribed, he may be said to descend from Hobbes and Hume.
About his relation to Hume there is no doubt, for he himself
refers to Hume's "Treatise" as supplying the refutation of the
theory that political society took its origin from an original
contract. And this rejection of the original contract is combined in Bentham with an assertion, essentially identical with
that of Hobbes, that the supreme power in the State, wherever
it may be placed, is absolute. These two positions are at the
ground of Bentham's "Fragment on Government" (1776), which
is an attack on Blackstone's view of the English Constitution as
consisting in an arrangement of checks and balances. The constitutional doctrine was worked out by Blackstone in relation to
a kind of contract theory; and it was, of course, likewise, a
continuation of those doctrines of limited monarchy which
Hobbes had attacked when they were put forth by the lawyers
of his time. Having thus cleared away the old constructions
and prepared the foundation, Bentham goes to work with
assumptions of his own. The legislator need no longer trouble

himself about fictitious "rights" of rulers and ruled against
each other, but must take for his end "the greatest happiness
of the greatest number," and make such laws, both criminal and
civil, as will best promote this end. His general formula for this
end Bentham adopted from Priestley. Happiness he proceeds

JEREMY BENTHAM, AGED THIRTEEN, BY THOMAS FRYE.
(National Portrait Gallery.)

to analyse into pleasures and absence of pains, regarding it as a
kind of algebraical sum in which pleasures count as positive and
pains as negative. From his conception of the end thus analysed
he begins to work out practical rules in his " Introduction to the
Principles of Morals and Legislation " (printed 1780, published
1789). Bentham's later writings, which are very extensive, were
for the most part put into shape not by himself but by disciples,
who took over from him the masses of manuscript he had a way
of accumulating on each particular subject. The expositions of

Dumont were of special service in diffusing Bentham's ideas on the Continent.

Bentham and Politics.

To Bentham's political influence, which dates from the early years of the present century, full justice has probably never yet been done. Exercised especially through James Mill and the other "philosophical Radicals," such as Grote and Molesworth, it was equally present, though in a more qualified form, in Whigs like Macaulay and Sydney Smith. The members of Bentham's school derived their political theory in part directly from Hobbes, but new application was given to it in accordance with Bentham's own doctrine. Bentham's later political, as distinguished from legislative, deduction from his general positions was to affirm "representative democracy" as the only form of government which in modern times can be trusted to promote the interests of the whole. The government of one or of a few will always try to promote its own interests at the expense of the community; and all mixed forms of government are necessarily unstable. "Balance of power" within a single State, if it means anything, means that the constitution has been made unworkable. Utilitarianism, of course, remains here the principle, and it is worthy of note that, both early and late, Bentham vehemently rejected the doctrine of "natural rights."

Science, Physics, and Chemistry. Cavendish.

At the end of the section on science in the last chapter Cavendish's theory of electricity was referred to (p. 332). Henry Cavendish (1731–1810) is our greatest name among the chemists and physicists of this period. Along with Black, he is one of the founders of chemistry as a quantitative science. In all the lines of investigation to which he paid attention, the exactitude of his work gave it special value during the formative period of the newer physical studies.

Cavendish's theory of electricity was thought out in relation to the newly discovered phenomena of induction. He had communicated it to the Royal Society before the publication by Æpinus of his "Tentamen Theoriæ Electricitatis et Magnetismi" (1759), but had delayed its publication. Having become aware of Æpinus's similar theory, he at length published his own in 1771, finding that, although he had been anticipated, he had carried the theory further than Æpinus. Both Æpinus and Cavendish proceed on the supposition of a single fluid with mutually repellent particles. Cavendish inclines to the true supposition as regards electrical attraction and repulsion—that they are forces varying inversely as the square of the distance.

By an application of electricity to chemical experiment, Cavendish proved water to be a compound. This discovery was published in the "Philosophical Transactions" of 1784–5 Oxygen and hydrogen ("dephlogisticated air" and "inflammable air" as they were then called) were mixed in various proportions and exploded in a close vessel by means of the electric spark. It was found that when they were mixed in a certain proportion the product of the explosion was pure water, and that water was also formed when a mixture of hydrogen and common air was exploded. In this last case the bulk of the air was diminished by about one-fifth, which corresponds to the amount of oxygen contained in the atmosphere. Thus water and atmospheric air were conclusively proved not to be simple bodies. In the same series of papers ("Experiments on Air") in the "Philosophical Transactions," the composition of nitric acid was established. This discovery had been prepared for by experiments of Priestley, in which he showed that the condition of common air is altered by the transmission of electric sparks.

Decomposition of Water.

Cavendish, like Priestley, though his discoveries had so important a part in overthrowing the theory of phlogiston, remained an adherent of that theory. He was, however, not quite so uncompromising an adherent as Priestley. And, though retaining phlogiston, he denied to heat the character of a substance, regarding Bacon's opinion "that heat consists in the internal motion of the particles of bodies" as "much the most probable."

In this period geology passes from the stage of description and collection to the beginnings of systematic theory. Geological specimens, particularly organic fossils, had long since excited curiosity and suggested speculations about past states of the earth during which there had been a different distribution of land and sea. Among the early modern speculations, those of the Italians were the most noteworthy. In 1695 William Woodward had founded his geological museum. This he bequeathed to the University of Cambridge, at the same time founding and endowing a professorship of geology. The construction of geological maps was proposed to the Royal Society by Dr. Lister,

Geology.

in 1683, and an example of a chart of the kind was published by Dr. Christopher Packe in 1743; but the idea was only that each portion of a country should be distinguished according to its soil or its predominant mineral. So far there was no thought of division into strata. The initiation of scientific geology in England was reserved for James Hutton and William Smith.

James Hutton. James Hutton (1726–97) was born at Edinburgh, and, like so many who contributed to the advancement of science at that

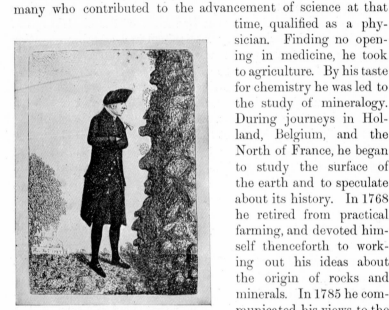

DR. JAMES HUTTON.
(*A caricature of 1787 by Kay.*)

time, qualified as a physician. Finding no opening in medicine, he took to agriculture. By his taste for chemistry he was led to the study of mineralogy. During journeys in Holland, Belgium, and the North of France, he began to study the surface of the earth and to speculate about its history. In 1768 he retired from practical farming, and devoted himself thenceforth to working out his ideas about the origin of rocks and minerals. In 1785 he communicated his views to the newly established Royal Society of Edinburgh, in a paper entitled " Theory of the Earth, or an Investigation of the Laws Observable in the Composition, Dissolution, and Restoration of Land upon the Globe." The " Theory of the Earth " was republished in an extended form in 1795. To the diffusion of Hutton's ideas his friend John Playfair, Professor of Mathematics at Edinburgh, contributed much by his " Illustrations of the Huttonian Theory of the Earth " (1802). Playfair had the gift of luminous exposition, in which Hutton was somewhat wanting.

The Uniformitarian Theory. From Hutton's ideas the geological doctrine known as uniformitarianism took its origin. According to this doctrine, the present state of the earth, and in particular the distribution of its rocks, is to be explained entirely by causes in kind and degree resembling those that are in action to-day. The present rocks, in Hutton's view, have been formed out of the waste of older rocks. The materials were laid down beneath the sea, consolidated under gréat pressure, and afterwards disrupted and upheaved by the expansive force of subterraneous heat. Molten rock was injected into the rents of the dislocated strata. The upheaved land, exposed to the atmosphere, is subject to decay, and the process of decay will not cease till the whole is again laid down on the sea floor, whence the consolidated sediment will be raised into new land by new upheavals. Geology is not cosmogony, but is concerned entirely with these alternate changes, beyond which it has evidence neither of a beginning nor of an end.

William Smith (1769–1839) was born at Churchill, in Oxford-shire, and became a mineral surveyor and civil engineer. From an early age his scientific curiosity had been drawn to the stratification of the earth; and in the course of his professional work he had opportunities of observing and comparing the strata of various districts. In his "Order of the Strata, and their Embedded Organic Remains, in the Neighbourhood of Bath" (1799), he at length put forward the scientific principle which had long been in his mind, and which his observations had gone to confirm. This principle was the identification of strata by the fossils they contain. Working by this principle, he was able to prove that there is a settled order of succession among the strata. After spending another period of several years in collecting and arranging data, he published his large "Geological Map of England and Wales, with part of Scotland," in 1815. Separate county geological maps were published later, constituting, when formed into a whole, the "Geological Atlas of England and Wales."

William Smith.

Though some previous geologists, both in England and on the Continent, had suggested views about fossils having some resemblance to those of Smith, his idea was developed quite independently; and he succeeded in carrying it further than anyone before him. At this stage of geological progress the way was prepared for Cuvier and others, who, from sufficient knowledge of comparative anatomy, were able to prove that there are fossil animals of different species from any that now

Palæont ology.

exist.   To make possible a science of palæontology, the work of many generations of naturalists and anatomists had been necessary.   Among those who contributed to this work may be mentioned John Hunter (1728–93, p. 574), the famous surgeon. Hunter had anatomised over five hundred different species of animals.   He had himself correct ideas about the nature of fossils, and recognised the importance of water as an agent in terrestrial changes.

Wider biological speculations now begin to appear.   Erasmus Darwin, in his "Zoonomia" (1794–96), put forth the opinion that species are evolved from one another, not separately created. On the causes of evolution he speculated in the spirit of his French successor Lamarck.   Thus he cannot be said to have anticipated the distinctive theory of his

ERASMUS DARWIN, M.D., F.R.S.
(*After the painting by J. Wright in* 1797.)

Evolutionism Begins. more famous grandson, by which, in our own time, the doctrine of evolution has been established to the satisfaction of all naturalists.   Instead of supposing transmutation of species to take place by the accumulation of "spontaneous" variations—that is, variations which are innate and of which the causes are not definitely assignable—he set out from the observation that the use of parts and organs causes them to develop, while disuse causes them to diminish or disappear; changes thus initiated, he went on to suppose, are transmitted to offspring, and, if the same external conditions continue, are gradually accumulated in succeeding generations, so that at length a form is arrived at which is so different from its remote ancestor as to constitute a new species.

THE period embraced by the years 1742 to 1802 was a momentous one for the science as well as for the art of medicine. With
the exception of John Huxham and William Heberden the
elder, there were no really great physicians in England in the
year 1742. Sir Hans Sloane, who had then recently retired
from the office of President of the Royal Society, was rather a
man of high scientific attainments than a pure physician, whilst
Cullen's reputation was gained wholly in Scotland.

D'ARCY
POWER.
Medicine
and Public
Health.

The surgeons were associated with the barbers as a City
Company, which had existed since the days of Henry VIII.
The only legitimate road to surgical practice in London and
within seven miles of the City lay through the portals of this
company. The Society of Apothecaries, another City company
which had developed in the reign of James I. as an offshoot
from the Grocers' Company, provided a subordinate order of
medical practitioners, but the Apothecaries' Society was itself
very much under the control of the College of Physicians, who
were apt to press their privileges with undue harshness. The
social status of the physicians at this time was good—that of the
surgeons was not yet defined. The condition of the apothecaries,
and of the members of the Scotch Colleges who were then
swarming into England, is revealed to us in Smollett's novels.
It was as low as it well could be.

A Surgical
Revolu-
tion.

Medicine consisted of empirical knowledge based upon an
incorrect pathology. Surgery of the rudest description had its
foundations in a very shallow knowledge of anatomy. The
Barber-Surgeons' Company did its best to teach anatomy and
surgery by a series of public lectures and demonstrations,
delivered by the most eminent and practical men of the time, but
the difficulty experienced in procuring subjects for dissection
rendered anatomy theoretical rather than practical. Midwifery
was chiefly in the hands of women, and the true mechanism
of a normal labour was not known to more than two or three
men in England.

Such was the condition of medicine in 1742 : in 1750 everything had changed. The College of Physicians indeed maintained for some time longer its supine attitude, but in 1745 the
surgeons, poor and penniless, seceded in a body from the
Company of Barber-Surgeons. They were reconstituted as the
Surgeons' Company. John Ranby, the king's Sergeant-Surgeon,

was chosen the first Master, with Cheselden as one of the Wardens. The new company was founded very much upon the lines of the united company, but its members had fewer expenses, and they were allowed the liberty of private teaching. The company soon acquired a hall in the Old Bailey, but as the barbers, with a' few trifling exceptions, retained the whole of the revenues belonging to the united company, the Surgeons' Company had to depend upon various extraneous sources of income. These were badly managed, and in 1780 the company was almost insolvent owing to the bankruptcy of its clerk, to whom it had incautiously advanced money. A new clerk, of approved business capacity, was appointed, and for a short time the progress of the company was satisfactory. It soon fell back into its former condition, however, and in 1789 its Master complained to the members that "your theatre is without lectures, your library, a room without books, is converted into an office for your clerk, and your committee-room is become his parlour. It is not always used even in your common business, and, when it is thus made use of, it is seldom in a fit and proper state." It is no wonder if this scandalous state of affairs led to disaster. The more active and radical members of the profession used the degraded condition of the company to "point a moral and adorn a tale." At length the Corporation found that it had destroyed itself by the illegal holding of a meeting to elect Mr. Cline its Master for the year 1796. An endeavour was made to reconstruct the company upon its old basis, but the opposition was too strong, and the Bill was thrown out by the House of Lords at its second reading, on 17th July, 1797. It was then determined, after much discussion, that the company should be revived by a Charter from the Crown rather than by an Act of Parliament. This Charter was granted on 20th March, 1800, to a new body called the Royal College of Surgeons in London. It gave the College extensive privileges in London, but it has since been amended in several important particulars, and the institution has been called since 1843 the "Royal College of Surgeons of England."

Nothing, perhaps, is more remarkable in the medical history of this period than the rise in the social position of the surgeon. The surgeon had always been subordinate to the physician, for in early days the physician was usually an ecclesiastic whilst the

AN INCIDENT IN THE RISE OF THE SURGEONS

(*From a satirical print of 1768.*)

surgeon was a layman, who performed operations at the command of the physician. This position of inferiority was maintained until quite recently. The College of Physicians procured an Order of Council in June, 1632, with a clause that no chirurgeon "doe either dismember (*i.e.* amputate), Trepan the head, open the Chest or Belly, cut for the stone, or doe any great operation but in the presence of a learned physitian"; and there are persons still alive who remember the time when a surgeon's prescription in a hospital had to be countersigned by the physician before it could be dispensed if it was for more than a black draught. It was only the energetic protests of Abernethy, at the beginning of the nineteenth century, which led to the surgeon gaining a complete control over his own patient. From time immemorial a few surgeons who were not barbers existed in London, and perhaps in the other large towns in England. In London they formed a guild or confraternity of surgeons from 1354 until they were united with the Barbers' Company in 1540. The numbers of this guild were few, not more than ten or fifteen at any one time, but they maintained the reputation of surgery, and its members appear to have been held in higher social estimation than the surgeons who were also barbers. The members of the united Company of Barbers and Surgeons never held a high social position; even Clowes and Gale, Banister and Woodall, the great surgeons of the end of Elizabeth's reign, never occupied a position at all comparable to that held by Caius, Butts, Harvey, or Theodore de Mayerne. The mere union of the surgeons with barbers sometimes led to troublesome mistakes, for it became impossible to ascertain officially who was barber and who practised surgery. The succession of great surgeons, Cheselden, Pott, and Hunter, and the formation of a Corporation of Surgeons apart from barbers, removed the stigma, and by the end of the eighteenth century the best surgeons occupied as good a position socially as the best physicians.

The members of the Surgeons' Company soon availed themselves to the uttermost of their liberty to teach. Percivall Pott began to deliver lectures at his house in Watling Street in the year 1747. They were private at the outset, being intended solely for the students who followed his surgical practice in the neighbouring hospital of St. Bartholomew. They were given at first with hesitation and reserve, but as the lecturer gained confidence his style improved, and the course eventually became so celebrated that all the most distinguished English practitioners of surgery and many foreign ones boasted themselves his pupils. John Hunter himself was an auditor in 1751.

The reform of midwifery in England is due to William **Obstetrics.** Smellie and to James Douglas, the friend of the Hunters. Smellie, who had been a humble practitioner in Lanarkshire, settled as an

THE ANATOMIST OVERTAKEN by the WATCH   CARRYING OFF MIST W— in a HAMPER

THE ANATOMIST IN TROUBLE.
(From a satirical print of 1773.)

apothecary in Pall Mall about 1739. He had spent a short time in France, and had there imbibed the spirit of the younger Grégoire's teaching. This teaching he reproduced in London in an improved form, and with such success that the battle of man-midwifery raged round him for many years. The men conquered, and their obstetric art is now based upon the best kind of knowledge, a thorough acquaintance with normal conditions.

Pathology, or the science of the cause of disease, did not exist **Pathology.** in the first half of the eighteenth century. Morbid anatomy itself, which is the basis of pathology, was as yet hardly known. Post-mortem examinations, indeed, were made, but the results were neither recorded nor tabulated, unless in exceptional cases.

The medical profession knew but little of the normal appearances met with in dead bodies; it is not surprising, therefore, that they made no advance in the knowledge of abnormal appearances. The genius of one man—John Hunter—created English pathology, and took it at once almost to the highest position, for he fortified it with clinical, anatomical, and experimental observations which are unassailable when they are combined.

John and William Hunter.

John Hunter was in some respects even more remarkable than William, his elder brother. He possessed greater singleness of purpose, and therefore greater concentration, greater depth of knowledge, greater determination, and that minute attention to detail associated with the power of generalisation which only coexist in the highest intellects. The minds of the two brothers in many respects were strikingly alike. Both had a mania for collecting. William accumulated the large museum which is at present housed in Glasgow. It was begun to illustrate his lectures, but it was not limited to anatomical preparations, for it contains an art department, books, coins, and specimens of natural history. John Hunter's museum, on the other hand, is severely scientific, but it is unique. It has long had the good fortune to be cared for by the Royal College of Surgeons of England, and it is magnificently housed in Lincoln's Inn Fields. The systematic teaching of medicine and surgery to students we owe in great measure to William Hunter. He established a small school to instruct a "Society of Naval Surgeons." The lectures were originally the continuation of a series delivered by Samuel Sharp, surgeon to Guy's Hospital. Hunter delivered his first course in 1746, at the house of his friend, Dr. James Douglas, in the Piazza, Covent Garden. This course proved to be the starting-point of regular instruction in every branch of medical science. The Hunterian or Great Windmill Street School of Medicine developed from it, and with varying fortunes continued until 1831. The first course of lectures resulted in a gain to Hunter of seventy guineas, a sum which he showed gleefully to his friends, saying that it was the first time he had seen so much gold. The school prospered exceedingly, and when Matthew Baillie, the Hunters' nephew, retired from its management at the end of the century, he received no less than £4,000 for his share in the goodwill. The success of the Hunterian school led in part to the multiplication of improved methods of teaching in England, and before the end of the century the outlines of medical education were fixed, and, with certain necessary modifications, are still carried out as William Hunter left them.

The medical schools attached to the hospitals also attained a

JOHN HUNTER, BY SIR JOSHUA REYNOLDS.
(By permission of the Royal College of Surgeons.)

greater prominence during the later years of the eighteenth **Medical** century. They began at St. Bartholomew's and at St. Thomas's **Education.** Hospitals about 1680, where the surgeons took pupils, or " cubs," whom they instructed in their art. No attempt, however, seems to have been made to give these pupils more than instruction at

the bedside until Pott began to lecture. Clinical instruction in
physic was of still later origin, and was derived from Scotland,
where it had been placed upon a satisfactory footing by Dr.
Rutherford, Sir Walter Scott's grandfather, a physician to the
Infirmary at Edinburgh.

The Hospitals. The students appear to have done their best to make up for
the deficiency of the official teaching which was given to them,
for in every hospital to which a medical school was attached
a debating society was formed. The idea of such a society
appears to have begun in the hospitals of St. Thomas and
of Guy, then united and situated side by side in the Borough,
almost on the site of what is now the London Bridge Railway
Station. The Physical Society was inaugurated there in
1771. It died in 1852 after a useful career, but its traditions
are still carried on by the daughter societies in the two hospitals, which are now separated. The Middlesex Hospital
Society was founded in 1774, and still flourishes, whilst in
1795 the Abernethian Society was founded in the Royal
Hospital of St. Bartholomew. The other hospitals followed the
example thus set them. The growth of the hospital debating
societies was coincident with the growth of the more important
medical societies for those who had completed their studies
and were actually practising their profession. Of these, the
Medical Society of London is one of the oldest, as it is
certainly one of the most flourishing. These societies have
done much for the advancement of medicine as a science, for
they have promoted free discussion, and have allowed a large
number of carefully observed facts to be recorded in a form
which is easily accessible to everyone.

The wave of philanthropy continued to rise throughout
England in exact proportion to the increase in the material
prosperity of the country. It took the very practical form of
building hospitals and infirmaries for the gratuitous treatment
of the sick. The London Hospital in Whitechapel began its
useful existence in 1740 as a small infirmary in Featherstone
Street. It was then moved to Prescott Street, Goodman's
Fields, a neighbourhood inhabited then, as now, by a large
Jewish population. Additional accommodation was soon required, and buildings were erected upon its present site in
1757. Every county town in England soon had its infirmary

THE LONDON HOSPITAL IN 1753.

(After a painting by William Bellers.)

235

Hospital Charities.

or local hospital. The York Hospital was founded in 1740, the Devon and Exeter a year later. The Newcastle-on-Tyne Royal Infirmary was established in 1751; the Leeds General Infirmary in 1767; the Radcliffe Infirmary at Oxford in 1770; the Norfolk and Norwich Hospital in 1771; and the Birmingham General Hospital in 1779. None were endowed; each had to be supported by the voluntary contributions of subscribers, who thus showed their genuine pity for the sick poor. It speaks well for the benevolence of Englishmen that none of these institutions, when once opened, have ever been allowed to close their doors for want of funds, but that through bad times and through good times money has always been forthcoming for their support.

Public Health.

Hygiene, or the science of public health and preventive medicine, arose from small beginnings during the latter half of the eighteenth century. We owe its origin in part to Sir John Pringle and in part to Sir Gilbert Blane. Sir John Pringle, in 1742, was physician to the Earl of Stair, then in command of the British army in Flanders. He was afterwards Physician-General to his Majesty's forces in the Low Countries, and eventually he became President of the Royal Society. Dr. Pringle published, in 1750, his " Observations on the Jail or Hospital Fever "; in 1752, the first edition of his " Observations on the Diseases of the Army "; and in 1783 an account of the method he had taken to preserve the health of the crew of his Majesty's ship *Resolution*

Naval Hygiene.

during her voyage round the world under the command of Captain Cook (p. 304). Scurvy had been for many years the curse of the Navy, but Pringle's rules were so good, and Captain Cook interpreted them so successfully, that he performed a voyage of three years and eighteen days with a crew of 118 men through every variety of climate, and only lost one man. The use of "sweet-wort," a rigid attention to diet, cleanliness, and the careful preservation of his company from wet and other injuries of weather, formed the chief part of Cook's hygienic code.

The condition of the sick and wounded in the Army was very bad at the beginning of the eighteenth century. The first improvement was introduced, doubtless at Pringle's suggestion, when the Earl of Stair proposed to the Duke of Noailles, in 1742, that the hospitals of the opposing **Military** forces should be considered as sanctuaries for the sick and **Hygiene.** should be mutually protected. This arrangement was approved, and was rigidly enforced during the campaign in the Low Countries. It had been usual, before this agree-

SIR JOHN PRINGLE, BY SIR J. REYNOLDS.
(By permission of the Royal Society.)

ment was entered into, to remove the sick to a considerable distance from the camp upon the approach of the enemy. This necessarily called away the medical officers from the fighting line, and so led to the death of many men for want of timely aid and skilful assistance. The good work begun by Pringle was ably carried out by Sir Gilbert Blane, who was first the physician to Lord Rodney's fleet, then a physician to St. Thomas's Hospital, and afterwards a commissioner to the Admiralty for the care of sick and wounded sailors. Sir Gilbert Blane made special arrangements for the provisioning of ships on foreign stations, and he was very particular that they should be supplied with an abundance of lemon-juice. He was also consulted on the subject of quarantine, the arrangement of hulks and some of the prisons on shore, as well as with respect to the transportation of convicts, on all of which his advice was conspicuously beneficial. The work of Pringle and Blane marks the beginning of a new science. Gaol fever is now unknown; the medical cure of our soldiers has been copied by the other nations of Europe; our Navy is the most healthy in the world; and scurvy has disappeared even from our mercantile marine.

Typhus and its Causes. The birth of sanitary science, however, was not out of due time. The Black Assize at the Old Bailey, in April, 1750, is still remembered. The persons of chief note who were in court at the time, and who afterwards died of the fever contracted there, were the Lord Mayor, one of the justices of the Common Pleas, one of the barons of the Exchequer, one of the aldermen of London, a barrister, one of the under-sheriffs, two or three students, an officer of the Lord Chief Justice, several of the jury, and about forty other persons whom business or curiosity had brought thither. The condition of the prisons throughout the country—and, indeed, in Europe generally—was most deplorable (p. 656). Overcrowding was the real cause of these outbreaks of typhus, but the window-tax (IV., p. 718) had much to answer for. This tax was originally imposed in 1696, and in 1710, houses with from twenty to thirty windows paid ten shillings, whilst those with more than thirty windows paid twenty shillings. It was replaced by the modern form of inhabited house duty, mainly in consequence of an agitation promoted by Mr. Reginald Orton, a surgeon living in Sunderland.

The public health during the second half of the eighteenth century was satisfactory, though it was not so good as it had been during the first part. Smallpox continued the prevalent disease. The deaths in London alone varied from a minimum of 522 in 1797 to a maximum of 3,582 during the great epidemic of 1763. A house of charity, called the Middlesex County Hospital

for Smallpox, was opened in July, 1746, in Windmill Street,
Tottenham Court Road. It was established for the gratuitous
inoculation of the disease, and in-patients were inoculated there
until 1821, though the inoculation of out-patients had been
replaced by vaccination in 1807. The operation of inoculation
soon became fashionable, and was reduced to a method. It was
considered to require a month's preparation, and subsequent
detention for a fortnight. It thus became a lucrative source of

Photo: Walker & Cockerell.
EDWARD JENNER, M.D., F.R.S., BY JAMES NORTHCOTE, R.A.
(National Portrait Gallery.)

income to those who, like Ranby, Hawkins, and Middleton,
performed the operation frequently upon patients in the upper
and middle classes of society.

The discovery by Edward Jenner, living at Berkeley, in
Gloucestershire, of the protective effects of cowpox marks a
distinct epoch in the history of smallpox. Vaccination was first
announced as a method of treatment in 1796, though the
industry of scholars has traced an allusion to the operation in
Sancteya Grantham, an ancient Sanscrit work attributed to

Vaccina-
tion.

Dhanvantari,[1] whilst Bruce and Humboldt say that it was not unknown in Persia and South America. It is certain that the dairy farmers in some parts of England and in Holstein held traditionally that cowpox protected from smallpox. Vaccination met with great and powerful support from the first. It was taken up voluntarily by the better classes in England, and its practice was widely extended amongst the poor by the labours of an enthusiastic band of workers, of whom John Ring and George Pearson were the foremost. The advance of the method was also furthered by the remarkable diminution in the number of cases of smallpox which followed the great epidemics of 1796, 1798, and 1800. This diminution was in part to be explained by the increasing number of persons who were vaccinated, but in part, no doubt, it was due to the enormous number of persons who had been protected by taking the disease itself during these epidemics, for one attack of smallpox usually renders a person immune more effectually than the most perfect vaccination with cowpox. Smallpox reasserted itself in the course of a few years with its original virulence almost unimpaired by vaccination. It was then ascertained that an attack of cowpox only conferred temporary immunity from smallpox, and that it was necessary to repeat the operation of vaccination if the fullest amount of protection was to be obtained. From its very commencement vaccination has been surrounded by the most bitter controversy. It has been attacked upon scientific grounds; it has been attacked from the lowest popular standpoint; statistics have been employed to demonstrate that it is useless. There remain, however, the stubborn facts that since it has been in general use the deaths from smallpox have sunk until they have almost reached a vanishing point in vaccinated—and especially in re-vaccinated—communities, whilst among the unvaccinated the disease still flourishes luxuriantly unless the most careful methods of isolating not only the sick, but also the members of invalid households, are enforced at an outlay which is economically prohibitive. Pock-marked faces, too, are now so rare as to excite our attention when they are seen, whilst formerly they were so frequent as to be the rule. All the more highly civilised

[1 But Baron, *Life of Jenner*, I., 575 (1817), states that the passage is a forgery, interpolated by the English introducers of vaccination into India to commend the practice to the natives]

THE COWPOX TRAGEDY: SCENE THE LAST.

(From a caricature by George Cruikshank.)

races of the world have rendered the practice of vaccination compulsory. In spite of the views of faddists and of all objectors to the preventive treatment of smallpox by vaccination, the plain and common-sense view to take of the subject, according to the present state of our knowledge, is the following : Every child ought to be vaccinated as soon as it is sufficiently strong to bear the operation, and usually the earlier it is done the better. Great care should be exercised in selecting the source of lymph, and the operation should not be looked upon as a trivial one, for the same dangers attend it as may follow upon any slight surgical operation. The vaccination should be repeated from time to time as its protective influence wears off. Too much, on the other hand, must not be expected from vaccination. It does not confer absolute immunity, and in a few cases it does not seem to confer immunity at all. In a large proportion of cases it protects the individual for a varying length of time from the worst effects of the disease, so that should he be exposed to its contagion, he either escapes variola, or has it in that mild form known to the medical profession as modified smallpox.

REGINALD HUGHES. Painting from Reynolds to Lawrence. IT will have been observed that the list of the earliest members of the Royal Academy (p. 387) contains the names of no fewer than ten foreigners. Of these, Cipriani, a painter of mythological inanities, Zuccarelli, the formal landscapist, Bartolozzi and Carlini were Italians ; Angelica Kauffmann was a Tyrolese ; Zoffany and Meyer were Germans ; Serres was a Frenchman. Moser the enamellist and his daughter Mary the flower painter, were Swiss, and Benjamin West came from the English colonies in America, which subsequently gave to England the more solid talent of John Singleton Copley. Nevertheless a good many English artists, not counting those who, like Romney, were intentionally excluded, were left out by inadvertence. The most celebrated of **Joseph Wright.** these was Joseph Wright of Derby. Like Reynolds, whose junior he was by eleven years, he was the son of a small professional man in the provinces, and was sent by his father to Reynolds's master, Hudson. He started as a portrait painter, but his special, if limited, gift lay in quite another direction. It was in rendering the tone and incidence of artificial light that he made his name, and for this he is deservedly remembered.

"Give me your firelight," said Richard Wilson to him, "and I will give you my daylight"; but the exchange, if not unfair from the point of view of art, would have been commercially disastrous to Wright, for while Wilson starved, Wright was never in want of paying patronage. He, too, visited Italy, and is said to have made a special study of Michael Angelo; but it is obvious that he found his account not so much in copying the old masters as in making studies of an eruption of Vesuvius, which came in the nick of time during his visit. Though only an occasional exhibitor at the Academy, he was elected an Associate in 1781, and a full Academician three years later; but owing to a quarrel, the details of which are obscure, his appointment was quashed. He was a defective colourist, but the tone of his candlelight is excellent, and he seems to have possessed considerable power as a draughtsman. He is finely represented in the National Gallery by "An Experiment with an Air Pump," reproduced at p. lxxxvii of Vol. I. of this work.

A few only of the less distinguished artists of the time of Reynolds can be here mentioned. One of these, Nathaniel Dance, himself an original member of the Academy, was a solid and somewhat stiff portrait-painter, and the author of numerous historical works of no great interest. John Wootton and George Stubbs, the latter of whom was a scientific student of the horse, and published a book on equine anatomy, were fashionable animal painters. They were succeeded by James Ward, born in 1769, whose "Bull" has rightly found a place in the National Gallery. **Minor Contemporaries of Reynolds.**

Benjamin West and James Barry represented the so-called historical art of the period, the former chiefly on the biblical and religious, the latter on the classical and mythological, side. West's pictures, though they now strike us as both vapid and exaggerated, had a great vogue in their day, and he succeeded Sir Joshua in the presidency of the Academy. He is credited with having brought about one beneficial change in English practice, viz. the abandonment of classic costume in the treatment of heroic subjects of modern date. Barry, who was an Irishman and had studied in Rome for five years, was a singular instance of a rather weak and limited talent determined to exercise itself on the scale and in the manner which demands unlimited strength. He finally settled in **West and Barry.**

London in 1771, and was elected two years later to the Academy, where he became professor of painting. He was anxious to be allowed to decorate the interior of St. Paul's, and when his proposals came to nothing, eagerly accepted the proposal of the Society of Arts to decorate their great room in the Adelphi. In a certain way this work, finished in 1784, shows a feeling of grandeur which was unknown to his contemporaries. There is a good deal of vigorous expression, and a management of light and shade that is not far from masterly. But the

LANDSCAPE WITH CATTLE, BY JAMES WARD, R.A.
(*National Gallery.*)

composition is frequently confused, there is a want of movement in the figures; and, as a decoration, it is not very decorative. Like Wilson, he was reduced to great penury, but unlike him, he could not bear his misfortunes with equanimity, and his attacks on Sir Joshua in his public lectures led to his expulsion from the Academy.

Copley.   Another Irishman, John Singleton Copley, remains to be noticed. He was born in 1737 at Boston, Massachusetts, a few weeks after his parents reached New England. There he learnt his trade, and it was not till 1775 that he settled in London. In the following year he was elected an Associate, and three years later an Academician. The elder Pitt died

THE VICTORS AT OLYMPIA, BY JAMES BARRY.

(By permission from the original etching for the painting at the Society of Arts.)

on the 11th of May, 1778, and the tragic incident of his fainting
fit in the House of Lords formed the subject of a picture by
Copley.   A crowded House of Lords, with its long series of
bewigged occupants, presented enormous difficulties, and the
comparative success of the artist is the measure of the enormous difficulties encountered.   More complete success attended
his representation of the death of Major Pierson, the gallant
defender of Jersey against the French.   The vigorous but dig-
nified realism of this work enables it to hold its own against
any work of its age, not in England alone, but in all Europe.
Even at the present day it would be difficult to name any
English historical picture to which it could fairly be asked to
yield precedence, and this notwithstanding that the painter,
though a sound, was not a great colourist, nor does he display
any special brilliancy of touch.   As regards its intrinsic truth,
as opposed to its dramatic power, it is of interest to recall the
fact that the great expert authority, the Duke of Wellington,
pronounced it the best representation of actual fighting known
to him.   The modern passion for truth of local colour and
minute accuracy of detail comes out in Copley's picture, the
background in the death of Major Pierson having been drawn
from the actual scene of the catastrophe.   To a like impulse
we may attribute his journey to Gibraltar, when commissioned
to paint the defeat of the Spanish attack by Lord Heath-
field.   Some of his portrait groups are admirable, but his
high place in English art belongs to him in virtue of his
success in that branch of painting where English success has
been most rare.

Reynolds's
Successors.   We come now to the numerous group of artists who represent
the generation after Reynolds, mostly born in or about the
third quarter of the century.   These men, who, for convenience,
may be described as the successors of Reynolds, were frequently
his imitators and followers, and occasionally his actual pupils.
Such a one was James Northcote, the son of a watchmaker, and
originally apprenticed to a watchmaker at Plymouth.   Probably
on the score of their common West-country origin, Reynolds
admitted him to his studio, first as pupil and then as
assistant, and he, more than anyone, should have imbibed the
master's spirit.   He was one of the most prolific and various
of the artists who were employed to draw for the Boydell

THE DEATH OF MAJOR PIERSON, BY JOHN SINGLETON COPLEY, R.A.

(*National Gallery.*)

Shakespeare. He painted in nearly every style; he was a clever writer, and has left us a valuable life of Sir Joshua Reynolds; and Hazlitt's record of his talk shows that as a conversationalist he was incisive and picturesque. But the mantle **Hoppner.** of Reynolds fell more on John Hoppner than on Northcote. He was the child of one of the German attendants of the Court at Windsor, and was born in 1759. He entered the Academy in his seventeenth year, obtained the gold medal, and became an exceedingly popular portrait-painter. His imitation of the President sometimes led him astray, even to the use of his unstable pigments. Some of his pictures which have stood the test of time are exceedingly refined in colour, and at his best he deserved the favourable verdict of his contemporaries.

Opie.   A far more individual talent was that of John Opie, the son of a carpenter, born at a village near Truro, in Cornwall, in 1761. His portrait sketches attracted the attention of Dr. Wolcot, the satirist and art-critic, better known as Peter Pindar. He was little more than a boy when he came to London, and in 1782 he exhibited in the Academy. Reynolds compared him to Caravaggio and even Velasquez, and the comparison, though flattering to Opie, indicates where we are to look for the strength and weakness of the painter. A certain savagery in expression and violence in the light and shade are common to both. But his portrait heads are frequently of singular force, and whatever may be urged against his "coarse and unsatisfactory execution," the vigour and facility of the self-taught "Cornish wonder" fix his position as one of the greatest of the "minor stars."

Beechey.   Another original artist, though his originality was somewhat thin and superficial, was William Beechey. He properly belongs to this generation, though he arrived somewhat later at celebrity. He was a Berkshire lad, intended for a lawyer, and came to London in 1771 to learn his business, being then eighteen. In the following year he threw up the law, and somehow managed to become an Academy student. When he had finished with the school he started as a portrait-painter in London. His attempts to obtain patronage for the time failed, and he went to Norwich, but, returning to London about 1780, he was fortunate in attracting the royal favour. The favour was obtained by a curious stroke of luck, which is only worth narrating because it shows how prodigious was the value of royal patronage at that period.   The portrait of a nobleman painted by Beechey was rejected by the Hanging Committee of the Academy, which so incensed the sitter that he complained to the king, who allowed him to send the picture to the palace. George III., being pleased with the artist, thereupon commanded portraits of himself and various members of his family from Beechey, whose fortune was thus made in a day.   He was, perhaps, little influenced either for good or otherwise by Sir Joshua or his greater contemporaries ; but his manner was showy, his colour was pleasing.   He was knighted in 1798, and died in 1839 at the age of eighty-six.   He had, at least, this much of insight into the character of his own gift, that during his long and prosperous career he never attempted an " historical " piece.

But perhaps the greatest of this generation was the Scotch- *Raeburn.* man, Henry Raeburn.   He was born in 1756 near Edinburgh, and apprenticed to a goldsmith of that city ; but he early quitted this employment, and, with some little teaching obtained from a Scotch artist named Martin, he started as a miniaturist and portrait-painter in his native city.   A fortunate marriage enabled him to come to London, where he was cordially received by Reynolds, who admitted him for two months to his studio and gave him letters of introduction to Rome, where he studied for two years.   On his return he set up in Edinburgh, where his commanding talents obtained him a position similar to that of Sir Joshua in London.   It is with him that Raeburn mainly comes into competition, but he had a power, or susceptibility of assimilation, not unlike that which is found in Vandyck ; and at times he caught the spirit, now of Sir Joshua, now again of Romney or Gainsborough, and—more often, alas !—of Sir Thomas Lawrence.   Though a most unequal painter, at his best he can hold his own, both for strength and elegance, with any of them.   At bottom he was a realist, though of a refined sort, and the gift of idealisation, " the painting of the very spirit," was not in him.   The technical quality of some of his work, the famous portrait of Mr. Wardrop of Torban Hill for example, is superb, and the masterly execution is backed up by the finest observation.   One may note, for instance, in this portrait with what subtlety he has rendered the light faintly piercing the thin nostril to the lip below, while the suffused glow, the melting colour, and broad certain brush work, recalls Northcote's famous saying about a still greater master of the brush—that it seems to have been painted by a wish. How sober and full of life it is, too, and how simply "all that should accompany old age" is set forth in this nobly realistic picture. This is a work of rich brown shadows, but Raeburn could do almost equally fine work under quite different conditions. Take, for instance, the blonde example of the "Greenwich Pensioner," that inimitable portrait of the old English sailor.

Lawrence.   None of these men, however, was really destined to take Reynolds's place, either in society or in the world of art. That was reserved for a younger man, afterwards known as Sir Thomas Lawrence. He was hardly out of the nursery when Raeburn was profiting by Sir Joshua's kindness. But Lawrence was the most prodigious of infant prodigies. Even as a baby, he was, in the intervals of riding on walking-sticks and similar childish amusements, engaged in taking likenesses. His parents were both children of country parsons, though at the date of his birth they kept the White Lion Inn at Bristol. The father was a rolling stone, and, after failing at Bristol, he went to Devizes, and thence successively to Oxford, Weymouth, and Bath. These continual changes made education difficult, but his fond parents insisted that their son's talents required no cultivation. At Bath, however, he had some instruction from William Hoare, R.A., a crayon painter of repute, and in that city he made crayon copies at second hand of various works of the old masters. One of these, a crayon of the Transfiguration, obtained the silver palette of the Society of Arts, and the society, with a prophetic insight into the young artist's career, had the palette "gilded all over." Before he was twelve he was a fashionable portrait-painter, and his studio "the resort of the fashion and beauty of Bath." In 1787 the family moved to London, and Lawrence was admitted to the Royal Academy. He was extremely beautiful, with his chestnut curls hanging over his shoulders, while there is official testimony to the fact that his proficiency in drawing was extraordinary.

It was while he was still well under twenty that his famous interview with Reynolds took place. Now the burden of Reynolds's sermons to the student, in season or out of season,

SIR JOHN SINCLAIR OF ULBSTER, BY SIR HENRY RAEBURN, R.A.
(National Portrait Gallery.)

was "Study the old masters"; but to Lawrence he adopted
a different tone. "Study Nature diligently rather than the
old masters," was his advice to him, showing, as an excellent
critic has pointed out, that " he had at once detected the danger
that lay in the path of the young aspirant." In two years
Lawrence leapt into unbounded popularity. His good looks, his
flattering pencil, his brilliant talk, his caressing manner, made
him the darling of the fashionable world. At the close of his
twenty-first year, the Academy elected him a supplemental
Associate, the rules not permitting regular membership to
anybody under the age of twenty-four. In February of the
following year (1792) Sir Joshua died, and the king immediately
appointed Lawrence to his vacant post of Royal Painter in
Ordinary. Then the Dilettanti chose him as their painter, and
no sooner did he reach the age of twenty-four than the honour
of the full R.A. was bestowed upon him. He was at the top of
the tree at an age when most men are bracing themselves for
the climb.

There must have been the making of a much greater painter
in Lawrence than fate allowed him to be, for though he was
most laborious, and had an unlucky passion for surface finish, a
few heads remain, seemingly painted at a single sitting, that are
full of fire. It is curious, too, to note how differently he was
judged by contemporaries. Thus Fuseli, the painter of night-
mares, who was a good draughtsman, declared that Lawrence
drew as well or better than Vandyck, and that his women were
" in a finer taste." Opie, however, was, we fear, nearer the truth
when he delivered the epigrammatic judgment that Lawrence
made coxcombs of his sitters, and his sitters made a coxcomb of
him. Wilkie, too, has pointed out that the features in nearly all
his heads were painted in the same position. His gift of flattering was sedulously cultivated, and he took amazing liberties in
altering and refining the features of his sitters. He has been
called " an attenuated Sir Joshua," but the phrase does not seem
particularly happy. Except occasionally in his earlier works, he
makes no attempt to get to the heart of the matter. In character, where Sir Joshua is specially strong, Lawrence is specially
weak. Richness and harmony he cares little for, nor for the
mass of light and shade; with him " drawing " is more esteemed
than painting, and purity more esteemed than tone. His skill

in depicting grace in dress, his delicate draughtsmanship, the beautiful hands, the brilliant eyes, all these must be accorded to Lawrence. But his deficiencies are no less obvious.

JOHN PHILIP KEMBLE AS HAMLET, BY SIR THOMAS LAWRENCE, P.R.A.
(National Portrait Gallery.)

Nevertheless, as the last portrait-painter in a great succession, as a most prolific artist in a great epoch if not an epoch of great men, Lawrence must hold an important place in the history of

English art. He reached the zenith of his fame in 1815 when the Regent knighted him. He visited Aix-la-Chapelle during the Congress, and painted a vast array of emperors and kings; but his pictures tell the tale of a gift growing ever more and more common, though occasionally the fine character of the sitter's face lights up the mechanical cleverness of the work. It must be said in his favour that his careful and laborious method —for he had quite lost in later life the childish gift of rapidly seizing a likeness—encouraged the practice of more careful drawing of the head, and that his abstention from bad vehicles and fugitive colours, discouraged imitation of the pranks which Sir Joshua used to play with his pigments. But, undoubtedly, in other ways his example was evil. His was a great gift, yet he reckoned it better to sit at home than to spend time in travel and study. He sought to flatter in the plain vulgar way of improving his sitter's features, not searching out, like Sir Joshua, some better quality of soul. We cannot but think that there was some congeniality between the nature of the man and the time with which he is identified—the time of the skin-deep refinement, the bastard elegance, the fine-ladyhood and fine-gentlemanliness of the Regent and his Court.

H. D. TRAILL. Literature. THE contrast between the fortunes of poetry and of prose during the eighteenth century has been briefly noted in the Introduction to this work. At the beginning of the period on which we are now entering that contrast had attained to its broadest incongruity of aspect and its strongest emphasis of expression. Our prose had been undergoing a steady development in its form, and receiving continuous additions to its resources from the days of Addison and Swift to those of Burke and Gibbon, in whose hands it became an instrument of literary achievements, distinct indeed in character but in their respective varieties **Poetry and Prose.** never before equalled. Poetry, on the other hand, declining as steadily in spiritual force, straying ever further and further from the living fountain of Nature into the desert of a lifeless art, was now at the furthest point of its aberration. The splendid service which Pope had rendered to the formal perfecting of the heroic couplet, and generally to the structural evolution of English poetry, had left indeed imperishable

benefits behind them; but by the operation of that stern law
of human affairs which exercised the mind of the dying King
Arthur, the once valuable example of Pope had become an
almost wholly mischievous influence.   In the words of a poet
who admired his genius, but was the pioneer of the new
movement destined to overthrow his sway, he had made poetry
a "mechanic art," till "every warbler" knew "his tune by
heart."   A few pages, nay, a few dozen lines of the most popular
poem of the day, will amply suffice to show how high time it was
that the old order should give place to the new, and how much
had been done by the "one good custom" of Popian "correctness" to corrupt the poetic world.

Yet even here it is only just to distinguish.   It has been too   **Pope's
common to condemn the frigidity and artificiality of the school   Influence.**
of Pope, and the divorce of his poetry alike from the truth
of eternal Nature and from genuine human feeling, as though
these were faults peculiar to himself and cultivated as virtues by
his imitators.   Again, this fashion of speaking has, as was
inevitable, made it equally common to talk of the leaders of the
Romantic and Naturalist revival as though they had brought
back the genius of our poetry from a false track adopted under
Pope's misguidance and had set its feet again on the true path.
But this is to show undue severity to the poet and excessive
leniency to his age.   The poetic spirit did not go astray under
anybody's misguidance during the eighteenth century; and that
for the best of all reasons—that it never moved at all.   It stood
waiting for that enlargement of the poetic faculty which the
close of the century was to reveal, and for that new birth of song
which the world was to witness, the appointed years being run.
Pope simply took the *matter* of poetry as he found it, being in
this respect abreast of his age, and not ahead of it, and devoted
himself with brilliant success to the perfecting of its form.
What we now consider prosaic in his matter derives from the
prosaic quality of his era.   His feeling for nature is neither more
nor less cold, his eye for nature neither less nor more true, than
the feeling and the eye of Addison, of Young, of Shenstone, or of
Thomson.   They and he alike surveyed it in the same scene-
painter spirit, with the same restriction of their vision to its
broader panoramic aspects, the same blindness to its more subtle
beauties, the same insensibility to its magic and mystery.   Even

in Gray there are but casual and fitful gleams of anything higher
and deeper ; and the " Elegy " itself, with all its satisfying
exquisiteness, contains perhaps but a single stanza — that
beginning with " The breezy call of incense-breathing morn "
—in which any voice reaches us from the heart of things.

Reaction against Pope. If the matter of poetry, then, improved not in Pope's hands,
neither did it deteriorate, and the demand of the New School
for a closer approach to Nature was a protest not against any
aberrations of Pope himself, but against the stationariness and
the limitations of Pope's period. All that can justly be alleged
against him—though that, to be sure, bears heavily enough
upon his influence as distinct from his genius—is this : that
the amazing brilliancy of his artistic method so effectually
concealed the poverty of his matter as to save it for many
years after his death from the discredit into which at last it
was inevitably doomed to fall. Many a poetaster had to show
his futile mastery of the art which Pope had made " mechanic "
before the machinery was detected ; a whole generation of
" warblers " had to repeat his tune before its empty jingle
could be recognised for what it was.

Pope's successors: Hayley. Nor in the year with which this period opens were there
any signs that such a discovery was at hand. Of all the
warblers to whom Cowper so contemptuously referred, and
among whom he doubtless never intended to include his
friend and subsequent biographer, none warbled with a thinner
and feebler note than William Hayley (1745–1820). Yet
Hayley's masterpiece, " The Triumphs of Temper," published
in 1781, was the " hit " of the day. Its author was a man of
considerable culture and intellectual refinement, and, as his
" Epistle to Romney " shows, of no contemptible artistic taste.
It is impossible to read his warblings, with whatever amount
of critical disdain for the warbler, without conceiving a genuine
liking for the man. His nature had all the simplicity in which
his art was so lamentably to seek, and his disposition was as
modest as his Muse was pretentious. His geniality and good
nature break out irresistibly even in his metrical attack upon
Hume, and even in his letters to the egregious Miss Anna
Seward he cannot heartily abuse even his rough critic Johnson,
but is continually slipping in admiring epithets which his fair
but fiercer correspondent amusingly entreats him to recall. But

Johnson, omnivorous reader though he was, declared himself
unable to get beyond the first two pages of ' The Triumphs
of Temper," and posterity perhaps has never got so far. Its
readability even to a seasoned critic is strictly limited to its
interest as a deliberate imitation, sometimes declining into a
downright parody, of its illustrious model. The frivolous
argument of the poem, its mock-heroic manner, its machinery

WILLIAM HAYLEY
(After George Romney.)

of boudoir *féerie,* and the incidents of the "drawing-room
supernatural" through which the fable is evolved, are all most
comically reminiscent of the " Rape of the Lock." Every device
of Pope's is there, only his inspiration is wanting—only the
aërial fantasy and gossamer grace of his inventions and the
intoxicating effervescence of his verse. Every now and then
you catch a faint far-off flavour of that lightest and brightest
of poetic champagne, but always therewith you get also the
disconcerting impression that you are drinking it in the
morning out of a bottle that was opened—and left open—the
night before. Taken as a whole, the poem is the most perfect

ot all imaginable illustrations of the inadequacy of the Popian tradition. Hayley is always faultlessly smooth in his versification, and careful in his workmanship, never slovenly, never inelegant. The errors of his poetic creed stand therefore conclusively proved in the hopeless reprobation of one, who, if poets could be saved by "correctness" alone, would occupy a high position among the blest.

ROBERT MERRY.
(*From a contemporary print.*)

And what Hayley was, that or worse than that was William Whitehead, the Poet Laureate, and his namesake Paul. Worse still, because wanting in Hayley's honesty and sincerity, and merely pretending to a culture which he actually possessed, were the members of that mutual admiration society of literary fribbles, known as the Della Cruscan School (from the

The Della Cruscans. pen-name assumed by one Robert Merry, a leading light among them), who had combined to publish an album of absurdities in which inanity of sentiment and affectation of style contended energetically but with varying fortunes for predominance. Hayley, and Hayley's friend, Miss Seward, coquetted with the school; and a few writers, who one would have thought had "too much wit to be there," like O'Keefe and Reynolds, were more or less formally attached to it. Mrs. Thrale, now Mrs. Piozzi, had relations with it; and among its other members were a ludicrous person of the name of Upton, in whose verses the habitual flattery of self and fellows became almost harmless by becoming wildly ridiculous; one Williams, a man of somewhat greater ability, but worse character and disposition than his colleagues; and a train of other simpletons and impostors whose very names are now as completely lost as those of the poetasters and pamphleteers of half a century earlier would have been if Pope had never written the "Dunciad."

In the first five or six years onward from 1785, when their precious album first appeared, this school of folly and pretence stood much in need of a Dunciad of its own; and this was at last launched at them from the hand of a rougher and less accomplished but still a sufficient Pope. William Gifford (1757–1826) was a man of humble origin, who by dint of great natural abilities, untiring industry, and the judicious aid of a benevolent patron, had educated himself into a competent scholar and acquired a position of some eminence in the literary world. His critical taste was none of the most delicate, but he knew nonsense when he saw it, and possessing a considerable fund of rough but genuine humour, together with the mastery of a satiric verse which stands to that of Pope in the relation of the oaken cudgel to the rapier, he turned the faculty and the weapon to such effective account in the "Baviad" and the "Mæviad," his two famous lampoons on the Della Cruscan school, as to reduce that incorporated society of idiots to its constituent atoms of individual imbecility.

The "Baviad" and "Mæviad."

ANNA SEWARD.
(*After George Romney.*)

The protest of William Cowper against the poetic errors of the time was of a more general and more serious, if of a less direct and conscious, character. Cowper was a scholar, a hymnodist, a writer of moral and satirical verse, before he presented himself to the world in that character of a true and genuinely if not very deeply inspired poet of nature in which alone his name survives. In the year 1784 he had not published—indeed he had not yet been moved to write— anything in the latter character at all. Whether he would have reached posterity as an important or commanding figure in English letters by the projective force of such poems as

Cowper.

the "Progress of Error," "Hope," "Charity," and other homilies
on the cardinal virtues, or even as "Table Talk," the most
vigorous of them all, it is now impossible to say. They were
poems essentially of a bygone *genre*—poems reminiscent of a
poetic past, and it was inevitable that they should be eclipsed
for us by that portion of his poetry which belonged to, or at
any rate foreshadowed, the poetic future. Yet they may be
read with profit, indeed they should not be omitted, by anyone who desires to take the full measure of Cowper's powers.
The last mentioned poem in particular, with its many
passages of stirring and occasionally even lofty rhetoric, of
admirably just and searching criticism, and its conspicuous
mastery of the difficult art of reasoning in rhyme, is a performance of extraordinary merit; but its purely technical
qualities are no less remarkable; and, though marred here
and there by occasional crudities of phrase and laxities of
metre, its rhymed couplet exhibits a masculine vigour of
versification which is hardly to be found elsewhere in English
literature, if we except a few brief flights of Churchill, since
the death of Dryden.

The
"Task."
But in 1785 his friend and admirer, Lady Austen, was
happily moved to make a suggestion, which he adopted with
memorable results. "Write on anything," she replied to him,
so the story goes, one day when he was at a loss for a subject.
"Write on that sofa." Cowper half jestingly accepted the
half-jesting commission, and the "Task," a poem in six books,
represents his execution of it. It would be too much to say
of this delightful and in many respects great poem that it
was animated by any deliberate intention to "testify" against
the school of Pope. Cowper does, indeed, abandon in it the
heroic couplet, but more for freedom of movement than with
any polemical purpose. There was, in truth, as little as possible
of the innovator about him, and nothing at all of the revolu-
tionist. He shows his essential conservatism by his contented
adherence to much of the old-fashioned convention of poetry—
its tiresome habit of personifying abstract qualities, its stiff and
periwigged ceremoniousness in the handling of common things.
Save for a few occasional—and not always fortunate—lapses into
familiarity, Cowper's manner of dealing with the domestic is still
the manner of the earlier century, still radically opposed to those

principles of "natural" poetic diction, on which Wordsworth was afterwards to insist with so much more zeal than discretion, and to delay for many years the acceptance of invaluable truth by exaggerating them in his preaching and rendering them ridiculous in his practice. Cowper is still far from that frank fraternal recognition of the common objects, ideas, and interests of life which is advocated in the famous preface to the "Lyrical Ballads." Poetry in his hands will unbend to common things, but it is always with a too vigilant dignity: she will take notice of the tea-urn and the silk-reels, and the modest indoor pleasures and employments of the country house, but it is all done with the conscious condescension of the squire's wife at the village school treat. And Cowper, moreover, clings still to that leisurely diffuseness of utterance which is so alien to the spirit of the greater poetry, pregnant with thought, and eager to bring it to the birth. One reads him sometimes divided between delight in his perfect literary finish and

Photo: Walker & Cockerell.

WILLIAM COWPER, BY GEORGE ROMNEY.

(National Portrait Gallery.)

irritation at its prolixity. Here, for instance, is the concentrated essence of a well-known passage in the Sixth Book: "It is cruel to tread wantonly upon a worm" (four lines); "You may accidentally crush a snail, but any humane man seeing the reptile would spare him" (four lines); "Unsightly and probably noxious vermin, if they invade the house, may be lawfully killed" (six lines), "but as long as they keep to their proper province out of doors it is wrong to destroy them" (seven lines). "In short, man may take their lives if his convenience, health, or safety require it" (three lines), "but not otherwise" (four lines). All these lines to be sure are in the matter of expression irreproachable: but in number they are twenty-eight.

**Cowper
and
Nature.**

When Cowper passes out of the garden into the open
country, and comes face to face with Nature, when he ceases
to moralise and begins to describe, we hear him much more
gladly. There is no magic, indeed, in his descriptions, but
they have the unmistakable accent of truth. To read him at
his best and simplest in this kind, after Pope at his most
pictorial, is like passing from a group of Watteau's shepherds
and shepherdesses in a perfumed picture gallery to the fresh
and breezy atmosphere of the field and fold. We feel ourselves to be at last in the hand of a poet who writes, in the
modern phrase, "with his eye upon the object"; whose
account of it is at first-hand, and not of hearsay—founded on
his own observation, and not on the report of tradition;
whose coldest and least illuminating adjective comes from
his own brain, and not from the Gradus; who describes
things as he sees them, and who feels what he sees. Undoubtedly he does not feel them with the spiritual solemnity
of a Wordsworth or with the emotional intensity of a Keats;
he strikes a note which wakens no mysterious echoes, but it
is at least one which, for almost the first time for more than
a century, rings clear and true.

Blake.

Another forerunner of the revival, though one who was
wholly without influence in it, having not, indeed, been
"discovered" as a poet at all until far on in the succeeding
century, was William Blake (1756–1827). As a follower of
nature, and a rebel against the artificial, Blake, by some years
preceding Cowper, went far to anticipate Wordsworth. His
"Poetical Sketches," though not published till 1783, a year
after Cowper's first volume made its appearance, were written,
it appears, between 1768 and 1776, the earlier in the author's
twelfth and the latter in his twentieth year. These were
followed by the "Songs of Innocence" in 1789, and the
"Songs of Experience" in 1794. Blake, who was an artist
before he was a poet, and perhaps one should add, a half-
deranged mystic before he was either, does not seem, as it
was not likely he would, to have caught the ear of a generation attuned to the song of Hayley and Anna Seward. And
indeed it must be owned that a singer of so faulty an ear,
and a writer of so shaky a grammar as Blake, was hardly
well equipped for a pioneer of literary reform. Even now a

considerable amount of the little that Blake has left must be
rejected by the impartial critic as neither poetry nor sense;
but the high poetical quality, the exquisite charm and freshness, of the residue are not to be denied. The affinity of

PAGE FROM "THE MARRIAGE OF HEAVEN AND HELL,"
BY WILLIAM BLAKE.

his highest work with that of Wordsworth's best is as striking as the resemblance of the two poets at their respective
flattest is amusing. He anticipated the creator of Betty Foy,
not in his noble simplicities alone, but in his irritating
puerilities also. If he led the way for Wordsworth up the
steep of Parnassus, he as certainly preceded him down the
slope on the other side into the valley of Bathos. Blake's lack
of humour seems to have been as complete as Wordsworth's

and in the elder poet there are lines of sudden descent
into prose which startle us almost like a prophetic parody
of the younger.

Burns.   To assign to Robert Burns (1759–96) the position of importance which no doubt properly belongs to him among the

Photo: Bara, Ayr.
ROBERT BURNS'S BIRTHPLACE.

great lyrists of the world is, in a work of this kind, of course,
impossible. Rare as was the poetic gift of Burns, and unique
in their quality of pure elemental passion as were his bursts of
song, the poet himself has no place in what is mainly a history
of influences and tendencies. Writing as he did—so long at
least as he wrote poetry and not somewhat inferior verse—in
the Lowland Scottish vernacular, he naturally could not con-
tribute anything directly to the development of English poetic
literature. Nor does it even appear that he directly influenced
those who were the main contributors to this work. The first
edition of his poems, published at Kilmarnock, appeared in 1786,
and the second at Edinburgh in the following year. Its success
with his own countrymen was instant, his fame during the last
ten years of his short life unbounded; and it has been growing
ever since on both sides of the border. But while Burns, who,
though he died two years before the publication of the " Lyrical
Ballads," was in ardent sympathy with the beginnings of the
new poetic movement in England as initiated by Cowper,
whose " Task " he described as a "glorious poem," it can

hardly be said that he attained to any general popularity among English readers until the Naturalist and Romantic school had fully established itself. Burns, in other words, did not help to lead English taste in poetry back to nature; it was nature that led it to Burns.

Wordsworth was but thirteen years old when Cowper's "Task" was published, and Coleridge only twelve. That they must have read and admired that poem in youth and early manhood may be taken as certain, but that they were much or at all influenced by him there is no evidence to show. Whatever direct external influence is traceable in their earliest productions came from Germany, but the development of the two poets proceeded, it should be remembered, though it is too often forgotten, at a very unequal rate. Coleridge, before completing his twenty-fifth year, had produced two of the finest and most mature of his lyrics, the "Ode to the Departing Year," and the other and even nobler piece entitled "France." Wordsworth, on the other hand, though two years Coleridge's senior, had published only those early pieces which, though no doubt they contained the germ and potentiality of his later and greater

Words-worth and Coleridge.

ROBERT BURNS, BY ALEXANDER NASMYTH.
(The National Gallery of Scotland.)

poetry, yet can hardly be said to have given assured promise of his future fame. It was not till just upon the close of our present period that the two young poets joined in the publication of that collection of poems whose appearance is conveniently, though in some respects not quite accurately, taken as an epoch-making event in the history of the Naturalist movement. The first volume of the " Lyrical Ballads " was issued in 1798, and the second, with Wordsworth's famous preface, in 1800. Our consideration of them, therefore, may be appropriately deferred to the next chapter.

Crabbe.   But poetical, like political, revolutions are never the work of one or two men. The revolt against the degenerate tradition of the school of Pope had been fermenting in many minds and took more than one specific form. With Wordsworth it was mainly a craving for a more honest report of external nature and a simpler form of poetic speech. But the poetasters of the Popian succession had not wandered further from truth to nature than from fidelity to the facts of human life. A demand for *realism* in the portraiture of humanity, and of the world in its relations to mankind, was as inevitable a product of the revolt against the dominant poetry as was the demand for veracity and simplicity in the poet's account of nature; and the former now found voice of almost brutal energy in the verse of George Crabbe (1754–1832). Crabbe, the son of a parish schoolmaster, who afterwards obtained a petty local office in the Customs, came up to London in 1789 with his poem of the " Library " in his pocket, but little else, and after coming within measurable distance of starvation, from which he only escaped through the providential interposition of Burke, was enabled by that kindly and judicious patron not only to publish his already written work, but two years later, in 1783, to bring out a second poem, the " Village," on which even more perhaps than on the " Parish Register," the " Borough," and the " Tales of the Hall," the fame of the poet rests. It is not a highly poetic fame; there are, indeed, " doctors of weight " in criticism who deny to Crabbe the name of a poet at all. But if he lacks that charm which is necessary to convert truth into poetry, his work has in it the root of the matter—truth itself. We do at least get away in it from the conventional world of Pope, and from the idealised rural life of Goldsmith. The " Village " set before us by " Nature's sternest painter but her best," as Crabbe has been called, is vastly unlike " Sweet Auburn "; but we feel, after near a century of the clogged and loaded poetry of the bygone era, that this bitter draught of realism is refreshing. And we get it nowhere else till Wordsworth's

rather turbid beverage has fined down. What remains of
poetry till then, is only the irreproachable didactic numbers of
the virtuous Mrs. Hannah More, and the dramatic commonplace of that other heroine of Scott's too easily captured
admiration, Joanna Baillie.

English prose in this, even more than in the immediately

GEORGE CRABBE, BY THOMAS PHILLIPS, R.A.
(*From a photograph, by permission of John Murray, Esq.*)

preceding, period is dominated by the two great names of **English**
Burke and Gibbon. This, indeed, might even have been the **Prose.**
case had their literary merit been far less eminent; for, in
fact, they were now almost the last survivors of that band of
distinguished prose-writers who had adorned the literature
of the previous generation. Johnson died in the year with
which this period commences; Hume and Goldsmith had
passed away several years before; Richardson and Fielding had
    237

preceded Hume to the grave—the one by fifteen, the other
by more than twenty years.   Gibbon and Burke had, therefore,
no prose contemporaries of the first rank, nor indeed, with
the exception of Mackintosh, any of the second.

Gibbon.   The four years from 1784 to 1788 witnessed the production
of the last volumes of the "Decline and Fall," and perma-
nently established its author in that position of supremacy as a
historian of which each succeeding generation renders his
tenure more secure.   It was, perhaps, not unnatural that his
favourite and sometimes rather fatiguing trick of hinting at,
instead of openly displaying, the vast stores of his learning
should have at first aroused suspicions of its reality, or at
least its depth; but that "allusive manner," by which the
smatterer of our own days so skilfully conceals the superficiality
of his knowledge, was with Gibbon simply a point of style.
Gibbon's "we could an if we would" is sincere, whereas the
smatterer's real position is that he would an if he could, but
that as a matter of fact he couldn't.   When the latter quotes
half a dozen words from some recondite authority, it is because
he does not know enough of the matter to fill a sentence; when
the former does so, it is only because he is resolved not to break
the flow of his narrative by expanding into half a dozen
sentences of digression what he can compress into a few words.
And invariably in his case, as never in the other, the few words
are found on fuller knowledge to be perfectly exact as far as they
go.   "Every careful critic of his own and other men's work
knows," it has been well said by Mr. Saintsbury, "that there
is no more dangerous point than this one of slight reference
or allusion to subjects imperfectly known, nor any one in which
sciolism or imposture is most certain to be found out.   Yet it is
scarcely too much to say that Gibbon has never been thus found
out.   There were some things—not many—which he did not and
could not know; but almost everything that there was for him
to know he knew."   And he used his magnificent wealth of
knowledge with a judgment in matters of detail and with a
breadth and sweep of generalising power which has seldom
been equalled and never surpassed.

His Style.   On the merits and demerits of his style it cannot be pretended
that the same consensus of competent opinion prevails.   It has
been reprehended by many who had some right to criticise it, and

by more who had not.   Coleridge, whose own prose style, with all
its eloquence, left much to be desired, condemned it in terms so
extravagant as to discredit the critic rather than the criticised;
but others, reviewing it with less bias, and expressing themselves
with more moderation, have managed to draw up a pretty long
list of objections to it.   It has been pronounced monotonous,
inelastic, affected, pompous; it has been called exotic in its
spirit, and un-English in its structure.   The most serious of
these charges is, perhaps, the second.   The last is not, indeed,
without a certain superficial plausibility, though, no doubt, it
would scarcely have occurred to anyone who was not acquainted
with Gibbon's admiration for the French as a medium of expression, or was ignorant of the fact that he actually began the
composition of his great work in that language.   When, however, the attention is called to it, the fact is found to be indis-
putable that the typical Gibbonian sentence has strong affinities
of construction and cadence with that of the *prosateurs* of
France.   Especially is this noticeable in Gibbon's apparent
determination never, if he can help it, to close his sentence
with a verb, adjective, or participle, and his uniform habit,
in itself the cause of a certain monotony, of bringing it to an
end, as often as may be, on a substantive governed by the
preposition "of."   Such sentence-endings would, no doubt, be
found upon inquiry to preponderate largely in all English
writers over any other single form or description of syntactic
clauses; but in Gibbon the preponderance is so excessive as to
make analysis almost amusing.   Out of thirty-five consecutive
sentences upon two pages selected from the "Decline and Fall"
by the arbitrament of the inserted paper-knife, no fewer than
twenty have this form of termination.   That is to say, it is of
more frequent occurrence not only than any one other, but than
all other forms taken together.

It will be found, we think, that what is felt as the
somewhat too monotonous uniformity of Gibbon's cadences is
due in great measure to a latent consciousness on the reader's
part of this inordinate uniformity of construction.   In any
case, however, the complaint is not a very serious one against
a prose writer of Gibbon's majestic power.   The sea is distinctly monotonous; that is one of "the defects of its qualities."
But there are those who can listen to the sound of its

waves for considerable spaces of time without being bored,
and similar enthusiasts are to be found who do not easily
tire of listening to the rolling surges of Gibbon's prose.
Those who do can find plenty of distraction in later English
writers.   By the shores of the sounding sea are many gay
kiosks and casinos, where they will find a band discoursing
selections from the masterpieces of lighter comic opera.

The charge of pomposity partly depends for its gravity
on that of affectation, or in other words of pretence, and partly
on the charge of inelasticity.   Loftiness of manner, when
displayed in social life by those whose position warrants it,
usually receives the more complimentary appellation of " stateliness."   It is not described as pompous till it is felt as
ridiculous.   And in Gibbon its approaches to the ridiculous
are comparatively rare, and when they occur are necessarily
due to an inelasticity of style which cannot accommodate
itself to the minor requirements of a historical narrative.
Gibbon (and this incidentally refutes the reproach of affectation) simply could not be familiar.   His stateliness was
not only natural to him, it was inseparable from him.   He
showed that in his " Autobiography," to which indeed it lends
much of the charm with which those inimitable confessions
are instinct.   When Gibbon " sighs as a lover, but obeys as
a son," the reader admires as a critic, though he smiles as
a man.   His condescensions to the insignificant or ignoble,
wherever he meets them in his history, have much the same
sub-comic effect as his handling of these domestic matters in
his autobiography.   But these, after all, are but infrequent
experiences with any serious historian.   For all other purposes—for those of straightforward narrative equally with
those of comment and disquisition—his style is, to say the
least of it, a satisfactory instrument : while as a vehicle of
wit, irony, eloquence, and richly yet soberly coloured description,
its measured manner makes it brilliantly effective.

Burke.   It was said, records Croker, by Sir James Mackintosh, that
Gibbon might have been cut out of a corner of Burke's mind
without Burke noticing it.   To determine Mackintosh's own
proportional relation to Burke by the same scale would compel
a resort to the calculus of infinitesimals.   The saying was, in
fact, an impertinence in every sense of the word, and as inept to

boot as any other attempt at the admeasurement of incommen-
surables.   But we can understand how a comparison between
the two men's minds should have produced such an impression
of their spatial disparity on a mind considerably less com-
modious than either.   It is undoubtedly true that after an
hour's walk with Burke through any abstract subject which he
found particularly stimulating, we do seem to have covered a

GIBBON OUTWEIGHING THE BISHOP.
(From a satirical print of 1788.)

considerably greater amount of intellectual ground than if we
had accompanied Gibbon for an equal period of time through
any even of the most philosophical parts of his history.   But
that is to some extent a deceptive effect of the greater number
and more rapid succession of ideas, or sometimes merely of
images, with which Burke will have filled our minds during the
walk.   In other words, it is not, as Mackintosh erroneously
supposed, in the wider reach and expanse of his intellect that
Burke had the advantage of Gibbon; it is in the greater

natural energy and the habitually much more active play of an extraordinary imagination expressing itself through a vocabulary the richest and most various that ever served the tongue or pen of man.

This, however, having been said by way of protest against an exaggerated and invidious comparison, let it be admitted

Photo: Walker & Cockerell.
THE RIGHT HON. EDMUND BURKE, BY SIR JOSHUA
REYNOLDS.
(National Portrait Gallery.)

that Burke, even if we cannot exactly cut Gibbon out of him, impresses with a combination of thought and expression at a higher power than Gibbon attains. Political writers both sagacious and eloquent have flourished at all periods of modern English history. The thought and the expression were often united in the same person, and in some instances with a profundity in the one gift matched worthily with distinction in the other. But it may well be doubted whether any writer on politics and the philosophy of politics has ever combined sagacity and eloquence in such measure, or anything approaching

DON DISMALLO RUNNING THE LITERARY GAUNTLET.

BURKE RECEIVING PUNISHMENT FOR HIS APOSTASY.

(From a satirical print of 1790.)

to such measure, as that in which they are combined by Burke. Of course he was not absolutely proof against the influences of tradition and training, and he allowed some Whig dogmas to pass with insufficient interrogation; but with these exceptions, and they were comparatively few, his brilliant general-ising faculty and splen-did theorematic powers were everywhere guided and held in check by a resolutely practical criticism of common sense. It was during our present period that this unparalleled array of gifts was to receive its most memorable illustration. In 1790 appeared the "Reflec-tions on the French Revolution," in which all the argumentative and all the rhetorical abilities which Burke had displayed in his earlier works were en-listed in a cause to which he was most passionately devoted. And the result was a masterpiece.

SIR JAMES MACKINTOSH, BY SIR T. LAWRENCE.
(*National Portrait Gallery.*)

Mackin-tosh.
To pass from Burke to Mackintosh is to make the descent from genius to talent with more suddenness, not to say violence, than one would naturally prefer. Yet Mackintosh is perhaps the only other prose writer who can be even mentioned in the period overshadowed by Gibbon and Burke; for Robertson, though an historian of merit, can hardly be said as a prose writer to be anything more than an echo of his English models. Mackintosh has undoubtedly more individuality. The "Vin-diciæ Gallicæ" can still be read with pleasure; and did it not everywhere challenge a disastrous comparison with the monu-mental work to which it is the very inadequate answer, it would win more admiration than it does. As it is, one cannot help

reading it with a feeling that with all its more than respectable merit it is thoroughly characteristic of that universal genius whom partial friends regarded as an Admirable Crichton and posterity has clean forgotten.

IN the first three quarters of the eighteenth century a striking advance had been made in farming ; the cultivation and rotation of crops were better understood, and stock-breeding had become a science. But this progress was partial and strictly local. Only in the Eastern counties and Leicestershire had the tillers of the soil profited by the new sources of wealth which men like Tull, Townshend, or Bakewell had revealed. The character of the farmers, the size of the holdings, and the comparatively small number of open fields, partly explain the superior enterprise of agriculturists in these favoured districts. Writers like Arthur Young and Marshall agree that, in Norfolk, farmers occupied " the same position in society as the clergy and smaller squires " ; in Lincolnshire, " many had mounted their nags and examined other parts of the country " ; in Leicestershire, they had " travelled much and mixed constantly with one another." Elsewhere, however, agriculture had made little or no advance for centuries, owing to the prevalence of wastes, the system of open-field farming, the absence of leases, the poverty and ignorance of hand-to-mouth farmers, the obstinacy of traditionary practices, the want of markets, and the difficulties of communication. Till these obstacles were overcome, agricultural progress could not be general. It is with the removal of these hindrances to advance that the name of Arthur Young is inseparably connected.

Vast districts, as has been already said (p. 131), still lay waste and unenclosed. So late as 1795 a report of the Board of Agriculture stated that twenty-two million acres lay waste in Great Britain, of which more than six-and-a-quarter millions were in England. Besides these tracts of uncultivated land, it has been calculated that in more than half the parishes of England the soil was in 1760 farmed in common by village communities on the system previously described. Thus in Cambridgeshire out of 147,000 arable acres, 132,200 were in open fields ; out of 438,000 acres in Berkshire 220,000 were similarly

R. E. PRO-
THERO.
Agricul-
ture.

Obstacles
to Pro-
gress.

Waste
Land and
Joint
Tillage.

cultivated. The Vale of Pickering, in Yorkshire, was farmed
by the township, the common sheep-walks and pastures were
overrun with weeds and bushes, the arable fields exhausted by
an unvarying succession of crops, the meadows mown year after
year without intermission or amelioration. At Naseby a few
pasture enclosures surrounded the mud-built village; the
open fields, tilled on the three-fold system, were crossed and
re-crossed by paths to the different holdings, filled with a
cavernous depth of mire; the pastures were in a state of
nature, rough, full of furze, rushes and fern. Similar to these
instances was the condition of almost every open-field farm.
No rotation of crops in which roots formed an element could
be introduced on land that was held in common from August
to Candlemas; among the underfed, undersized, and under-
bred flocks and herds of the commoners it was impossible to
practise the principles of Bakewell. It was not without reason
that Arthur Young came to the conclusion that "the Goths
and Vandals of open-field farmers must die out before any
complete change takes place."

**Land
Tenure.**

Without some security for his outlay no tenant could be
expected to invest capital in his farm. But the tenure by
which land was most commonly held, except where it was
freehold or copyhold, was an agreement voidable on either
side at six months' notice. In Essex and Suffolk leases for
terms of years, with clauses as to management, were not
unknown. But elsewhere leases were regarded with suspicion
not only by tenants, but by landlords, because they "told the
farmer when he might begin systematically to exhaust the land."
Where a good understanding existed between landlords and
tenants, a simple tenure at will, or from year to year, practically
secured the farmer in his holding; yet its nominal uncertainty
undoubtedly checked all enterprise on the part of tenants.
Leases for lives were also common; but, though they gave fixity
of tenure to the farmer, their utility was marred by the
absence of any clauses as to management or any provision for
the maintenance of farm buildings. Without long leases, no
tenants would invest their capital in the land; without careful
provision for management and repairs, no landowner could
safely surrender to an occupier the entire control of his holding
for a lengthy period.

Other formidable obstacles to progress lay in the ignorance and poverty of farmers, the mass of local prejudices, and the obstinate adherence to antiquated methods. Open-field farmers lived from hand-to-mouth, and the antiquated system on which their land was tilled was only adapted to supply the producers themselves with their daily food. Their ambitions did not rise beyond sustenance to profit. Where farms were enclosed and tilled by individual tenants, or copyholders, or yeomen, traditional practices were treasured as agricultural heirlooms.

MOUSEHOLD HEATH, NEAR NORWICH, BY JOHN CROME.
(*National Gallery.*)

Thus, for instance, in Kent, in the time of Hartlib, and, a century and a half later in the time of Young, it was not unusual to see twelve horses and oxen to one plough. In Hampshire, Lisle, writing in the eighteenth century, says that it was the practice to employ from eight to ten oxen to each plough. A trace of the practice survives in the ancient crooked ridges which may be seen on grass-lands. The enormous length of the team and the unwieldy plough required a vast width of head-row on which to turn. To obviate this difficulty a deflection or curvature was made in the furrow, and the result is the curved ridge which may still be seen. In Gloucestershire, at the close of the eighteenth century, two men and a boy and six horses were employed for ploughing. A Norfolk ploughman, with a pair of horses and a Norfolk plough, was sent into the county who did the work in the same time at a saving of £120 a year. But it was twenty years before any of the neighbours profited by the example. Young, writing in 1768, says that clover and turnips were unheard of in many parts of the country. Clover was not sown in Northumberland till 1752. In the same county turnips were sown broadcast till 1780. Horse-hoeing, till nearly the close of the century, was rarely practised outside the Eastern counties. In 1811 Davies wrote an agricultural report on Wiltshire; but, though sheep were the sheet-anchor of the county, turnips were still almost unknown.

Difficulties of Locomotion. The difficulties of dissipating local prejudices and disseminating new ideas were enormously increased by defective means of communication (p. 468). Turnpike roads had been established in 1663, and, at least as early as the reign of George II.,

> "No cit nor clown
> Can gratis see the country or the town."

Yet, in the eighteen miles of turnpike-road between Preston and Wigan, Arthur Young measured "ruts four feet in depth and floating in mud only from a wet summer," and passed three broken-down carts. In Essex "a mouse could barely pass a carriage in its narrow lanes," which were filled with bottomless ruts, and often choked by a string of waggons buried so deep in the mire that they could only be extracted by thirty or forty horses. "Of all the cursed roads that ever disgraced this kingdom in the very age of barbarism, none ever equalled that from Billericay to Tilbury," cries Young in 1769. In country districts, in fact, roads were mere lanes, generally engineered on the principle that "one good turn deserved another." During the winter many were almost impassable except by well-mounted horsemen. The bells on waggon horses were not in those days merely an ornament; but were a necessary warning when two teams could not pass each other.

Effect of the Industrial Revolution. Shut off from their neighbours by impassable roads, and impelled to raise no more from the soil than their own needs demanded, farmers had little stimulus to improvement. But Watt, Arkwright, and others changed the face of society

with the swiftness of a revolution. Population advanced by
leaps and bounds in crowded manufacturing centres. Huge
markets sprang up for agricultural produce. ✗Hitherto there ✓
had been few divisions of employment, because only the
simplest implements of production were employed; cloth-
workers and weavers combined much of their work with the
tillage of the soil. But the rapid development of manufacture

THE WINDMILL.

(After Thomas Gainsborough.)

caused its complete separation from agriculture, and the application of machinery to manual industries completed the
revolution in social arrangements. A division of labour was
an economic necessity; farmers and artisans became mutually
dependent. How was the change to be met? How was a
country, with a strictly protective policy and at war with
Europe, to raise food for a rapidly growing population concentrated in the coal and iron fields? It was evident that
farms must be made efficient manufactories of beef and mutton
for the million; that large farms, capitalist tenants, long leases,
must sweep away every obstacle to good farming; and that,

compelled to make a choice, England must sacrifice to the artisan her wastes and commons, her farming communities, her small yeomen and copyholders, and exchange the picturesque varieties of the peasantry for the monotony of wage-dependent labour.

The Work of Arthur Young.

In this agricultural revolution Arthur Young played a conspicuous part, though it may be doubted whether his spirited crusade against bad farming would have produced any result if it had not been supported by industrial necessities. To him, more than to any other individual, were owing the enclosure of wastes, the extinction of the open-field farms, the partition of commons, and the consolidation of holdings, which changed the face of rural England with the rapidity of an earthquake. To his energy, again, were mainly due the dissemination of new ideas on agriculture, the collection of agricultural statistics, the diffusion of the latest results of experiments, the creation of the Board of Agriculture, the establishment of farmers' clubs, ploughing matches, and agricultural shows.

Born in 1741 at Bradfield Hall, near Bury St. Edmunds, Arthur Young began his career by failing as a practical farmer. In 1767 he commenced those farming tours in the course of which he drew his graphic sketches of rural England, Ireland, and France. From this date until 1810 his efforts on behalf of good farming were unremitting. His brain was never weary ; pamphlets and reports flowed from his pen, and his " Annals " were a farming periodical to which George III. often contributed. In 1793 the Board of Agriculture was created, and he acted as its secretary till his retirement in 1810. He died in 1820, having been for ten years totally blind. For half a century after his death the completeness of his success obscured his fame. He recognised the absolute necessity of providing food for a growing population, and offered a common-sense solution of the difficulty. His general aim may be summed up in the policy of developing to the full the resources of the country, the reclamation of wastes, the partition of commons, the break-up of open-field farms, the consolidation of holdings, the investment of capital in the land by both landlord and tenant, long leases, large tenancies, and the most improved methods of cultivation and stock-breeding. More produce, as he puts the case, meant more profit—higher rents to landlords, larger incomes to farmers,

better wages to labourers, and more food to the nation. **The**
system which he advocated, aided as he was by the pressure of
war-prices and the gigantic increase of the manufacturing
population, was established with such completeness that men
forgot the previous existence of any other conditions. It is only
of recent years that his name has been revived in England by
the renewal of the struggle between large and small farmers,
while in France, where the contest between capitalist farmers
and peasant proprietors
has never been decisively
terminated, the discussion
has always centred round
his name.

The two most im-
portant changes in rural
England which belonged
to the closing years of
the eighteenth century
were the reclamation of
wastes and the partition
of commons. Enclosures
aimed at bringing into
cultivation all the im-
provable land of the
country, and they resulted
also in destroying the
open-field system which
was dependent on com-
mons. / The old method

ARTHUR YOUNG, F.R.S.

(After a portrait by Rising.)

of enclosing commons and wastes was by writs of partition and
admeasurement. But the proceedings were too costly to be
used on any large scale. In more modern times commons were
divided by consent of the interested parties or by private Acts of
Parliament. Here, again, the difficulties were so great as
practically to prevent enclosures. It was almost impossible to
obtain the consent of all the parties interested, and four-fifths of
the commoners, the lord of the manor, and the tithe-owner, were
obliged to agree before a Parliamentary sanction could be
obtained. Under the pressure of social changes, many private
Acts were obtained as the century drew to its close. But the

Reclama-
tion and
Enclosure.

process of enclosure was greatly accelerated after 1801, when the first general Act was passed. Between 1793 and 1809, it has been calculated that 4½ million acres of land were added to the cultivated area of England and Wales. There can be no question that, viewed in an agricultural and economical aspect, enclosures were profitable to the country. But socially the advantages of the change are less conclusively proved. It is probable that " A Country Gentleman," who, in 1772, wrote a pamphlet on " The Advantages and Disadvantages of Enclosing Waste Land,' expressed the truth when he said that landlords, farmers, and the nation gained by the change, but that the common field farmer must suffer by becoming " a hired labourer."

The result of enclosures, which were the great social feature that marks the closing years of the eighteenth century is, in fact, the extinction of the common-field farmer, and his transformation into a wage-earner. The disappearance of the yeoman and the small freeholder was the result of different causes, and, in the main, belongs to a later date. Against individual losses must be placed the national gain. Without the enclosure of her wastes and commons, and the break-up of open-field farms, England would never have fed her growing population, supported the strain of the Napoleonic wars, and gained the first place in the race for industrial supremacy.

"Where," asks Young, with perfect truth, "is the little farmer to be found who will cover his whole farm with marl at the rate of 100 or 150 tons per acre? Who will drain all his land at the expense of £2 or £3 an acre? Who will pay a heavy price for the manure of towns, and convey it thirty miles by land carriage? Who will float his meadows at the expense of £5 an acre? Who, to improve the breed of his sheep, will give 1,000 guineas for the use of a single ram for a single season? Who will send across the Kingdom to distant provinces for new implements, and for men to use them? Who will employ and pay men for residing in provinces where practices are found which they want to introduce into their farms?"

The new system of farming was, in fact, a necessity of the times. Landlords and tenants put their capital into the land, and found it the most profitable investment. Farming began to make a rapid and general advance. Mr. Coke of Holkham is, perhaps, the most conspicuous instance of a great landlord devoting himself, by the expenditure of capital and personal energy, to the development of his estate. His long and useful career extended far into the nineteenth century, and will be more appropriately noticed at a later stage. But the movement which, from 1772 onwards, he headed in the Eastern counties found its representatives among large landowners in every part of England and Scotland. With the close of the eighteenth century commences the system of farming with which we are to-day acquainted, and the threefold division of the landed interest into landlords, tenants, and labourers.

ALTHOUGH it is wrong to imagine that before the days of Watt the steam engine was not a practical working machine, yet it was only useful in a strictly limited way. It was useful for pumping, and that was practically all. One reason of its limited application, namely, its cost, has been explained in a previous section (p. 427). But there was another reason, which was that the capability of combining the longitudinal movement of the piston rod with the rotatory movement of the wheel was not clearly grasped, although the crank had long been in use for lathes. It is true that in 1736 Jonathan Hulls had placed a pair of paddle wheels in the stern of a boat, and had employed a Newcomen engine to work them. But this gear was very clumsy, and the boat when tried on the Avon was a failure. In all the pumping engines the power was applied to a beam, and a pump rod attached to the other end. This suited the immense length and the slow pace of the Newcomen engine. But the time was now come for something better, and the man who made the manifold improvements necessary was James Watt.

G. TOWNS-
END
WARNER.
Machinery
and Manu-
factures.
The Steam
Engine.

In 1756 Watt, then a mathematical instrument maker, was endeavouring to set up in Glasgow. Obstacles were put in his way by the town guilds, as he had not served his apprenticeship there, but the University gave Watt the use of some rooms in one of their buildings where the town guilds had no power of molesting him. A model of the Newcomen engine came into his hands for repairs in 1763, and he began to experiment with it. He soon perceived that the source of failure of the New-comen engine lay in its waste of heat, due to condensing the steam in the cylinder itself. No less than three-quarters of the heat was wasted. This waste would be solved by keeping the

James
Watt.

238

cylinder always as hot as the steam that entered it; palliatives, such as steam jackets, non-conducting cylinders, and so on would not go to the root of the matter. He hit on the plan of having a separate condenser in which a vacuum might be created, so that the steam would rush into it, and be there condensed, and made a model on these lines, which worked well. The problem was theoretically solved, but it was long years before the practical difficulties were overcome. One of these was to provide a good vacuum in the condenser. For this Watt used an air pump worked by the engine. He also covered in the top of his cylinder to prevent loss of heat when the piston descended, and made the piston-rod pass through a stuffing-box. This would have prevented the atmospheric pressure acting on the piston at all, but Watt had determined to dispense with atmospheric pressure, and so he admitted steam above the cylinder, and made it do the work of driving down the piston. When this was done a way was opened between the upper and lower part of the cylinder; the pressure of steam thus equalised above and below, the weight of the pump gear

ORIGINAL MODEL
OF A SEPARATE
CONDENSER, BY
JAMES WATT.

(*Victoria and Albert
Museum.*)

drew the piston up again, and the steam left below being condensed in the separate condenser, the engine was ready for another stroke. Thus, instead of the old atmospheric engine, there was created the steam engine. Watt only used low pressures at first, for so long as the condenser and vacuum were used a low pressure would do the work. But even now Watt had two great foes to struggle with—expense and bad workmanship. The first of these was overcome by a partnership with Roebuck, of Carron, entered into in 1767, by which Roebuck contracted to pay debts incurred to the extent of £1,000, and find money for further experiments. In return he was to take two-thirds of the profit. Watt took out a patent,

JONATHAN HULLS'S STEAM TUG BOAT.

(After the drawing attached to his specification for the patent.)

and went on experimenting. But even the Carron workmen did not work nearly true enough for him. His cylinders drove him to despair; he tried copper, block tin, lead, cast iron; the hard ones were not made true, and the soft ones soon worked out of shape. The engine built by Watt at Kenneil could not be persuaded to go properly. And, to make matters worse, Roebuck

PUMPING ENGINE OF 1777, BY JAMES WATT.
(From a photograph, by permission of the Birmingham Steam Navigation.)

got into financial difficulties, and in 1773 went bankrupt. He owed £1,200 to Matthew Boulton, of Birmingham, and in payment of this Boulton took the two-thirds share in Watt's engine. The Kenneil engine, "Beelzebub," as Watt called it, was taken to pieces, packed up, and sent off to Birmingham.

Boulton and Watt. Matthew Boulton, Watt's new partner, had begun as a manufacturer of small metal articles, buttons, links, shoe-buckles and the like. He had money to start with and had prospered. In 1762 he had built works at Soho and enlarged his business, adding to it the manufacture of plate and articles in ormolu. In 1769 he had been offered a share in Watt's patents, but had not taken it up. He was energetic, enterprising and hard-headed, and was particularly honoured for his determination to try to

remove the reproach from " Brummagem " goods by sending out
everything of the best quality. With his help Watt soon began
to make progress. Wilkinson, of Bersham, cast an eighteen-inch
cylinder and bored it true. The Soho workmen worked with
accuracy. In 1776, Watt's engine, built for Wilkinson at
Broxley, was a success.
Orders came in fast. " Pray
tell Mr. Wilkinson," writes
Boulton, " to get a dozen
cylinders cast and bored from
twelve to fifty inches diameter,
and as many condensers of
suitable sizes. The latter
must be sent here, as we will
keep them ready fitted up,
and then an engine can be
turned out of hand in two
or three weeks. I have fixed
my mind upon making twelve
to fifteen reciprocating and
fifty rotative engines per
annum." In 1777 Watt
himself went to Cornwall
to set up pumping engines
there, of one of which,
built at Chacewater, he
writes : " The velocity,
violence, magnitude and
horrible noise of the en-

MODEL OF INVERTED STEAM PUMPING
ENGINE.
(*Victoria and Albert Museum.*)

gine give universal satisfaction to all beholders." It " forked "
water as no engine had done before. The news spread rapidly
over the country. In 1781 Boulton wrote to Watt, " The people
in London and Manchester are all *steam-mill* mad." In 1783
Watt built a steam-hammer capable of striking 300 blows a
minute, with a stroke of two feet and a hammer head of seven
and a half hundredweight ; but his and other steam-hammers
of the eighteenth century, were all " tilt " hammers—that is, the
hammer was fastened at the end of the shaft and the head raised
by the action of cams or some such plan ; thus the head moved
on a curve and would only strike a full straight blow on a com-

paratively small object, for a big object did not leave the hammer room to do any effective work.   In this way the machine was unsatisfactory, for the heavier and bigger the job, the less the hammer could do.   Watt in no way forestalled Nasmyth, whose hammer is on a different and better principle.   In 1786 Watt

MODEL OF COMBINED FORGE
AND TILT HAMMERS.
(*Victoria and Albert Museum.*)

made double-acting engines of considerable size, which were set up at the Albion Mills, near Black-friars Bridge.   The engines were of fifty horse-power each and worked with a steam-pressure of five pounds to the inch.   They drove twenty pairs of mill-stones, and could grind 150 bushels of wheat an hour, and the steam-power was also used for fanning, sifting, loading and unloading, hoisting and so forth.   The gear for these celebrated mills was designed by John Rennie (afterwards the engineer of Waterloo and London Bridges), and was a novelty, being made entirely of cast or wrought iron. Hitherto wood had been used almost universally, though Smeaton had made an iron wheel at Carron in 1754, and Murdock had fitted rough iron gearing to a mill in Ayrshire.   Watt himself had suggested the use of iron — this is proved by a letter from Boulton in 1781, saying, " I like your plan of making all the principal wearing parts of tempered steel and the racks of best Swedish iron, with the teeth cut out. Query: Would it not be worth while to make a machine for dividing and cutting the teeth in good form out of sectors ?   The iron would be less strained by that method of cutting."   But in excellence, ingenuity, and accuracy of workmanship, Rennie's gear was remarkable, and it was the beginning of a complete change in millwork.   To return to Watt's engines.   Saw-mills in America, sugar-mills in the West Indies, paper-mills, flour-mills, engines for flint grinding in the Potteries, were ordered in quick succession. In 1785 one was ordered for a silk-mill in Maccles-field, and one was built for Robinson's cotton mill at Papplewick, in Nottinghamshire. The first engines in Manchester and Glasgow were set to work in 1789 and 1792 respectively. In fact between 1780 and 1800 the steam-engine was established as the motive power of the day. When wind-mills lay idle and water-mills were frozen up Watt's engines worked on and worked economically.

The inventor himself was never tired of improving his own work. His suggestion of iron gear has already been mentioned. He was the first to use steam expansively, cutting off steam at half-stroke. He invented the "governor" to regulate the throttle-valve and so keep the power developed steady. As the crank, an old mechanical device, was patented for use with the steam-engine by Pickard,[1] and so wrested from him, he designed a new plan for securing rotary motion—the sun and planet wheel. He made his engines double-acting, ad-mitting steam in turn above and below his piston. Improve-ments came fast from Soho. His assistant, Murdock, made the first oscillating engine, though he did not bring it into practical use, and he was also the first to apply coal gas as an illuminant. From 1794 till 1802 Murdock carried on trials. At the celebration of the Peace of Amiens, in 1802, Soho was lit up by gas, and in 1803 the works were regularly lighted by it. Other firms soon followed the example of Soho, and in 1805 Watt found gas in pretty general use in Glasgow. Mr. Smiles notes as an illustration of how slowly knowledge spreads and how permanent is illusion, that the gas in the pipes was long believed to be on fire, and that when the House of Commons was first lit by gas, members were to be seen cautiously feeling the pipes and wondering that they were cool.

By 1783, as far as smelting was concerned, coke and pit coal had practically driven their rival charcoal from the field; but for one purpose charcoal still held its own, and that was for

Watt's Inventive Powers.

Gas.

Coal and Iron.

[1 There is a story, repeated in the *Dictionary of National Biography*, that Watt, having invented or readopted the crank, explained it at the local ale-house, drawing diagrams on the table with a finger wetted in his mug; and that James Pickard, a stranger who happened to be present, hastened to patent the device as his own. Another account is that one of Watt's workmen supplied Pickard with his information.]

making malleable iron. This fact held back the iron trade just
as the scarcity of yarn had held back the textile industries.
The first person to make a success of using coal for malleable
iron was Henry Cort. Like most other inventors he was not
really the first in the field, but rather one who brought to
perfection what his predecessors had left in an unfinished state.
The advantage to be gained was so obvious that every ironmaster must have turned his thoughts to it. It is stated that
Roebuck, at Carron, worked out his bar iron with pit coal in
1763, but the bar iron here mentioned can hardly have been
malleable, for Watt writes that he went to Carron and showed
them how to make tough iron, and that before that they had
never turned out a ton of it. In 1766, however, two brothers
named Cranege, employed at Coalbrookdale, told Reynolds
that they thought pit coal might be used in a reverberatory
furnace, that is a furnace where the flame alone reaches the
iron, instead of the iron and fuel being in contact as they
are in a blast furnace. Now the idea of a reverberatory furnace
was not a new one, as one of the pioneers in the use of coal,
a German named Blewstone, had tried smelting in a reverberatory furnace in the latter years of the seventeenth century.
But the brothers insisted on the probability of success in the
attempt to turn cast into malleable by this method, and as the
event proved they were right. The problem was to get the
iron in a purer state, in which it is tough instead of being
brittle as cast iron is, and to do this it was necessary to get
rid of impurities such as silicon, sulphur, and phosphorus, and
at the same time to reduce the amount of carbon. Reynolds
allowed the Craneges to try their idea at Bridgnorth, and
the experiment was successful. He says "the iron put into
the furnace was Old Bushes, which are always made of hard
iron, and the iron thrown out is the toughest I ever saw. A
bar, $1\frac{1}{4}$ inches square, appears to have very little cold short
in it." "Cold short" is the technical term for brittleness in
iron when cold, caused by the presence of phosphorus. No
blast was employed and the fuel was pit coal. Although the
first experiment was promising, yet there must have been
something wrong somewhere. Reynolds was not a man to
neglect a new idea, and the fact that Coalbrookdale did not
make a reputation by the Craneges' process is a sufficient proof

that complete success was not attained. In fact, the quality of the iron turned out varied so greatly that no reliance could be placed on it. Another attempt was made by Peter Onions of Merthyr Tydvil in 1783. His furnace was charged with pig iron, the doors luted up and a blast used. The fire was to be kept up until the metal became less fluid, when it was to be stirred by a workman, gathered into a lump and then forged. This process turned out good malleable iron, but just at the same time Cort was able to offer a better.

MODEL OF SUN AND PLANET GEARING.
(*Victoria and Albert Museum.*)

Henry Cort, who was born in Lancashire in 1740, had set up as an ironmaster at Fontley, near Fareham. As Russian iron was mostly used for the purpose of making malleable iron in England, and as Russia had just raised the prices from 70 to 220 copecks the ton, Cort was led to try if something could be done with English pig. As the result of his experiment he took out, in 1783, a patent for the use of grooved rolls for rolling out iron into bars or plates instead of putting it as before under the hammer; and in 1784 he patented his process of puddling. The reverberatory furnace was used with a hollow bottom to contain the metal when fused. Pig iron

Puddling and Rolling.

was put in and the heat provided by pit coal. The furnace
was kept closed till the metal was fused. An aperture was
then opened and the fused metal stirred by a workman with
long bars of iron, when an ebullition took place and a bluish
flame was given off. During this the iron was decarbonised:
that is, the excess of carbon was burnt off and the iron was
left in a purer state. The flame was so managed that the
iron was brought at the last to a pasty consistency, so that it
could be collected in lumps or "blooms," these being raked
about in the furnace till of a sufficient size to be taken out.
They were then put under the hammer or into the squeezer,
after which they went into Cort's rollers. The saving effected
by Cort's process of puddling combined with rolling may be
judged by the fact that before his time an out-turn of twenty
tons a week of malleable iron was as much as any works could
manage. The hammer had to be kept hard at work to work
out a ton of average-sized bars or plates in twelve hours, while
with the rollers fifteen tons could be worked in the same time.
Cort sent plates of his manufacture to the navy contractors,
who approved of them and gave him orders for the Navy.
He set up works at Gosport. The great ironmasters of South
Wales, Homfray and Crawshay, heard of his invention, came
to inspect it, and agreed to pay Cort royalties for the use
of it. The process became still more widely adopted in
consequence of Cort's bankruptcy and the seizure of his
patents by the Government. Substantially the same process
is still in use. No change has been made in principle,
although, with increased knowledge, some modifications have
been made in detail. One defect in Cort's furnace was
that, the bottom being made of sand, it was necessary
for a fresh "hearth" to be made for each puddling, and as
but a small quantity of iron could be puddled at a time
the output was kept small. In fact a puddler could only work
four hearths a day. The process had been much accelerated
by substituting for the sand a hard bottom of cast-iron plates,
on which a layer of cinder is melted so as to form the bottom or
the furnace chamber on which the iron is worked. The stimulus
given to the iron trade by Cort's invention was wonderful.
Malleable iron became cheaper and more widely used. To
take one example only: Crawshay, at Cyfarthfa, in 1787, was

making forty tons a month, while in 1812 the same works were turning out 200 tons each week.

As coal or coke could now be with advantage substituted for charcoal in all the main processes of iron manufacture, the necessity of carrying on iron works in the neighbourhood of forests came to an end. The full effects of this will call for remark later on when it is possible to regard the migration of industry which accompanied the industrial revolution as a whole. The iron industry set itself down where there was coal: that was now the first requisite. Water communication was also of importance; and at first water power. Roebuck placed his works as far as possible near water power. South Wales, too, was convenient in this respect. So little known were the mineral riches of this part of the kingdom that in 1765 Bacon was able to get a ninety-nine years' lease of the mineral rights extending over forty square miles of country round Merthyr Tydvil for £200 a year. In less than twenty years Bacon was able to retire on the profits coming from his furnaces and the sale of his rights.

RICHARD CRAWSHAY.
(From a photograph, by permission of W. T. Crawshay, Esq.)

Cyfarthfa, Pen-y-darran, and Dowlais all owe their beginnings to this sale. The small operations of Crawshay, at Cyfarthfa, have been already mentioned. But Crawshay had been connected with the iron trade in an even humbler way. He was a Yorkshire lad, and had been sent up to London, apprenticed to an ironmonger, who, finding that among his customers the sharpest at driving a bargain were women who came to buy, or (if occasion offered) to steal, flat-irons, set young Crawshay to manage the flat-iron business. His natural sharpness raised him step by step, till the ironmonger's apprentice became the "Iron King" of South Wales, whose progress through his countryside was the signal for all

the people to turn out and wonder at his unofficial majesty.
The era of great ironworks had begun. The Carron Company
(p. 420) had five blast furnaces, sixteen air furnaces, a clay
mill, an engine raising twenty-eight tons of water a minute to
work the blast, and four boring mills. In 1784 Coalbrookdale
had sixteen fire engines (as steam engines were then called),
eight blast furnaces, nine forges, and more than twenty miles
of iron railway. This last was due to Reynolds. Wilkinson's
operations have been already mentioned. Ironmasters all over
the country gave Boulton and Watt orders for steam engines
to work the blast, and as the power of the blast grew, the
size of the furnaces built increased very much. The furnaces
used by the charcoal masters had been from twelve to eighteen
feet high, but they were now built much larger. One built at
Butterley, in 1790, was forty feet high, made square and
entirely of stone. One of seventy feet was built in Wales, but
this was found to be too big, and it was reduced in working
height to forty feet by knocking a hole in the side. The
generality were from ten to twelve feet wide at the boshes
(the widest part), diminishing to four feet or so at the top. This
was afterwards found to be too narrow for the best results.
One tuyère was generally used. With the steam-blast ironmasters had no longer to think of anything but coal, iron ore,
a flux, and, where possible, water communication. The ironworks in the charcoal districts came rapidly to an end. In
the Forest of Dean coal could be obtained easily enough, but
the days of the Sussex furnaces (Vol. IV., p. 178) were
numbered. By 1788 there were only two still in blast, at
Farnhurst and Ashburnham, and these stopped work soon
after; while in their stead, furnaces flared in parts of Wales,
Scotland, and the North of England, where hitherto there had
been nothing but a little coal mining. The well-known Bowling
Inn Works started in 1780, and were followed, before the end
of the century, by those of Low Moor and Farnley. " Best
Yorkshire" iron, the produce of these companies, was made
by substantially the same process as is in use to-day. The
coal used was the " Better Bed " coal, and this, when coked,
yields the purest coke in the world, sulphur being present in
very minute quantities. The ironstone found above the " Black
Bed " coal was brought to the surface, weathered to detach

MODELS OF CABINET STEAM ENGINE.

(Victoria and Albert Museum.)

the adhering shale, calcined, smelted, and run into pig. The pig was then refined by melting under cinder, with a blast directed on to the surface. This leaves almost all the carbon contained in the pig, but much reduces silicon, sulphur, manganese, and phosphorus. In the final process of puddling the carbon is reduced and the iron left exceedingly pure. The refinery was also in use in South Wales at about the same date, and was generally supposed to have been the invention of Samuel Homfray. In 1791 there were in England seventy-three blast furnaces using coal and making annually 67,548 tons, and twelve in Scotland making 12,480 tons. There were only twenty-two charcoal furnaces still in blast. Still there were 20,000 tons of Oregründ iron imported from Sweden, and 50,000 bars and slabs from Russia. By 1796 the total number of blast furnaces had risen to 121 with an average annual make of 1,000 tons.

Textiles.   From 1740 to 1783, thanks to the inventions of Hargreaves, Crompton, and Arkwright, the supply of yarn became plentiful, more in fact than the weavers could do with. In this chapter we shall see a corresponding advance made in weaving, owing to the application of power, either water, or, later, steam to the loom. With the exception of Kay's invention of the flying shuttle, the hand-loom had remained substantially the same machine for centuries. Kay's invention (p. 410), while enabling the weaver to weave wider cloths, and to weave faster, had not revolutionised weaving in the way that the invention of the jenny, the mule, and spinning by rollers had done in

The First Power Loom.   spinning. The revolution in weaving was begun by Cartwright, the inventor of the power loom. This person, who was a clergyman, visited Arkwright's mill in 1784, and, the conversation turning on the possibility of making machines to weave, maintained that it could be done. He was ridiculed, but stuck to his idea, saying that there were only three motions required. He went away, thought it over, and with the aid of a blacksmith made the first power loom. It was an extraordinarily clumsy machine, but this is perhaps not astonishing if Cartwright's statement is to be believed, that prior to the completion of his own power loom, he had never even seen an ordinary hand-loom at work. In his power loom the warp was placed perpendicularly, and he adds, " the reed fell with the weight of half a hundredweight, and the springs which threw the shuttle would have thrown a Congreve rocket." In fact it required the strength of two powerful men to work the machine even at a slow rate. However, encouraged by his success, he took out a patent in 1785, and then did what most men would have done first of all, namely, inspected and got to understand the action of the ordinary hand-loom. After doing this he was able to make several improvements which he combined in a new patent, and set up a factory at Doncaster. He was not the first to hit on the idea of machine weaving; nor was he actually the first to put it into execution. M. De Gennes had made a power loom of some kind in the seventeenth century, and in 1678 a patent was taken out for "a new engine to make linen-cloth." But Cartwright was the first to attain a measure of practical success, especially in the weaving of wide goods. Cartwright's first machinery was worked by a bull, but his Doncaster factory was furnished with a steam engine in 1789. In 1791 a Manchester firm contracted for 400 of his power looms, but the factory was burnt to the ground, probably by the workmen, who thought they saw machinery taking work out of their hands and bread out of their mouths.

Cartwright did not rest content with his patent for the power loom, but also patented a machine for woolcombing in 1789, though here, again, he was preceded by Isaac Mills, who took out a patent for the same object in 1723. The effect of this upon the worsted industry was very great. In woollen manufactures, properly so-called, the wool is of short staple, the fibres of which are matted closely together, and so the yarn owes its strength not to the length, but the tenacity of short fibres closely intertwined. Worsted is made of

Machine Wool Combing.

MODEL OF ROLLING AND SLITTING MILL,
BY JAMES WATT.
(*Victoria and Albert Museum.*)

wools with long staple, and these had to be combed or straightened out by hand. The industry was thus dependent on the hand-combers, who got plenty of work and good wages, so good that, like the hand-spinners of an earlier day, they could and did indulge in a considerable amount of idleness. Cartwright's invention put a term to their prosperity. By his machine the first operation opened the wool, and made it connect together in a rough sliver, but did not clear it. The clearing was performed by the second or a

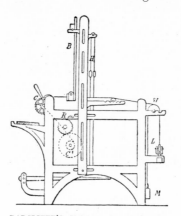

RADCLIFFE'S IMPROVED HAND-LOOM.

(*From Barlow's " History of Weaving."*
Sampson Low & Co., Ltd.)

third operation if necessary. Three of his machines with an overlooker and ten children would c mb a pack of wool in twelve hours. As neither fire nor oil was necessary for machine combing, the saving in these alone generally paid the overlooker and children, so that the manufacturer himself pocketed what he used to pay the handcombers, while for machine spinning the machine-combed wool was said to be 12 per cent better than the hand-combed since it was better mixed and the slivers uniform. Cartwright said that it did the work of twenty hand-combers, but according to a verse of the time the machine familiarly known as " Big Ben " could do more than that :—

" Come, all ye Master Combers, and hear of our Big Ben,
    He'll comb more wool in one day than fifty of your men,
    With their hand-combs and comb-pots and such old-fashioned ways,
    There'll be no more occasion for old Bishop Blaize."

St. Blaize, it may be explained, is the patron saint of woolcombers. Cartwright's machine was not entirely satisfactory, and improvements and alterations in combing machinery were made by Toplis, Hawksley, and Wright. The wool-combing machines excited great opposition. A Bill was brought into the House of Commons to forbid the use of the machines altogether.

but it was thrown out. In fact, the days for such interference were passed. Parliament was taking a wider view of what was good for industries, and now declined to cripple a growing trade in order that men who possessed a certain specialised skill should be exempt from the competition of machinery.

Two other improvements remain to be noted, not exactly **Bleaching.** textile processes, yet closely connected with textile arts. They are bleaching and cylinder printing. The old process of bleaching necessitated immersions in numerous leys and the

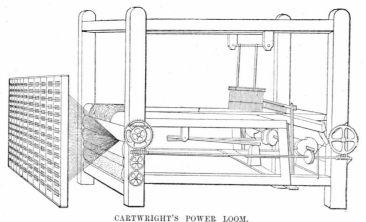

CARTWRIGHT'S POWER LOOM.
(*From Barlow's "History of Weaving." Sampson Low & Co., Ltd.*)

subsequent exposure of the goods to the air for long periods. The Lancashire towns were surrounded by vast bleaching fields. To persons unaccustomed to the sight of these white fabrics in great numbers side by side and length by length, they have all the effect at a distance, especially in sunlight, of extensive and brilliant sheets of water. Linen required six months to bleach. In 1774 Scheele discovered chlorine, and the bleaching properties of this gas and some of its compounds were demonstrated by Berthollet in 1789. It was shown that by the new process bleaching could be performed in forty-eight hours. A good deal of experiment was required before the process was at all perfect, but by 1800 it was used by many, including Tennant, of Glasgow, who made considerable improvements. The saving in time was enormous, although the new bleaching process was injurious to

239

the lasting power of the things to which it was applied, and this defect has not been overcome even in our own day.

Cylinder Printing.

An equally great saving was brought about by the invention of cylinder printing. Printed calicoes had been forbidden by the Act of 1721 (pp. 149, 185), as it was presumed that it was impossible for them to be of native make. In 1736, by the so-called Manchester Act, printing was permitted on fabrics which had a linen warp, as these were of native make. This was the Act which impeded Arkwright until its alteration in 1774, when colour printing on calico again became legal. But the old process of colour printing was excessively slow. The colour was applied by hand to a wooden block and the block to the material. The blocks were very small, mostly about ten inches by five. To print a piece of calico 28 yards in length required the application of the block 448 times. If another colour was required, the whole operation had to be gone through again. Block printers got 40s. to 60s. the week; pattern drawers wore fashionable clothes and were called " Mr." The usual patterns were leaves variously disposed, small circles, pippins, clubs, dice, diamonds, spots, and flower-heads of the daisy or buttercup. It was from his use of the parsley-leaf as a pattern that Peel (the grandfather of the statesman) got his name " Parsley Peel." Colours were crude and staring—the cheapest print cost 3s. to 3s. 6d. the yard. In 1764 Fryer, Greenhow, and Newbery projected a machine for printing, staining and colouring silks, stuffs, linens, cottons, leather, or paper by copper cylinders, on which the colour was laid by other cylinders. In 1765 there was " a gentleman " (indefinite) of Paris who printed 200 ells of calico per hour, or said that he did. The practical use of cylinder printing in England began in 1783 with a machine made by a Scotchman, Bell. The great firm of Livesey, Hargreaves, Hall & Co. took it up in 1785. The machine was made with six cylinders, on which the pattern, or part of the pattern, was cut. The colour was supplied to each cylinder by what is called the " box doctor," and was removed from where it was not required by an elastic steel blade. The machine could do as much as a hundred block-printers and a hundred tear-boys working in the old style. Prints rapidly increased in elaboration and fell in price, and a great use was made of the cheap novelty.

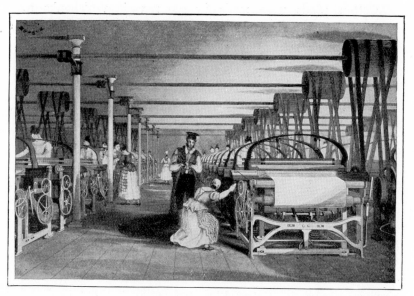

WEAVING BY POWER LOOMS.

CALICO PRINTING.

(*Baines, " History of the County Palatine of Lancashire."*)

Kinds of Goods.

Cotton goods were made in great variety. Thanks to Crompton, the English muslin trade grew rapidly to large proportions. Muslins were made in Lancashire of several kinds: book-muslin, mull-muslin, leno and lighter muslins in Glasgow; they were also striped and checked. Pullicat and Bandana handkerchiefs came from Glasgow, dimities from Warrington and Yorkshire; cotton cambrics, sewing thread, and vast quantities of calico from Arkwright's mills, and from Lancashire. For many purposes cotton superseded silk.

Cotton.

In 1775 the import of cotton was 4,764,589 lb., in 1785 it was 11,482,083 lb., in 1789 it was 32,576,023 lb. Out of the twenty-three million pounds imported in 1787, nearly seven millions came from the West Indies, six millions from French and Spanish colonies, nearly six millions from Turkey, two-and-a-half millions from Brazil, and about a million and a half from Dutch colonies. The American import was practically nothing. In 1784 an American vessel with a cargo of cotton was seized by the Custom-house officers, who sought to condemn it under the Navigation Act, on the ground that cotton was not produced by the United States. The cotton imported from America in 1871 was more than five thousand times as much as the import of 1791.

Linen.

The spread of machinery from the cotton industry into its neighbour linen was not long deferred. The principles to be applied were, widely speaking, the same, but technical difficulties, springing from the difference in nature between flax and cotton, took some time to overcome. The records of the Scotch Board of Trustees for Manufactures from 1760 onwards contain frequent mention of improved machines, but these were not practically successful. In 1787 Kendrew and Porthouse, of Darlington, took out a patent for a machine to spin hackled flax, by adapting Arkwright's drawing rollers in use in the cotton industry. Two important linen firms took out licences to use this machine—Marshall & Co., of Leeds and Shrewsbury, and James Ivory & Co., of Brigton. The latter firm built a large mill in 1789, and is said to have carried on work successfully till 1803, when the firm failed. One of the partners started the concern again in 1804, but it had a chequered existence, failing again in 1815, and being for sale in 1817 for £2,000 without finding a purchaser. The Kendrew patent may have worked but it was not a commercial success. Marshall & Co. had the same experience with it, but they had the aid of Matthew Murray, who made several improvements. Still, during the years 1788–1793 the firm found that flax spinning by machinery had not, so far, proved remunerative. Fresh inventions, an improved spinning frame and a carding engine for tow patented by Murray in 1793, were more successful, and from this time flax spinning was a commercial success. In the last years of the century John Marshall, who had been left as sole partner in the firm, was joined by capitalists. New mills were built at Leeds and Shrewsbury, the latter 150 ft. long, 36ft. wide, and five storeys high. In 1793 the firm had 832 spindles running, and in 1810, 5,796. In the same year the finest count of yarn spun was 30 leas, 25 leas, having been spun for at least six years before that. In 1809 one of the partners took out the first patent for hackling by machinery. It is worth while being somewhat explicit about the early flax spinning, on account of the fact that the invention is sometimes claimed for a Frenchman, de Girard. In 1810 Napoleon offered a million francs for the invention of flax-spinning machinery, and it is said that de Girard, with wonderful promptitude, invented his machine the very next day. Prompt as he was, he was some twenty years behind the English firms above-mentioned. In fact, his chief claim to be reckoned the inventor of flax-spinning is that his machinery brought him into bankruptcy—a fate too often shared by his kind.

WHEN Pitt first came to power he found a deficit of six millions in the national Budget, and a National Debt of unheard-of proportions. The American war and other causes had raised the country's debt in twenty-eight years from seventy-four millions to two hundred and forty-four millions. Pitt had, however, three great advantages. England was at peace ; the industrial revolution, though still in its infancy, had already greatly increased the production of wealth ; and Pitt had studied Adam Smith, and had gathered many valuable hints from the " Wealth of Nations." In his first Budget (1784), in spite of the existence of a heavy deficit, he boldly reduced the duty on tea from 119 per cent. to 12½ per cent. on its value. He saw that the excessive duty had led to such extensive smuggling that the revenue

J. E. SYMES. The National Economy.

was defrauded, and that the reduction would stimulate consumption. Some new taxes must, however, be imposed to choke the deficit and make up for the loss. He decided to impose various licence duties, to tax horses whether kept for riding or driving, and also silver plate (gold was already taxed), and windows. The last of these proposals was probably unwise. It was a discouragement to the due lighting of houses. Pitt's object was to get money out of the classes that could best afford it, and in a manner that could not be evaded without considerable inconvenience. He was also anxious not to add to what we should call "protective" duties, and, no doubt, his choice was somewhat limited. The Budget of 1785 introduced extensive changes. These were mostly of the nature of readjustments and reforms in the methods of collection. Pitt had learnt from Adam Smith to attach great importance to diminishing the cost of the collection of taxes and to reducing to a minimum the temptation to fraud. The chief of the new taxes fell immediately on shopkeepers. Pitt, however, believed that they would ultimately be paid by the customers, and that it would be convenient in the first instance to levy them on the shopkeepers. These taxes were, however, violently denounced, and were mostly dropped in 1789, probate and legacy duties being substituted for them.

By the year 1786 the national finances were so far restored that Pitt felt himself in a position to begin redeeming the National Debt. He proposed that one million pounds **Pitt's Sinking Fund.** should be set aside from the revenue every year to accumulate at compound interest for this purpose. He was apparently not altogether unaffected by the familiar fallacies conspicuously illustrated in a well-known work by the moralist, Dr. Price (p. 328), growing out of the fact that a small sum set aside annually at compound interest will in time accumulate to a gigantic amount. He tried to make careful provisions against any interruption of the working of his automatic sinking fund. It was to be vested in Commissioners, and withdrawn as far as possible from the control of Parliament. But what was to be done if Parliament authorised new loans for which a higher interest would have to be paid than was being obtained for the sunk millions? Any child could see that in such a case the fund would be worse than useless. Yet Pitt attached so much importance to the almost futile attempt to tie the hands of subsequent governments, and his opinion had so much weight with the country, that, in order to keep the fund intact, the nation went on putting money to accumulate at 3 per cent. and at the same time borrowing

PITT CRUSHING THE SMUGGLER.
(From a satirical print of the year 1784.)

at 6 per cent. The fund was kept up till 1807, in spite of the growing debt and the increasing rate of interest.

As was to be expected in a disciple of Adam Smith, Pitt was a convinced Free Trader; but there was, as yet, no chance of getting Parliament to assent to what is still called by many "onesided Free Trade." So he had to content himself with negotiating commercial treaties, of which the one concluded with France in 1786 was the most important. Under this treaty most of the protective duties between the two countries

Treaty of Commerce with France.

were either diminished or swept away. It is interesting to note that the opposition to the treaty came chiefly from manufacturers, the support chiefly from landlords; a curious inversion of what happened in the Free Trade controversy of the nineteenth century.

Finance, 1787–1792.

Pitt's Budgets during the next few years introduced no important changes. There happened to be an extraordinary series of bad harvests from 1789 to 1792, and the prosperity of the country depended then far more upon the harvest than it does at present. Nevertheless, industrial progress and the wise finance of Pitt were introducing such results that in 1792 a number of bold remissions of taxation were introduced, especially in the interests of the poor and of the lower middle classes. Thus the taxes on women-servants, and on candles, were now abolished, and the tax on windows was limited to houses that had at least seven windows. England was now on the verge of the great war, but our great minister had so little expectation of such a catastrophe that he thought he could afford some loss of revenue.

Crisis of 1793.

The war came, and with it a severe financial crisis. This would, no doubt, have occurred, even if the country had remained at peace. Its fundamental cause was the over-trading encouraged by the recent prosperous years. An immense amount of capital had also been locked up in the new machinery, factories, and canals. The bank-note circulation had nearly doubled in the eight years, 1784–1792, and the reserves and credit of many of the banks were very inadequate. Then came a bad harvest, and a sudden increase in the number of bankruptcies, which rose to 105 in the November of 1792, as against a previous monthly average of fifty. There was a slight improvement in December. On February 1st came the declaration of war, and it was almost at once followed by heavy failures. Of the four hundred country banks, one hundred stopped payment, and most of the others were in serious straits. Everyone began to call in his money and to refuse to lend. The locked-up capital could not be realised, and the Bank of England, in spite of appeals from the Government, insisted on contracting its issues. Many solvent firms were now in grave peril. A Committee of the House of Commons was hastily formed, and at once recommended the issue of Exchequer Bills to the amount of five millions. Under this scheme loans of over two million pounds were made; but the mere knowledge that the Government was prepared to lend to anyone of assured solvency had probably more effect than the actual loans. The panic ceased. Every penny that had been lent was repaid, and Government made a clear profit on the transaction.

THE DOG TAX.
(*From a contemporary satirical print.*)

When the crisis had once passed, the war exercised at first a far less harmful influence on trade than might have been expected. Our naval supremacy enabled us to take possession of much of the business that France would otherwise have done. In 1795 the Republic dominated Holland, and this enabled us similarly to annex much of the trade that had hitherto been in Dutch hands. The removal of our two great competitors went far to counterbalance both the loss of our trade with France and the increased perils to

The War and Commerce.

our merchant vessels. Moreover, we captured many French and Dutch ships with rich cargoes. The value of such prizes taken during the war of 1793–1802 is estimated at above fourteen millions.

THIRD OF A GUINEA OF 1797 (GOLD).

The commercial advantages we should otherwise have gained were, however, much diminished by the necessity of conciliating neutral powers. By the " Rule of 1756," a neutral had no right

Rivalry of Neutrals. to relieve a belligerent by trading that was illegal at the outbreak of the war. This brought on disagreements with states who complained that we were interfering with their trade from ports in the West Indian colonies of France. The rule was, therefore, modified in 1794, and again in 1798. Neutrals were then allowed to carry the produce of enemies' colonies to their own ports or to England. It was found, however, that this gave much scope for evading the objects of the rule. Trade was carried on, especially in American ships, between hostile ports by using American ports as nominal destinations or places of exit. Thus, an American vessel would ship a cargo

A SIXPENCE OF 1787.

from a French colony, carry it to an American port, and thence to some place whence it could be easily introduced into the enemies' country.

A still more serious blow to English trade was the threatening attitude of the Baltic Powers (p. 512). Their contention was, in effect, that neutral vessels might conduct the trade of belligerents, except that in contraband of war. Such goods as timber, hemp, etc., were not strictly contraband, but they were useful for warlike purposes, and there were strong political as well as commercial reasons for our objecting to such a claim. There were further disputes as to what constituted an effective blockade. Russia, Sweden, and Denmark, entered into a convention to enforce their views, and Russia laid an embargo on all British vessels within her ports. England, in retaliation, adopted a similar policy in the case of Russian, Swedish, and Danish vessels (1801). The Battle of Copenhagen followed (p. 512). But for our present purpose it suffices to notice that the attitude of the Northern Powers was a fresh check to English commerce.

A SHILLING OF 1787.

As time went on the **The Distress.** burden of the war began to be severe. Our population was growing very fast. The census of 1791 had shown an increase of nine per cent. The census of 1801 showed an increase of eleven per cent. in ten years.

This was during a period when the war was raising the price of agricultural products, when the industrial revolution was displacing many labourers by its changes in manufacturing processes, and when taxes were being steadily increased. Pitt remained, on the whole, faithful to the teachings of Adam Smith. He tried to keep down the burdens laid on the poor, and to derive his taxes from property and successions. He even adopted the principle of graduated taxation. His expenses were enormous.[1] He was obliged to increase the Customs and other duties that fell largely on the poor, and the landlord interest in Parliament was so strong

A SHILLING COINED FOR DORRIEN AND MAGENS, 1798.

that real property was exempted from some of its legitimate burdens. We cannot wonder that there was much suffering among the working classes, and that the king,

---

[1] The revenue of Great Britain and Ireland rose from 18·9 millions in 1792 to 33 millions in 1800.

as he drove through the streets, was greeted with shouts of "Bread" and "Peace" (1795; p. 668).

Inconvertible Currency.

In 1796 the fear of a French invasion caused a run on the country banks. These withdrew their reserves from the Bank of England. The specie in the latter sank below a million in February, 1797, and Government had again to interfere. This time they adopted the sweeping policy of making the Bank's notes inconvertible, except in certain specified cases. One of the chief objects of this new departure was to set free gold and silver for exportation. In addition to the expenditure on our own expeditions, we were sending large subsidies to our allies. In 1795 we sent £478,000 to Hanover, £317,000 to Hesse Cassel, £150,000 to Sardinia, and smaller sums to Brunswick, Baden, and Hesse-Darmstadt. Pitt seems to have under-estimated the tendency of the precious metals to flow back, after such exportation, to a country which was producing more commodities than it consumed. This excess was the real measure of our capability to conduct an expensive war. Still, there can be no doubt that the use of inconvertible paper for currency gave a temporary relief, and the disadvantages were, perhaps, worth incurring, so long as the issue was carefully limited. The bank directors were quite alive to the importance of such limitation. The recent experience of France under the *assignat* system had illustrated the evils of an excessive paper currency, and the Bank of England used its powers with so much prudence and moderation that for eleven years (1797–1808) their notes were not seriously depreciated, as compared with gold, except occasionally and temporarily. It is probable, however, that the use of inconvertible paper helped to cause a general rise of prices, which aggravated the misery of the poor.

Budgets, 1796–1801.

Meanwhile the difficulty of meeting the expenses of the war and the subsidies to allies was leading to more and more taxes. In 1796 a second ten per cent. was put on the assessed taxes. Additions were made to the duties on horses, wines, tobaccos, and hats. The succession duties were made more productive, especially by compelling executors to pay them before handing over the property to the legatees. In 1797 there were fresh additions and increases, especially in the duties on transfers. Most of the stamp duties were doubled.

Every sale by auction was taxed, and a duty of ten per cent. was laid on all legal deeds. Still there was a deficit, and in 1798 Pitt appealed to the country to submit to what was called a triple assessment, under which all persons should pay *at least* three times as much as they had paid in assessed taxes in the previous year. Those who had paid more than £25 were to have their tax more than trebled. Those who had paid £50, or more, were to have the charge quintupled. An alternative was offered of an income-tax of ten per cent. on all incomes of over £200 per annum. Incomes under £60 were to be exempt. Incomes between £60 and £200 were to have abatements.   Pitt's next scheme was to raise capital by allowing landlords to redeem their land-tax, on terms so very favourable that the tax on nearly a quarter of the land of the kingdom was redeemed in 1798 and 1799. Next he appealed to all who could afford it to subscribe voluntarily towards national expenses, and he actually obtained in this way more than £2,000,000. Finally, he definitely substituted an income tax for the complicated triple assessment scheme, which had proved almost unworkable, and had led to much fraudulent concealment (1799). In view of this, he made a **The** calculation of the income of various classes, which may be **National Income.** thus summarised :—

Landlords (as such) (England and Wales)	£20,000,000
Tithe-owners and Tenants (from land)	£10,000,000
Houses, Mines, and Canals	£8,000,000
Professional Earnings	£2,000,000
Scotch income under above four heads	£5,000,000
Income from Over-sea Possessions (Great Britain)	£5,000,000
Income from Public Funds	£12,000,000
Profits from Foreign Commerce	£12,000,000
Profits from Domestic Trade	£28,000,000
	£102,000,000

This estimate takes no account of working-class wages, and most likely under-estimated the incomes of other classes. But it is interesting, even though it must be regarded as only a rough approximation. Owing to various deductions, the tax was only expected to bring in seven-and-a-half millions, and it actually produced only six millions, and so in 1800 and 1801, fresh taxes on commodities had to be

imposed. Pitt had tried to meet each year's expenses out
of taxation. He had taken alarm at the growth of the debt
and the decline of the national credit; but in spite of all
his endeavours he had added two hundred and seventy-one
million pounds to the National Debt by the close of the
war (1802), by which time it is calculated that the annual
charge for the debt was equivalent to 10 per cent. of the
total income of the nation, and the taxation absorbed another 20 per cent. of that income.

We have already noticed the influences of the " Wealth of
Nations" on the financial policy of Pitt, especially in connection with the Commercial Treaty of 1786 and the national

**Economic
Doctrine:
Adam
Smith.**
Budgets both before and during the war (p. 449). In other
respects Adam Smith's relation to the economic history of
this period is rather that of a skilful analyst than of a powerful
influence. "Division of labour" continued to develop. Production was more and more carried on on a large scale, but
the employers of labour were probably not so much influenced
by the arguments of the Scotch professor as by the evidence
of practical experience. Our industrial evolution had now
reached a point when it was inevitable that the factory system
should spread, and that manufacturing towns should increase
both in number and size. This increase was naturally promoted
by new mechanical inventions and applications. It was further
facilitated by the war, which, while disorganising industry, made
many openings for ingenious, able, or lucky persons to build up
fortunes by availing themselves of the exceptional conditions.
It was not till a later time that Smith's influence again became
very important. Another economist was, however, now beginning
to produce a considerable effect upon national thought. This

Malthus.
was Malthus, whose first essay on the "Principle of Population"
appeared in 1798. Hitherto it had generally been assumed that
an increased population was a rational object of hope. Now
England's population was increasing at an unprecedented rate
(p. 651), but with it the poverty of the working classes was also
increasing. Economic theories are generally the outcome of
special economic conditions. In this case the injurious effects
of a growing population were largely due to three sets of
circumstances, viz.: (1) The disorganisation caused by the
industrial revolution, with the special inducements it offered

to child labour from the point of view of immediate wages, and the absence of any protective influences of Factory Acts, Education Acts, etc. (2) The high price of bread aggravated by the war, which made the importation of food dangerous and expensive, and cut us off from some of the markets which would otherwise have supplied us with food. (3) A defective poor law (of which more will be said in the next chapter), which

THE REV. T R. MALTHUS, AFTER JOHN LINNELL.

directly encouraged the reckless multiplication of the poorest classes. The doctrines of Malthus also fitted in with another tendency which lay almost outside the sphere of economics. The reaction against the French Revolution included a reaction against the high hopes of human perfectibility—of a golden age that would reign on earth when once political tyrannies were overthrown. To cherish such hopes now was to be suspected of French sympathies, of lack of patriotism, and of the desire to promote a reign of terror. Malthus struck the hardest blow that had yet been struck at political utopias, for he maintained that there was " a cause intimately united with the very nature of man," fatal to all such utopias, namely, the tendency of population to increase more rapidly than the means of subsistence. We need not discuss the general truth of this proposition. It must suffice to say, that in the year 1798, when the "Essay" appeared in its first form, it was literally the case in England that, while wealth in other forms was probably increasing more rapidly than the population, wealth, in the form of food, was not keeping pace with the number of mouths that had to be filled.

ARTHUR GRIFFITHS.
Prison Reform: Howard.

PRISON reform, or rather the crying need for it, began with John Howard. Until the advent of the great philanthropist towards the end of the eighteenth century, every form of atrocity and abuse had flourished unchecked in the gaols of the United Kingdom. Howard, however, aroused people who had hitherto remained callous to less eloquent invective. Earlier, in 1728 that is to say, and at the instance of the Society for the Promotion of Christian Knowledge, Parliament had made a feeble inquiry into the state of gaols. Again, Mr. Popham had brought forward a Bill to abolish gaolers' fees, which became law in 1774. But now John Howard entered upon his self-imposed labours, and at great peril to himself commenced his visitation of prisons. He travelled all over the country, penetrating the most noisome dungeons, bringing fearlessly to light the widespread horrors he found.

State of the Gaols.

From one end of the kingdom to the other our prisons were a standing disgrace to civilisation. Imprisonment, from whatever cause it might be imposed, meant consignment to a living tomb, an existence of acute suffering. Gaols were pest-houses; a fell disease peculiar to them, but akin to our modern typhus, was bred within their foul limits, and flourished constantly, often in epidemic form. The gaol fever slew more than the hangman, and its ravages extended to the courts, to judges, juries, barristers, witnesses, and all who approached the poisonously affected assize (Vol. III., p. 768). What wonder, when hundreds of hapless folk were huddled together in narrow underground dens, practically deprived of light, air, water, and an adequate supply of food?

Gaols were mostly private institutions, or at least worked

so as to pay their way, leased out to ruthless, rapacious keepers who used every menace and extortion to wring money out of the wretched beings committed to their cruel care. Gaol fees were imposed upon all, even the untried; men declared innocent by the law were hauled back to prison until they could satisfy these monstrous charges. The use of fetters was universal, although even then deemed illegal; all alike, tried and untried,

Photo: Walker & Cockerell.

JOHN HOWARD, F.R.S., BY MATHER BROWN.
(*National Portrait Gallery.*)

male and female, young and old, were laden with chains so that the gaoler might secure another perquisite, the bribe he demanded for easement of irons. Prisons were dark because their managers objected to pay the window tax; water was costly, and therefore scantily supplied; sanitation, as we understand it, did not exist in those days anywhere, least of all in gaols. Pauper prisoners, by far the largest proportion, were nearly starved, for there was no regular allowance of food; their beds, of old littered straw, reeked with filthy exhalations; if they

240

were ill the doctors feared to approach them; chaplains held aloof, and the dying were left to the ministrations of an occasional self-devoted layman.   Worse even than the cruel neglect of the authorities was the active oppression exercised by the stronger over the weaker prisoners; there were gaol customs such as that of "garnish" or "footing," exacted from new comers who were called upon to "pay, or strip." In default, their clothes were torn off their backs, and they were left naked to eke out a wretched existence, forbidden to approach the fire, to lie on the straw, or share in the daily doles of food made by the charitable.

Debtors in Prison.

It must be borne in mind that most of the inmates of gaols were not even criminals.   Debtors formed a very large proportion of the population; the victims, that is to say, of the existing commercial code which gave the creditor his debtor's body but no chance of recovering his debt.   These debtors often brought their families with them, and the already limited space was further crowded by weak and unoffending women and children.   Untried prisoners made up the rest of the numbers incarcerated; people still innocent in the eyes of the law, whose detention was only defensible on the ground that they must be produced to plead, and who yet, under the apathy of judges and the rarity of gaol deliveries, rotted in gaol for years awaiting trial and possible acquittal.   To those actually found guilty the law gave but a short shift.   Prisoners did not long cumber the gaols when once they received sentence; all who were not hanged out of hand were sold into servitude, were sent to hard labour on the American plantations, to endure hideous tortures under a semi-tropical sun, with no hope of emancipation under seven or fourteen years.   The price of one of these white slaves was £20, and the contractors who traded in this human flesh often complained that their merchandise was so much deteriorated by ill-usage as to entail serious loss upon them.   Howard found these wretched "transports" awaiting deportation in prisons chained to the floor.   Many were kept under the most abject conditions in hulks on the Thames, and an extraordinary mortality prevailed amongst them always.

White Slavery.

Howard's Influence.

Happily Howard's crusade against prison mismanagement and its shortcomings soon produced tangible results.   The matter was taken up by Parliament, and the energetic philanthropist was examined at the bar of the House. Some few public-spirited people did their best to apply a remedy at once. The Duke of Richmond built a new prison for Sussex under Howard's advice and guidance; others were erected on an improved plan for Oxford, Stafford, and Gloucester, by which some of the worst evils were removed. A more comprehensive scheme of reform, one of which indeed contained the germ of our best modern practice, was contemplated by the Government, and its execution was to be entrusted to Howard. The great philanthropist

A PRISON INTERIOR.
(*" Humours of the Fleet,"* 1749.)

was far in advance of his age. While inveighing loudly against the prevailing ill-usage, he clearly realised the true principles of criminal treatment as we understand it to-day. These as advocated by him were embodied in an Act, that of 19 Geo. III. c. 74, in which the hope was expressed that " if offenders were ordered to solitary imprisonment accompanied by well-regulated hard labour and religious instruction, it might be the means, under Providence, not only of deterring others, but also of reforming individuals and training them to habits of industry."

Howard was no visionary; his philanthropy was practical, the suggestions he made were sound and feasible. It was the main idea in this new and most enlightened scheme to establish Penitentiary Houses in various parts of the country, and these Howard proposed should be built " in a great measure by the

The Penitentiary Plan.

convicts themselves." It is remarkable how he foretold our modern practice. There was first to be a boundary, then within the enclosure all the necessary operations were to be carried forward; the foundations were to be dug, bricks made, timber sawn, stone dressed exactly as has been done at Wormwood Scrubbs within the last twenty years. Each prison house was to be spacious, with a sufficient number of separate cells to allow one for every individual; the food was to be ample, the supervision intelligent and reformatory without pauperising or lavishing undue tenderness upon those who had broken the law. Had Howard's views been accepted and borne fruit the movement of prison reform would have been anticipated by at least half a century. But many obstacles interposed to ruin the enterprise; difficulties in obtaining suitable sites delayed it, and then followed dissensions between Howard and the colleagues associated with him to give effect to the scheme. He at last declined to act, and other supervisors were appointed who actually bought land about Wandsworth, entered into building contracts, and would have begun the work, when the Government suddenly stopped all proceedings.

Although the plan of Penitentiary Houses was approved in theory, it had never been very cordially adopted. Really the best and soundest, as we now fully believe it, in those days it **Trans-** was accounted only a *pis aller;* in spite of Howard's warm **portation.** approval, the Government still preferred exile to a distant land, if that land only could be found. Now the recent discoveries of Captain Cook at the antipodes opened the vast territories of Australia, in lieu of the lost American colonies, and the Government embarked at once upon a new and more extensive system of transportation beyond the seas. There was something peculiarly attractive in the theory which gave offenders the chance of redeeming misdeeds by becoming useful members of society in a new country, remote from the memories and temptations of the old. Although now quite exploded, the idea still fascinates our neighbours the French, who see only the results, and forget or cannot estimate the evils that transportation entailed. To some minds its admitted failure has been neutralised by the precious jewel it has added to our Colonial crown. It was a means of making men outwardly honest, of converting vagabonds into active citizens, and it has produced

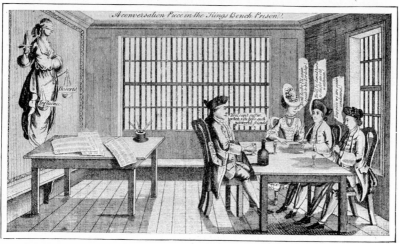

LIFE IN THE KING'S BENCH PRISON.

("*Humours of the Fleet*," 1749.)

Australia. Whether that new and splendid country has so greatly prospered because of transportation or in spite of it need not be now discussed. At least, the colonies themselves condemned it, and since that first great and no doubt highly successful experiment, it has never again been tried. Of the many and great evils it induced, its extravagant costliness, and its inequality, uncertainty, and general futility as a means of criminal repression, there can be no doubt, and we may have occasion to speak of this again. But these momentous questions belong to a later date.

Bentham's "Panopticon." Meanwhile, the revival of penal exile on a more guarded, but still objectionable plan, put an end to the Penitentiary Houses. Only one more effort was made, about this time, to follow in Howard's footsteps and give effect to his views. Another eminent Englishman, Jeremy Bentham (p. 562), devoted himself to prison reform, and in 1791 made a definite proposal to Government to turn prison constructor ; he was to erect a Panopticon, or gaol of a peculiar form from plans of his own, and charge himself with the employment, discipline, and control of a certain number of criminals. This Panopticon, or Inspection House, was to be a building so contrived that its inmates could be "kept within reach of being inspected during every moment of their lives." It was to be circular, "a species of iron cage, glazed—a glass lantern as large as Ranelagh, with the cells on the outer circumference"; this arrangement, assisted by blinds to be let up or down to conceal the warder inspectors, was to constitute a sort of "invisible omnipresence" of authority, by which the criminal himself, in solitude or limited seclusion, yet came under constant supervision. The idea was somewhat far-fetched, but Bentham also contracted to deal fairly with his charges; engaged to give wholesome food, good bedding, sufficient clothing, light, air, warmth, and a separate cell. In return for all this he was to have the exclusive right to the products of the prisoners' labour, only his responsibility towards them was not to end with their release. After discharge, he was to find work for them "outside," and by retaining a portion of their prison earnings, he was to lay a foundation stone of a provision for their old age.

Promise and Performance. Prison reform would indeed have made giant strides had these great promises been kept. But to this day even,

although the principles that underlie them are sound, they
are not exactly fulfilled.   Bentham's scheme was, however,
accepted by Parliament, and an Act was passed in 1794
empowering him to proceed.   Still the project hung fire,

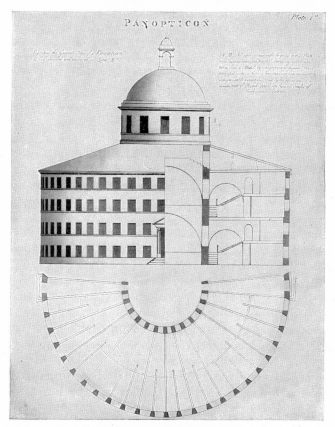

JEREMY BENTHAM'S "PANOPTICON."
(*After the original drawing of* 1791.)

and for many years.   Public money was advanced for the
preliminary expenses, and Bentham was himself a good deal
out of pocket, yet nothing definite was done.   He certainly
purchased a site for his prison in the district of Tothill Fields,
but that was all, except a nearly interminable litigation over
the disposal of the Treasury funds.   Later, when the proposal

to build Penitentiary Houses was revived, Bentham's land was utilised for the erection of the well-known Millbank Penitentiary. This was, in a measure, therefore, the legacy of the Panopticon; but Bentham did no more for prison reform.

Elsewhere in the kingdom, while Howard survived the daily dangers he encountered, the great question was kept alive. The local magistracy were anxious, in many cases, to do their best; but Newgate, the chief prison in London, continued infamously mismanaged, and altogether inadequate for the numbers crowded into it. After Howard's death, the cause of prison reform soon dropped, the old evils revived, and at the beginning of the nineteenth century were everywhere visible.

Howard's Successes. Again and again the voice of philanthropic protest was heard, but none spoke with the energy and directness of Howard. Still, his mantle had fallen on worthy men, such as Neild and Silas Told, while the Quakers of the Eastern counties were soon to do admirable work, headed by Mrs. Fry. Presently, a prison discipline society was started by Fowell Buxton, and, composed of many benevolent and influential people, took the matter in hand. A longer and more consistent effort was now made to compass reform. This movement and its fruits will be dealt with in the next volume.

MARY BATESON. Social Life. BURKE, writing of the fateful October 6th, 1789, says that from that day may be dated the most important of all revolutions, "I mean a revolution in sentiments, manners and moral opinions," a revolution which was in his opinion wholly mischievous. He was writing of France, but his words may also be applied to England, for English sentiments, manners and morals were affected by the events which were happening in France, and changed, perhaps, less for the worse than Burke would have us believe.

Effects of the French Revolution. Of the revolution in political sentiments Burke's own life is the best example. Overwhelmed with horror at the course of events in France, and believing those events to be the outcome of democratic views, such as he himself once held, he left his former friends to warn the world of "the danger of their wicked principles and black hearts." He carried with him the majority of Englishmen, but he was not immediately followed by Pitt. For another four years Pitt quietly held his own course, refused to interest himself in French affairs, and devoted his time to England's financial difficulties. But in 1793 he, too, succumbed to the prevailing influence, and revolutionised himself. With him went many who had with-stood the torrent of Burke's eloquence. There still remained a minority, which was swept by the revolutionary tide into an opposite direction. Political parties now divided on a new principle; a democratic party began to form, claiming that "delegated authority was the only legal power," while those who had long been striving against certain class privileges and immunities were inspired by the French example to pursue larger schemes of reform.

The effects of the Revolution can scarcely be separated from those of the war which was its result. The war, with its famine-prices and heavy taxation, excited popular agitations, and these were more or less allied to or confounded with the agitations of constitutional reformers. Both kinds of agitation called forth repressive measures, for the one expressed itself in riots, the other in seditious writings. It was found hard to distinguish the man who attacked a butcher's or a baker's shop, crying "Peace and no Famine" as he forcibly carried off food, from the politician who held merely theoretical opinions on the rights of man. All persons who cried peace were Jacobins and dis-affected persons, and the many tumultuous excesses for which the well-affected were responsible were forgotten in the prevail-ing excitement. The disturbance at Birmingham, excited by the cry of "Church and King" in 1791, reached larger proportions than any excited by the cry of Reform. At Nottingham, too, until the scarcity riots began, there were no tumults or attacks on property but those excited by the Blues or loyalists, who were daily busied in burning Tom Paine's effigy, ducking and pumping on the readers of his works, and smashing the windows of supposed Jacobins.

Sedition.

In November, 1792, the French Republic issued its Edict of Fraternity, inviting all nations to follow the French example, and promising help to those who obeyed the call. Here was direct encouragement offered to the many democratic societies existing, it was supposed, for one dark purpose or another. It seemed to many that the English Government did well to

Causes of Alarm.

publish a proclamation warning people against wicked and seditious writings industriously dispersed among them, and ordering magistrates to prosecute those concerned in issuing them.

Political Societies.   There was known to be a flourishing Revolution Society, and though it existed to commemorate the Revolution of 1688, and not that of 1789, to toast the memory of William III., and not to drink to the fall of kings, its name laid it under suspicion. There was the Society for Constitutional Information and the

THE RIGHTS OF MAN.
(*From a satirical print of* 1792.)

Society of Friends of the People, both engaged, nominally at least, in working for parliamentary reform. Some of their members advocated universal suffrage, so it was thought not improbable that they were, like the London Corresponding Society, secretly negotiating with French Jacobins.

Tom Paine.   Paine's book on the "Rights of Man" was known to have an enormous circulation, and he was prosecuted for it under the proclamation of May, 1792. Paine's counsel argued in vain that it had never been held criminal to express opinions on the problems of political philosophy; in vain he dwelt upon his personal disapproval of the theory of human equality; Paine was condemned. A further proclamation was issued stating that the militia must be called out to repress the dangerous

spirit of tumult excited by the evil-disposed, who were acting
in concert with persons in foreign parts, with the intention to
subvert all order and government.

Then, as if to prove that the fears of the Government were

FASHION before EASE,
or, A good Constitution sacrificed for a Fantastick Form

TOM PAINE LACING BRITANNIA'S STAYS.

(*From a satirical print of* 1793.)

not unfounded, came the discovery that 3,000 daggers had **Daggers**
been ordered at Birmingham. But in spite of the general **Ordered.**
alarm, some ventured to think that Burke's " dagger scene "
in the House of Commons was a fiasco. The discovery,
however, was thought to necessitate the Traitorous Correspondence Act, intended to stop Anglo-French intercourse ;
at the same time voluntary societies were formed, and

the members made it their business to listen to conversation in public places, in the hope of hearing something of a seditious character, which could be reported and punished. A great conspiracy to overthrow the Government was believed to be on foot in 1794, and then followed the suspension of the Habeas Corpus Act, and a number of trials for sedition. The juries were remarkably fortunate in excluding seditious persons from their number, for unanimous verdicts were obtained upon the slenderest thread of evidence.

The King Attacked.   In October, 1795, the king's carriage was pelted by the mob as he was on his way to open Parliament, amid cries of "Give us bread! No war! No famine!" for the war had begun to make itself felt among the poor. There followed a new Statute of Treasons, dispensing with proof of any overt act of treason, and also a Seditious Meetings Bill, which forbade any meeting of more than fifty persons to be held without previous notice to a magistrate, who was to attend and prosecute any speaker whose words tended to excite hatred or contempt towards the Government.

Industrial Disturb-ance.   In 1797 Fox moved for the repeal of these Acts, arguing that "in proportion as opinions are open they are innocent and harmless," but in vain, for although all fear of a revolution in England was over, the industrial disturbances called for suppression. Bad harvests and the closing of foreign markets had raised the price of corn at the beginning of 1796 to 79s. a quarter. The changes in the nature of manufacturing industries, and the consequent hardships endured by those who were thrown out of employment, increased the number of malcontents. In 1799 accordingly came the Corresponding Societies Act, which made all societies unlawful which held secret proceedings or required their members to take an oath, and with it came the Act against Combinations, which was directed against Trade Unions.

Acts against Trade Unions.   The Combination Acts, hastily passed in 1799 and 1800, say nothing concerning the circumstances which called them forth, but from their terms it is clear that they were required to suppress the trade unions forming among the textile workers of Yorkshire and Lancashire. The object of the unions was to enforce the unrepealed laws of the Tudors, especially the Statute 5 Elizabeth c. 4, which required the seven years' apprenticeship. After the Institution had been formed at Halifax, in 1796, the journeymen became aware of the protection which the old laws gave them against the intrusion of

THE DAGGER SCENE IN THE HOUSE OF COMMONS.
(From a caricature by J. Gillray.)

workers who had served no apprenticeship. The unions undertook to prosecute employers breaking the old law, and endeavoured to fix a minimum scale of wages. To prevent this, the Combination Acts made all trade combinations illegal, whether on the part of the masters or of the men.

The journeymen calico-printers alone entered a protest, urging that "no one journeyman or workman will be safe in holding any conversation with another on the subject of his trade or employment," but their complaint was not heard.

As yet, however, the popular agitation on the subject of trade and wage regulations did not express itself in violent acts. Even among the framework knitters, who were in a state of chronic disturbance after the rejection of the proposed Bill to regulate their wages (1779), there had been no violence since 1790. Nearly all the riots that took place in large towns at the end of the century were not trade but scarcity riots. In 1800, wheat being at 115s. 11d. the quarter, popular dis-content was at its height. It was not only the price of bread that had risen; in seven years the price of meat, butter, and sugar had doubled.

Scarcity Riots. In Nottingham, in spite of a large public subscription for the relief of distress, the food stalls in the market-place were attacked, and the granaries at the canal wharves were broken open. " It was really distressing to see with what famine-impelled eagerness many a mother bore away corn in her apron to feed her offspring." The volunteers were called out to quell the disturbance. In London there was continued rioting, with breaking of windows and attacks on corn-dealers. Popular hatred was directed chiefly against the " forestallers, regraters and engrossers' of corn and meat. Forestallers were persons who anticipated the market by buying goods outside; regraters bought to sell again in the same market; engrossers bought standing corn. The poor believed that the rise in the price of corn was entirely due to the action of these persons, who were buying corn cheap and holding it back to raise the price. The judges encouraged the people in this belief. Chief Justice Kenyon congratulated the jury when a verdict against a forestaller was brought in, saying, " You have conferred by your verdict almost the greatest benefit on your country that was ever conferred by any jury." Numbers of associations were formed to prosecute those who could be charged with offences under the old Acts. In September, 1800, when the quartern loaf was at 1s. 9d., a great meeting was planned to assemble at the London Corn Market, the handbills declaring that bread would be at 6d. a quartern if

HINTS TO FORESTALLERS.

(From a satirical print of 1800.)

a sufficient number assembled. "Fellow countrymen," the address runs, "how long will you quietly and cowardly suffer yourselves to be imposed upon and half-starved by a set of mercenary slaves and Government hirelings? Can you still suffer them to proceed in their extensive monopolies while your children are crying for bread? No! Let them exist not a day longer. We are the sovereignty, rise then from your lethargy," and so forth. About 2,000 gathered at Mark Lane, hissing mealmen and corn factors, and pelting Quakers. The Lord Mayor appeared and read the Riot Act, constables charged the mob, which did not finally disperse till the Tower Ward Volunteers and East India House Volunteers cleared the streets. After this the Lord Mayor issued notices requesting London citizens to keep away from the windows and to stay in their back rooms when the military were ordered out to quell tumultuous assemblies. In November it was believed that a great meeting of mechanics was to gather on Kennington Common. The Privy Council hastily met to consider measures to suppress it; when the time came the common was peopled with police and military, and the assembly was nowhere to be found. The quartern loaf was at 1s. 10½d. when at last peace was declared, and then for a while all was quiet.

The Revolution in Manners.

There were revolutions in popular sentiments, there were also revolutions in manners. Foreign travel was impossible, so it became fashionable to go to the sea-side, to Margate, Weymouth, or to Brighthelmstone, as Brighton was then called. Since the royal family set the example, it was easy to believe in the merits of sea-bathing. When the income-tax fell at the rate of £20 on an income of £200, it was not possible to indulge in expensive amusements.

Food.

The scarcity of flour necessitated a change of diet. In July, 1795, the Privy Council implored all families to abjure puddings and pies, and declared their own intention to have only fish, meat, vegetables, and household bread, made partly of rye. It was recommended that one quartern loaf per head per week should be a maximum allowance. The loaf was to be brought on the table for each to help himself, that none be wasted. The king himself had none but household bread on his table. The rich were recommended to make no soups or gravies, to take only the prime cuts, and leave the others that the poor might buy them. The poor were to be taught to make soup and rice-pudding. Rice was a new and as yet little used commodity, and the Government agreed to give such a bounty on its sale that its price should never exceed 35s. a hundred-weight. In 1801 the Government offered bounties on the importation of all kinds of grain and flour, and passed the Brown Bread Act (1800) forbidding the sale of wheaten bread, or new bread of any kind, as stale bread would go further.

BATHING MACHINES AT BRIGHTON IN 1789.
(From a drawing by Rowlandson.)

The scarcity of flour, together with Pitt's tax on powder **Dress** (1795), caused a total change in the personal appearance of both sexes, for men ceased to wear powdered wigs, and women had no more powdered "heads." Both sexes allowed the natural hair to be seen. This was but part of the revolution in dress that took place between 1784 and 1795. As Fox had led the fashion in his macaroni, red-heeled-shoe days, he led it when carelessness of dress became the mode. Wraxall's "Memoirs" speak explicitly on this point, and his evidence may be trusted. "Mr. Fox and his friends, who might be said to dictate to the town, affecting a style of neglect about their persons, and manifesting a contempt for all the usages hitherto established, first threw a sort of discredit on dress." From Brooks's Club, the club of the opposition, "it spread through the private assemblies of London." White's, the Government club, had no control over fashion. Even the Prince of Wales wore Fox's famous Westminster colours, blue and buff, and although it is little likely that he ever showed a contempt for neatness in dress, he wore the blue and buff morning-dress on occasions when full dress would at one time have been required. Court-dress and swords had been the rule in Parliament till Fox sat in top boots and a great-coat. When the Coalition Ministry of 1783 was formed, Lord North's full dress and Blue Ribbon looked out of place "among the great-coats, buff waistcoats, and dirty boots of his new allies." Swords being no longer worn in Parliament, they ceased to be worn at social gatherings. The plebeian umbrella displaced the clouded cane, and gentlemen could walk in the streets protected from the weather without calling immediately for a chair or a coach. Fox was the first to propose the tax on hair powder to Pitt, and long before his suggestion was accepted he renounced its use. "But," Wraxall says, "though gradually undermined and insensibly perishing of an atrophy, dress never totally fell till the era of Jacobinism and of Equality, 1793–1794."

Men's Hair.

Already in 1791 Walpole wrote, " I do not know the present generation by sight," the young men "in their dirty shirts and shaggy hair have levelled nobility as much as the mobility in France have." He finds that the result of the revolt against wigs is that " all individuality is confounded," when to modern eyes it would first seem to have been restored. It was, however, still only the younger and wilder spirits that wore the hair short. They went by the name of the Crop Club, or the Bedford Crops, because in a famous scene at Woburn Abbey the Duke of Bedford and a party of young noblemen formally renounced the use of powder, and retired to the " powdering-room " to have their heads washed and cropped.

Men's Dress.

A change in the cut of breeches and coats was obvious at least as early as 1785, when knee-breeches, buckled at the knee, were no longer worn by those anxious to be in the latest fashion. Instead pantaloons were worn, buttoned or tied with long strings below the knee, at first as far down as the middle of the calf,

A Natural Crop.
(*By Gillray.*)

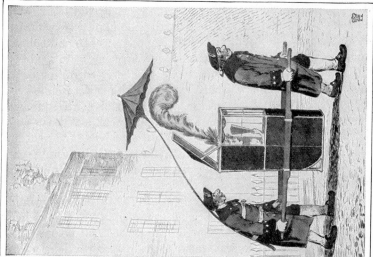

A Belle at Bath, 1796.
(*By Gillray.*)

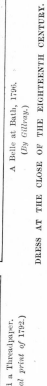

A Spencer and a Threadpaper,
(*From a satirical print of 1792.*)

DRESS AT THE CLOSE OF THE EIGHTEENTH CENTURY.

where they were met by Hessian boots, and in 1793 they had reached the ankle. The buckled knee-breeches were still used at Court, where now for the first time superannuated fashions reigned. It was not there that the close-fitting buckskin breeches were to be seen, nor anything else that was "immense taste." There shoe-buckles were still worn, and not "the unmanly shoestring" which had come in, to the dismay of the Birmingham buckle-makers.

Tail Coats and Panta loons.   The wide-skirted coat had shown a tendency to slope more and more both upwards and downwards from the waist, where it fastened with one button. In 1786 the "sparrow-tail" began, and before long none but tail-coats were worn by the beaus and the bucks. The side pockets, once with wide flaps, were now set close together at the back, with little or no flap; cuffs and collars were small. On dress occasions coat and breeches were made of striped silks. Brown and blue stripes, mulberry-colour, or dark olive were used. The waistcoat was of white silk, richly embroidered. The Ranelagh frock-coat of plain or corded tabinet (between cloth and silk) was for ordinary wear. A coat and waistcoat of superfine cloth, in 1795, cost £3 8s.; Florentine or satin waistcoat and breeches, £3 3s.; Cassimere waistcoat and breeches, £1 16s.; Manchester cotton breeches, from 16s. upwards. A very fashionable outdoor coat was the Spencer, so called from Earl Spencer's bet, in 1792, that he would wear a coat which should become the fashion. It reached only to the waist, and showed the coat-tails below. In complete contrast to it was the "thread-paper," a long close great-coat with "watchman's capes," resembling a Newmarket coat in cut. In 1800 the "Jean de Bry" coats were in date. They were padded on the shoulders, and fastened with three large buttons. They were cut too short to reach the trousers in front, and a smart waistcoat filled the gap. Bunches of seals dangled from the two fobs; one fob was out of fashion. No lace or embroidery was any longer worn; shirt-ruffles were behind the fashion. The coat now buttoned higher, and a large muslin cravat was worn, either tied in a loose bow or swathed in many folds about the neck, and almost covering the chin.

Hats.   In masculine dress length, not width, was the rule, and the long breeches and long coats brought with them the tall hat in place of the three-cornered hat. The "sugar-loaf" hat had a

small flat brim, and was made of beaver or of silk in dark
colours. Then, to make his costume complete, the buck
required his "quizzing-glass."

A JEAN DE BRY COAT.
(*From a satirical print of* 1799.)

But it was not in this costume that the ordinary citizen Ordinary
or the countryman went to his business. The wide-skirted Dress.
coat and knee-breeches were still the ordinary wear. At a
shop for ready-made clothes the average price for a great-coat
was 13s.; a waistcoat, 6s. 6d.; stout breeches, 3s. 9d.; stockings,
1s. 9d.; dowlas shirt, 4s. 6d.; strong shoes, 7s.; a hat "to last

three years," 2s. 6d. Linens and cambrics were still comparatively high in price. A woman's shift was 3s. 8d., when a stuff gown was only 6s. 6d. A linsey-woolsey petticoat was 4s. 6d.; pair of shoes, 3s. 9d.; stays "to last six years," 6s.; and a hat of the cheaper sort, 1s. 8d.

Women's Dress. In the dress of fashionable women the short transition stage from the extreme of artificiality to the extreme of simplicity is believed to have been due to the influence of the portrait-painters. In 1785 Leghorn picture-hats and hair in curls began to replace the huge "mobs" and "heads." In 1788 the hoop was small, the bodice tight and very low, the bust being covered by the "buffont" white muslin kerchief. Then came the classical period, certainly traceable to French influences. The long ringlets were confined *à la victime*, or *à la guillotine;* the dress fell from the shoulders and disregarded the waist. The "Caroline wrapper" of 1795 resembled a carter's smock; if the waist was indicated at all it was by a sash under the arm-pits. Only flimsy stuffs were suit-

THE EXTENDED DRESS OF 1786.
From a contemporary print.)

able for dresses of this cut, and to secure a diaphanous "aërial" appearance the weather was wholly disregarded, and drapery was adopted which Wraxall says was more suitable to the climate of Greece or Italy. The Greek honeysuckle pattern or borders from Pompeian furniture were the favourite trimmings. Gloves to the elbow or mittens and a scarf were the protection allowed out of doors, and while the body was thus scantily clad the head and face were closely covered, at first in the "peasant bonnet" tied under the chin over a "mob," and later in a poke-bonnet with a "valence" or pendant lace curtain, little in harmony with the wearer's supposed classical appearance. Madame de Récamier had too much sense of congruity to dress thus. In 1802 she created some sensation in Kensington Gardens when she

Caroline Wrapper, July, 1795.

Poke Bonnet and Dunstable Hat, September, 1797.

FASHIONS FOR LADIES, 1795 AND 1797.

("The Gallery of Fashion," 1794–1802.)

appeared dressed *à l'antique* in muslin which "clung to her form like the folds of the drapery on a statue; her hair in a plait at the back, and falling in small ringlets round her face, and greasy with *huile antique;* a large veil thrown over the head." In evening dress English women completed the Grecian or Roman coiffure by a *panache,* or bristle-plume, or a bunch of feathers standing erect in front. The "buffont" kerchief

FULL DRESS FOR FEBRUARY, 1799.
(From a contemporary fashion plate.)

went out, and for a short time it became the fashion to wrap the neck up to the chin in folds of muslin in imitation of a man's cravat. This was succeeded in 1795 by the low-necked bodice exposing the shoulders. As the waist was placed abnormally high, the bodice measured only two or three inches in depth.

The Revolution and Morals.   With this total change in externals there came also that revolution in "moral opinions" of which Burke speaks. Even the changes in a fashionable woman's dress serve in some ways to show it. The movement in dress was in part a movement from artificiality to simplicity, and in morals it

LADIES IN EVENING DRESS.

("The Gallery of Fashion," June, 1796.)

was paralleled by that simplification of life which the national
poverty necessitated.   In a sense, it is true, female dress merely
passed from one form of artificiality to another; the same may
be said of the nation's ideas of morality.   Till 1793 the prosperity of the nation had so steadily grown that the sufferings
caused by the war were the more severely felt by all classes.
The manufacturers whose industries were developing, and the
farmers who had corn to sell, alone escaped.   Intellectually and
morally the upper and middle classes were affected by what
they endured.   When the news of the death of Louis XVI.
reached England, the audiences left the theatres before the
curtain fell, the nation put on mourning.   And so in the
years that followed; Ranelagh is heard of no more, its
masquerades were at an end, and in 1803 it finally closed.
The Pantheon promenades and masquerades and operas were
over; the building was still used for concerts and lectures till
1812, when it was taken down and reconstructed.

Places of Amusement.

Popular feeling was now for the first time excited against
gambling.   In 1796 Chief Justice Kenyon, in giving sentence
at a trial to recover £15 won by gambling, threatened that he
would set in the pillory any who were brought before him for
gambling, "though they be the first ladies in the land."
Thereupon Gillray (p. 777) caricatured two ladies whose Faro
banks were notorious as "Pharaoh's daughters," standing in
the pillory.   In 1797 Lady Buckinghamshire, Lady Elizabeth
Luttrell, and others were summoned for playing at Lady
Buckinghamshire's house in St. James's Square.   They were
fined £50, and not condemned to the pillory; but from this
time gambling was no longer public and reputable.   At a
time when so many stirring events were happening, conversation was more interesting than cards.   Political excitement
began to take the place of "pleasure" and "diversion" in the
social world.   There were military, naval, parliamentary, financial, and literary careers to be made, and made quickly.   It
was a time to rouse ambition in young men, who now found
themselves compelled to act, not to travel with a tutor,
educating themselves to gain distinction as professional idlers.
It was a time of great inventions, a time when genius in
whatever class it was found quickly gained reward.

Gambling.

Never were the sufferings of the poor more patent to the

casual observer. It was impossible that philanthropic and
humanitarian schemes should not be in the air. Thinkers
were devoting their minds to the new problems which the
state of the industrial world required men to face. Political

Exaltation of FARO'S Daughters.

THE EXALTATION OF FARO'S DAUGHTERS, 1796.
(From the caricature by J. Gillray.)

economists sought to solve them, and charitable persons sought
to alleviate the distress. It was an age of both voluntary and
involuntary self-denial. Besides philanthropic schemes for
temporary relief there were schemes for educating the poor in
habits of thrift, and numerous savings-banks and friendly
societies were started. The missionary societies renewed their
activity: in 1808 the British and Foreign School Society began.

MUSICAL INSTRUMENTS OF THE LATE EIGHTEENTH CENTURY.

1, Irish or Union Pipes, with bellows. 2, Hurdy-gurdy (Vieille), by Louvet of Paris. 3, Northumbrian bagpipes, with bellows. 4, Musical glasses on Benjamin Franklin's system. 5, Piano by Zumpe, London, 1770. 6, Dulcimer, with beaters.

(By permission of the Rev. F. W. Galpin.)

Sunday Schools were everywhere established. The sufferings of children began to excite sympathy; in 1803 an "Association for improving the situation of infant Chimney-sweepers" was formed.

The strict observance of Sunday had the support of nearly all the advanced moralists of that day. As if to show that the reformers of 1800 stood exactly where the reformers of 1700 stood (IV., p. 810), there was Wilberforce's new society with the old title "for the Reformation of Manners," and an "Association for the Better Observance of the Sabbath." In 1787 the king had issued a proclamation against vice, as William and Mary had done before him. Wilberforce seized

BAKERS' TOKEN COMMEMORATING
SUNDAY OBSERVANCE, 1795.

the moment to start his society. He found the Archbishop of Canterbury "deeply impressed with the torrent of profaneness which every day makes more rapid advances." Both archbishops and all the bishops joined, six dukes, and many of the nobility. The society no longer encountered any hostility.

It was a serious, self-conscious time, a time when seriousness of purpose told to the full. Finish of manner was at a discount, but an outward moral decorum was expected. "Private indulgences" were suffered so long as the public was not insulted by their exhibition. In 1768 a few persons "of delicacy" had considered it shocking that the Duke of Grafton, then First Lord of the Treasury, should lead his mistress, Nancy Parsons, in triumph before the queen. In 1802 Fox had to announce his marriage to Mrs. Armistead before she could be received in society. Even the vices of the Prince of Wales and of the Duke of York were considered matter for regret.

THE appointment of Henry Dundas as Lord Advocate (1775) JAMES
COLVILLE.
Scotland. had introduced to power the most remarkable man Scotland had yet given to the political life of the kingdom. He came of an old Mid-Lothian stock that, for the three immediately preceding generations, had won for itself the highest distinctions of bench and bar. Until his fall and impeachment in 1805, by which time he had been made Viscount Melville, he ranked in public notice with Pitt, Fox, and Burke He won his spurs as a debater in resisting all compromise with armed colonists in America. The admirer and friend of Pitt, he The
Dundas
Régime,
1783-1803. stood by him stoutly through the summer of 1783 in facing the attacks of the powerful Whig Opposition. Whether as Treasurer of the Navy, War Secretary, or First Lord of the Admiralty, he was the life and soul of the national defence, earning indeed almost the entire credit for the successful Egyptian campaign. Throughout he was a tower of strength to the triumphant Tories. The first move towards parliamentary reform, Dunning's resolution on the growing power of the Crown (1780), was opposed by him; and when the French Revolution quickened the forward movement, he proved himself a thorough Anti-Jacobin. In Scotland his repressing hand was most effective. A mere fraction of the population could exercise the franchise. Self-elected town councillors would meet in some dingy corner of their Tolbooths and quietly choose their members as Dundas ordered. In counties *parchment barons* on a bogus qualification swamped the legitimate freeholders. The election of 1790, when his power was at its height, passed with but nine county contests. The total county electorate was then 2,652. Edinburgh was the only burgh with a member to herself, and he was elected by thirty-two votes. The control of the elections was easy for a minister whose position gave him the patronage of hundreds of good posts at home and abroad. Cockburn calls him "the Pharos of Scotland: whoever steered on him was safe." There was no political sentiment abroad; public spirit slept the sleep of indifference. Great writers like Robertson and Blair, philosophers like Hume and Adam Smith, scientists like Maclaurin, Cullen, and Black, all being voteless, stood absolutely outside the public life of the country. During the last decade of the eighteenth century the statistical accounts were drawn up by nearly a

thousand parish ministers, not one of whom expresses dissatisfaction with the political situation. But for a few poor
visionaries and discontented Dissenters, Scotland would be
the best of all worlds.

The bogeys of Atheism, Jacobinism, and invasion were
powerful aids to the rule of Dundas. They staved off the two
pressing questions of the hour—burgh and parliamentary reform.
As early as 1783 artisans and small traders were agitating for
reform of abuses in burghs,
and in 1787 an appeal was
made to the parliamentary
leaders. Pitt gave no answer,
whereas Fox and Sheridan
offered eager support. But
Dundas always resisted such
a blow to his influence, and
his attitude was the only
unpopular one in the whole
course of his career in the
eyes of the mass of his
countrymen. The question
was shelved for the more
important one of parliamentary reform. It was in this
cause that the first blow was
struck at the power of Dundas. The Jacobin movement
found a response in the As-

LORD BRAXFIELD.
(*From a caricature by J. Kay,* 1793.)

sociation of the Friends of the People. The Scottish Branch,
Parlia-
mentary
Reform.
at a meeting in Glasgow (1792), pledged itself to equal representation and shorter parliaments. Government had spies everywhere. Even Dugald Stewart's lectures at Edinburgh University
on Political Economy were suspiciously watched by the Crown
officials. Dundas urged his nephew, the Lord Advocate, to
adopt strong measures. Obsequious juries, under the notorious judge Lord Braxfield, eagerly disposed of the leaders of
the people. Muir, vice-president of the Association, the
friend of Barras, Condorcet, and Lafayette, and a gentle,
humane, and cultured member of the Scottish Bar, was sentenced to fourteen years' transportation. Fysshe Palmer, a

Dundee clergyman, was banished for seven years. Skirving, secretary to the Society of United Scots, and Gerald and Margarot, English delegates, were transported for fourteen years. Their friends, Sheridan, Whitbread, and Fox, with Stanhope in the Lords, fought hard to save them, but Government was too strong. The saddest feature of such political martyrdom was the panic, following on the long-sustained deadening of public opinion, that blinded the outlook of the moneyed and governing classes to the real condition of the nation, and led judges and juries alike into senseless re- pression of which the right thinking were speedily to be- come ashamed. The State trials hastened reform and strengthened the Whig oppo- sition, which had survived the rule of Dundas. The brothers Erskine formed the life and soul of this party. Thomas, while at the English Bar, from which he rose to be Lord Chancellor, was one of the original fifty "Friends of the People," and defended Tom Paine on his trial. His brother Henry remained in their native

Photo: Walker & Cockerell.
LORD CHANCELLOR ERSKINE.
(National Portrait Gallery.)

Edinburgh, where his Whiggism excluded him from public life and the highest rewards of his profession, despite the beauty of his character and the wit and eloquence of which his countrymen were so proud. The Tory reign fostered a generation of privi- leged mediocrities, whereas the cold shades of opposition pro- duced the band that founded the *Edinburgh Review* (1802; p. 802), Brougham, Jeffrey, Horner, and Sydney Smith.

A treatise would not exhaust the marvellous story of the **Rise of** making of industrial Scotland. The first solid start in material **Industry.** progress came with the close of the Seven Years' War (1763). Pioneers had been at work here and there ever since the union **Agricul-** under the impetus of Dutch and English examples. The Duchess **ture.** of Gordon, daughter of the Earl of Peterborough, was the first to bring ploughs from the South, and men used to the new methods of sowing grasses, making hay, planting waste lands, and draining morasses. On the Borders a ploughboy, Dawson, applied lessons which, in a spirit of adventure, he had travelled to learn under Bakewell (p. 406), and about 1764 sowed seventy acres of turnips. In the same district the famous judge, Lord Kames, began his career as the most notable of improvers. With every step forward he was directly or indirectly connected. Colonies of veteran soldiers were tried (1752–59) on his reclaimed lands in Perthshire, but without success. The poor feudal tenants, however, driven out of the upland straths, were turned to excellent account. Kames did more: his *Gentleman Farmer* (1777) marked an era in agricultural progress. To him is also due the first technical instruction in husbandry, when he selected Wight, a Midlothian farmer (1773–74), to report on the annexed estates. His six volumes (1778–84) form a business-like, intelligent, and extremely interesting picture of this period of momentous change. Kames planned the Board of Agriculture which Sir John Sinclair realised, and founded the Highland Society (1784). The Statistical Accounts and the County Reports of the last decade of the century show that an eager spirit of progress was abroad among intelligent landholders. Rural life and customs were being revolutionised, and cultivators of the old school like Robert Burns had to go to the wall. Meikle's threshing-mill (1787) soon superseded the flail, saving at least one per cent. of the total produce of the country, while Small's plough, in full vogue about the same date, banished for ever its old ox-drawn cumbrous rival. The marketing that followed new wants and increased production soon produced made roads instead of bridle-paths, and neat carts to take the place of clumsy sleds and wooden-wheeled wagons. In spite of all this the Highlands and the Isles remained till quite recently

The High-lands. in their primitive condition. Climate, inaccessibility, overpopulation fostered by a vicious land system, the pride and poverty of landlords—these all contributed to this result. The middlemen, or tacksmen, who had so long secured the advantages going, were driven out with the rise of rents and the decay of clan sentiment. The landless peasants, long virtually serfs, had to emigrate in thousands to find a Caledonia in the virgin forests of New England and the Lower St. Lawrence. The advent of sheep-farming (1767) hastened emigration and secured big money rents. The change was attended with little agrarian disturbance. In 1792 there was a blind spasmodic rising in Easter Ross to drive the sheep into the sea, but it was easily suppressed. The much-debated Sutherland evictions (1812–14) made a great sensation. They were the outcome of well-meant efforts to settle the dispossessed peasantry in fishing villages newly-erected; but the farmer-fisher proved a failure, and the Highland question is not yet settled.

Fiscal laws sorely hampered local industry. The heavy

SHIELING IN THE ISLAND OF JURA, WITH VIEW OF THE PAPS.
(" *Britannica Curiosa,*" Vol. II., 1787.)

taxes and intolerable restrictions on the movement of salt, coal, **Taxes.** corn, wool, made all coast-dwellers daring and active smugglers. The expenses of collection exceeded the total revenue. Only about one-third of the salt dues went into the public purse. The social and industrial discomfort made government odious, while the general demoralisation was pernicious in the extreme.

Despite unwise legislation industry developed by dint of **Manu-** energy and intelligence. Under such native guidance as that **factures.** of Forbes and Kames and a band of self-sacrificing improvers, the face of the country was so altered that according to a contemporary, one returning to Scotland in 1800 after forty years' absence would find his direction only by the neighbouring hills. The Board of Linen Manufacturers (1727) fostered the time-honoured industry of the fireside by premiums

242

on the finished stuffs, the annual value of which rose from £293,864 in 1748 to £936,453 in 1805, diffusing valuable resources among many industrial villages. The British Fishery Society (1786) strove to create the net and line fishing in deep waters, paying bounties till 1830. But the greatest triumphs in industry were won by Glasgow. Provost Ingram established the first calico print-field at Pollokshaws in 1742, and before the end of the century there were thirty in and

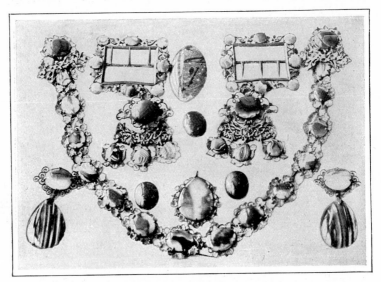

AN EIGHTEENTH-CENTURY NECKLACE, WITH EARRINGS AND BUCKLES.
(*National Museum of Scottish Antiquities, Edinburgh.*)

around the city. The inventions of Hargreaves, Crompton, and Arkwright led, about 1785, to the cotton industry and a vast trade in muslins. David Dale, a practical philanthropist of advanced type, secured land about this time on the estates of Judge Braxfield, and with Arkwright's help laid out the novel industrial village of New Lanark, near the Falls of the Clyde. His water mill was the first of the kind in the island. Here he made use of the labour of the expatriated Highlanders, boarding the young in barracks and employing teachers to instruct them at a time when elementary education was thought a distracting luxury. Rapidly cotton mills were set up wherever labour and water power were to be had. When Arkwright's patent ran out (1785) a fresh start was possible. Watt had made his first model in 1763 in a room of his house near the Broomielaw in Glasgow, and when a fellow-citizen[1] worked the mule jenny by machinery instead of hand labour (1792) Watt applied steam to the process, so that Todd was able in the same year to spin cotton by the new motor. Before 1818 there were fifty-four cotton mills, with 600 spindles, in and around the city. Robert Miller of Glasgow patented a

power-loom in 1796, and a factory was at once set going with 200 looms. Dyeing grew up alongside of cotton weaving, and with it is identified the name of Mackintosh, famous for his water-proofing process. Finding a Rouen dyer, Papillon by name, in London, he took him north (1785), and with the help of Dale set up the Turkey Red industry. The population of Glasgow, at the rise of the cotton industry

DAVID DALE.
(After John Henning.)

(1785) only 45,889, rose to 147,197 in 1819, the date of the first exact enumeration of the inhabitants. The spirit of enterprise spread to other towns, Paisley being the most successful imitator of Glasgow with its thread, tape, and gauze. Here, in 1785, many houses paid as much as £500 a week in wages. Dundee began to import much flax from Holland and the Baltic for coarse linen and sailcloth. A Quaker from Glasgow established (1735) bleaching and dyeing in Perth, where the trade has vastly flourished. Dunfermline gave up ticking for diapers about 1750, and by 1792 had 1,200 looms at work. In Aberdeenshire there

---

[1] Robert Muir was the first to make an engine in Glasgow for moving machinery. It was started in a cotton mill in 1792. Watt's engine was first used for spinning cotton at Manchester in 1789 (p. 631).

was an enormous development of stocking-knitting and pork-pickling for the Navy.   Even remote Shetland turned out stockings to the annual value of £17,000 (1801).   Mineral wealth was not overlooked.   At Cramond, near Edinburgh, Cadell had long forged Swedish iron by water-power.   The works were erected in Carron (1760) for the manufacture of native ore, and rapidly the iron industry extended into Lanark-shire.   Newer methods had to be employed to reach the deeper seams of coal.   At Shettleston the first engine for drawing water from pits (1764) marks the beginning of such efforts.

P. W. JOYCE. Ireland.   AFTER 1782 the only connection between the Parliaments of England and Ireland was that they had the same sovereign for head.   "Grattan's Parliament" was completely independent, and was absolutely free to make any laws it pleased for Ireland. But it stood sadly in need of internal reform ; for, free as it was, it was as bad a type of parliament as could well be conceived. Of the 300 members of the House of Commons, not more than seventy-two were returned by the free votes of the electors ; all the rest were, directly or indirectly, nominated by lords or other powerful persons, who commonly sold the seats for cash at election times.   The spurious boroughs fabricated in the times of the Stuarts (IV., p. 270) still existed, whose electors, being very few, could easily be brought up when the Government wanted one of their own supporters elected.   And lastly, the Roman Catholics, the great bulk of the people, were wholly unrepresented.   The Parliament did not represent the nation ; it did not represent even the Protestant people.   It contained within itself the elements of decay and dissolution, which nothing but a thorough reform could avert.

Parlia-mentary Reform.   The two antagonistic parties still subsisted, with the line of cleavage as distinctly marked as ever.   The Patriotic Party were eager for Parliamentary reforms ; the Government party obstinately resisted reform of every kind ; and by means of the corrupting influences at their command they were generally able to secure a majority.   The Volunteers took up the question ; and in 1783 Flood brought in a Bill embodying their demands ; but the Government proved too strong, and after some violent scenes the Bill was rejected.   There were now fears of a collision between the Volunteers and the Government; but through the influence of Lord Charlemont the convention was adjourned without any day being fixed for next meeting. This was the death-blow to the influence of the Volunteers, who never again took any leading part in the political affairs of the country.

Though many of the ruinous restrictions on Irish trade had been removed, there were still enormous prohibitory duties on Irish goods exported to England, and but little or none on English goods brought to Ireland; a state of things which greatly repressed all that remained of Irish manufacture and commerce. On this point the Irish Government were for reform; but when their very moderate proposals were brought by Pitt before the English Parliament in 1785, a violent outcry was raised all over England by companies, manufacturers, and merchants, who insisted on maintaining the unjust monopolies that enriched themselves and impoverished Ireland; so that the whole scheme fell through. *Irish Trade and English Interests.*

The liberation of the Irish Parliament had no effect whatever in ameliorating the condition of the country; the same causes continued to produce the same effects; and distress and discontent prevailed everywhere. Secret societies again arose among the peasantry, and the whole country began to be fearfully disturbed. In the South there was a revival of the White-boys. In the North there were "Peep-o'-day Boys," all Protestants and Presbyterians, who directed their hostilities chiefly against Catholics, while the Catholics, on their part, banded themselves as "Defenders"; and battles were fought, in which numbers on both sides were maimed or killed. Grattan moved, in Parliament, for inquiry with a view to remedy, but he was overborne; and instead of this the Government had a crushing Insurrection Bill passed in 1787, which was followed by the usual crop of transportations and executions; after which, instead of improving, matters became worse than before. *Social Unrest.*

About 1790 the minds of the higher classes began to be stirred profoundly by the French Revolution. Clubs were formed in Dublin and Belfast, whose publications and speeches exposed unsparingly the evil systems and the corruption of the Government; but the Government was inexorable, and never deviated from its course. Lord Charlemont, Lord Moira,

Hamilton Rowan, Theobald Wolfe Tone, and Napper Tandy, all belonging to the Protestant gentry, were members of these clubs. In 1791 Tone founded the Society of United Irishmen, in Belfast, which was to include all classes and religions in its ranks; its chief fundamental objects, which were quite legal,

The United Irishmen.

WOLFE TONE.
(By Hallmandel, 1827.)

being to break down the corrupting influence of the Government by Parliamentary reform, and to remove the disabilities of all religious persuasions.

Catholic Disabilities.

The association called the "Catholic Committee," composed of the leading Catholics of Dublin, had been in existence for many years. Their purpose was to look after the Catholic interests in general, and especially to obtain the repeal of the remaining penal statutes; but beyond this they did not mix themselves up much in any political movements. Considerable success attended their efforts. In 1793 a Bill was passed through the Irish Parliament restoring the franchise to the Catholics, opening up to them almost all situations, civil and

military, and granting them permission to open colleges. But
several heavy restrictions still remained, the most serious of
which was that no Catholic could be a Member of Parliament.

The leading spirits among the United Irishmen were now
very active both in Dublin and Belfast, held meetings and
circulated bold addresses, for which some of them were prosecuted, fined, and imprisoned. Secret negotiations were carried
on regarding a French invasion, the chief agent being the
Rev. William Jackson, a Protestant clergyman. But there
were spies among the body, and the Government was made
aware of all their plans. Jackson was arrested, tried, and
condemned; but he managed to take a dose of arsenic and
dropped dead in the dock. Hamilton Rowan, who was also
implicated, escaped to America.

Intrigues with France.

Towards the end of 1794, William Pitt took measures to
have the Catholics of Ireland completely emancipated; and
with this object in view, Earl Fitzwilliam, a just, liberal,
and enlightened man, was sent over as lord-lieutenant, which
caused great joy in Ireland. He at once applied himself to
the task, and with his concurrence, an Emancipation Bill was
brought in by Grattan, early in 1795. But an unexpected
obstacle disconcerted the whole intended reform. The king,
persuaded it seems by certain mischief-makers from Ireland
that the Protestant religion was in danger, interposed his
veto and stopped the whole measure. Fitzwilliam was recalled,
and the bad old policy of force and coercion was resumed.
Whatever may have been the cause, that cruel disappointment
spread sorrow and indignation, not only among Catholics, but
among Protestants; and it was in great measure answerable
for the tremendous evils that followed.

Pitt's Attempt at Eman- cipation.

The people were now exasperated and desperate, and they
resolved to attempt revolution and the establishment of a
Republic. The United Irishmen, abandoning their legal
methods, banded themselves as a secret, oath-bound society.
Wolfe Tone, compromised by some disclosures, had to leave
the country; he went to America with the intention of
negotiating for help from the United States, and from France.
In Ulster, as usual, the disturbances took the form of bitter
religious strife. The Protestants formed themselves into a
new society called Orangemen, openly expressing their deter-

An Irish Republic Projected.

mination to expel all the Catholics from Ulster; after which
the Catholics were attacked everywhere through the province,
and suffered great persecution. Wolfe Tone had long before
endeavoured to bring the two religious bodies to a mutual
good understanding, but his efforts were unavailing.

One great object of the Government at this time was to
prevent the spread of revolutionary doctrines in Ireland; and
it did not escape their notice that all young Catholics who
aspired to the priesthood were forced to go to France for their
education. The Government feared that the young priests
might import into Ireland the ideas of the Revolution, to
prevent which they founded the College of Maynooth in 1795,
with an annual grant of £8,000 for the education of the
Catholic clergy.

The Rebellion of 1798. The United Irishmen continued to increase till they ultimately numbered 100,000; among other important persons, they
were joined by Lord Edward Fitzgerald, brother of the Duke
of Leinster; and towards the end there were many Catholics
among them. In December, 1796, through the influence of Tone,
a French fleet of forty-three ships of war under General Hoche,
with 15,000 troops, and 45,000 stand of arms, sailed for Ireland;
but they were dispersed by storms, and only sixteen vessels
entered Bantry Bay, which, as the wild weather continued, soon
returned to France. After this came another Insurrection Act;
many of the leaders were arrested; and military, yeomen, and
militia were let loose on the country and committed horrible
and unspeakable brutalities on the inoffensive peasantry, so
that thousands of peaceable people were driven to join the
ranks of the United Irishmen. There was another attempt at
invasion in 1797, by a Dutch fleet with 15,000 men, under
Admiral de Winter; but the expedition, having first been
delayed by unsuitable weather, was finally defeated by Admiral
Duncan at Camperdown.

The rebels at last determined on action, and fixed on the
23rd of May, 1798, for a general rising. But the spies within
their ranks kept the Government well informed of their proceedings. In March, several of the leaders were arrested, among
them Lord Edward Fitzgerald, who received a mortal wound
while resisting. Two brothers, Henry and John Sheares, barristers, were arrested, tried, and hanged. When the actual rising

came it was only partial, being confined to the counties of Kildare, Wicklow, and Wexford; in this last-named county it took a religious character, which it had not elsewhere, and nearly all the rebels were Catholics, though many of their leaders were Protestants. The peasantry of Wexford were a peaceable, industrious people, among whom secret societies had made no headway, and who had no wish to rise; but they were driven to rebellion, simply by the terrible barbarities of the military, yeomanry, and more especially of the North Cork militia.

They rose up in desperation, without arms, or plan, or leaders, and in their blind fury committed many terrible outrages on the Protestant loyalist inhabitants, in retaliation for the worse excesses of the militia. The Rev. John Murphy, a parish priest, whose little chapel had been burned, at last placed himself at their head; and under his leadership they annihilated a company of the North Cork militia, on the 27th May, at Oulart. On the day previous, a body of 4,000 rebels had been defeated at Tara. The rebels captured Enniscorthy and Gorey, after which they fixed their chief

LORD EDWARD FITZGERALD.
(After the painting by William Hamilton, R.A.)

encampment on Vinegar Hill, beside Enniscorthy. On the 30th of May, a detachment of military was attacked and destroyed at the Three Rocks, near Wexford; and the rebels took possession of Wexford, where they drank and feasted, and committed great outrages on those they considered unfriendly to them. While here, they placed at their head, as general, a Protestant gentleman named Bagenal Harvey. In June they took Newtownbarry and New Ross, from both which, however, they were soon after expelled by the military. An irresponsible rabble, flying from New Ross, seized a number of inoffensive loyalist prisoners at a place called Scullabogue, and having murdered thirty-seven of them, followed up the massacre by setting fire to a barn in which the rest—more than 100—were confined,

and burned them all to death. The rebels next attempted
to march on Dublin, but they were intercepted and defeated at
Arklow, by General Needham. On the 21st of June General
Lake marched on their chief encampment at Vinegar Hill,
with 20,000 men, and after some hard fighting, defeated and
dispersed the rebels. This virtually ended the rebellion; many
of the leaders were arrested and hanged, among them Bagenal
Harvey and Father Murphy. The whole country was now at
the mercy of the yeomen and militia, who perpetrated dreadful
atrocities on the peasantry; while straggling bands of rebels
traversed the country free of all restraint, and in retaliation
committed terrible outrages.

In the North the rebellion broke out in June. But the
rebels were defeated in two battles, and their leaders, Henry
Joy McCracken and Henry Munro, were captured and hanged,
Munro at his own door.

Lord Cornwallis, a humane and distinguished man, was
appointed Lord-Lieutenant in June. He put a stop to the
cruel military outrages, and succeeded in restoring some
degree of quiet. After the rebellion had been crushed there

**French
Invasion.**

were two small hostile expeditions from France—still in 1798:
one under General Humbert landed at Killala, and the other
under Admiral Bompart entered Lough Swilly; but both were
repelled without much difficulty. Wolfe Tone, who was on
board one of Bompart's vessels, was taken and sent prisoner to
Dublin, where he was tried and sentenced to be hanged. But
on the morning fixed for the execution he cut his throat with
a penknife, and died of the wound a short time afterwards.

**The
Union.**

William Pitt believed that the proper time had now
arrived for carrying out his favourite project of a Parliamentary union of Ireland with England. At this time Lord
Cornwallis was Lord-Lieutenant, and Lord Castlereagh Chief
Secretary. Under Pitt's directions elaborate preparations were
made for passing the measure next session. The Irish Government had been all along corrupt; but corruption was now
carried to an extent never experienced before. The proprietors of the " rotten " or " pocket " boroughs were bought
off for large sums, the whole amount expended in this part
of the business being £1,260,000, which Ireland herself was
made to pay. There was bribery everywhere, with scarcely

an attempt at concealment; and votes were bought for peerages, promotions in peerage, pensions, judgeships, situations of various kinds, and direct cash. Lord Cornwallis, a high-minded man, expressed the utmost abhorrence at being obliged to take part in such disreputable transactions.

The session opened in January, 1800. Grattan, who had been for some time out of Parliament, had himself elected and took his seat. Dublin was in a fearful state of excitement, so

THE UNION COACH.
(*From a contemporary satirical print.*)

that the exasperated crowds had to be kept in check by the military. Lord Castlereagh brought forward the motion for Union; it was opposed most vehemently by the anti-unionists led by Grattan, who pleaded with all his old fire and eloquence; but in spite of all their efforts the measure was carried. The one bright spot in the dark record is that there were over 100 members who stood proof against the corrupting influences, and opposed the project to the last.

In order to lessen the hostility of the Roman Catholics to the measure, it was conveyed to them that the union would be immediately followed by Emancipation. But this promise was not kept; for the Act emancipating the Catholics was not carried till after the lapse of twenty-nine years.

Lecky, *History of England in the Eighteenth Century ;* Sir G. C. Lewis, *Administrations of Great Britain ;* Erskine May, *Constitutional History ;* Cunningham, *English Industry and Commerce ;* Bright, *History of England ;* Mahan, *Influence of Sea Power on the Wars of the French Revolution ;* biographies of Pitt by Lord Stanhope, Lord Rosebery, and Lord Ashbourne; John Morley, *Burke ;* Wakeman, *Charles James Fox ;* Wilberforce's *Life.* Among contemporary authorities, Burke, *Reflections on the French Revolution* and *Appeal from the New to the Old Whigs ;* Arthur Young's *Tours ; Memoirs of the Life of Sir Samuel Romilly, Diaries and Correspondence of the Earl of Malmesbury, The Grenville Papers, The Paget Papers.*

SPECIAL SUBJECTS.

Military History.—Seeley, *Expansion of England ;* Innes, *Britain and her Rivals ;* Norman, *Colonial France ;* Malleson, *Decisive Battles in India,* and *Final French Struggles in India ;* also his *Dupleix* and *Clive,* "Rulers of India" Series ; Orme, *History of India ;* Lyall, *British Dominion in India ; Regimental History of the Madras Fusiliers ;* Mahan, *Sea Power* (see above); Wellington, *Supplementary Despatches ;* Dundas, *Drill Regulations ;* Bunbury, *Narrative of the Campaign in Holland ;* Wilson, *Campaign in Egypt ;* Elmslie's prize Essay in *Journal of United Service Institution,* 1895.

The Navy, 1742–1815.—Dr. John Campbell, *Lives of the British Admirals* (continued by H. R. Yorke and W. Stevenson, 1817) ; Charnock, *Biographia Navalis* (1798); James, *Naval History of Great Britain* (continued by Chamier, 6 vols., Lond., 1837) ; Marshall, *Royal Naval Biography ; Letters of Sir S. Hood,* 1781–83 (Navy Records Society) ; E. Thompson, *Sailor's Letters written to his Select Friends* (Ind. ed. 1767) ; *The History of Edward and Maria* (also by Thompson, published anonymously in the *London Magazine,* 1774–75) ; Thompson's journal, ed. Hayman, in *Cornhill Magazine,* May, 1868 ; Beatson, *Naval and Military Memoirs of Great Britain* (1804) ; C. Derrick, *Memoirs of the Rise and Progress of the Royal Navy* (1806) ; Mahan, *Influence of Sea Power on History ; Influence of Sea Power on the French Revolution and Empire ; Life of Nelson,* and *Types of Naval Officers: Logs of the Great Sea Fights,* 1794–1805 (Navy Records Society) ; Sir W. Laird Clowes, *The Royal Navy : a History.*

Exploration 1642–1802.—For Dampier: Harris, *Collection of Voyages ;* Hacke, *Voyages* (1699) ; *Voyage of Captain Bartholomew Sharpe,* 1684 ; Public Record Office, *Minutes of Court-martial,* vol. x., *Captain's Letters* D. L. ; British Museum, Sloane MSS., 46A and B, 49, 54, 3236, 3820 ; but especially Dampier's own narratives, with Funnel's, reprinted in 4 vols., as *Dampier's Voyages.* For Morgan and the earlier Buccaneers: Exquemelin, *Buccaneers of America,* 1654 (partly republished in the "Adventure Series," 1891) ; British Museum, Add. MSS., 27968 ; *Present State of Jamaica,* 1683 ; *Journals of Jamaica Assembly,* vol. i. ; *History of Jamaica,* 1774. For Narborough and others, Narborough, *Journal ;* Charnock, *Naval Biography.* Anson's *Life,* by Sir John Barrow, very unsatisfactory ; Walter, *Account of Anson's Voyage round the World* (1748) ; Pascoe Thomas, *Journal of a Voyage to the South Seas* (1745). For Cook, *cf.* his *Life,* by Kippis, in *Biographia Britannica ;* Accounts, of his *first* voyage in Hawkesworth's *Voyages,* vols. ii. and iii. (1773) ; of his *second* voyage, by himself, in 2 vols. (1777), and also by George Forster (1777); of his *last* voyage, by himself and King, in 3 vols. (1784) ; *cf.* also the *Narrative of Cook's Death,* by David Samwell, surgeon of the *Discovery* (1786) ; British Museum, Egerton MSS., 277A, which contains the *Journal* of his last voyage to 6th January, 1779; Banks' *System of Geography,* and, above all, the edition of Cook's *Journals* by Wharton, and his Letters among the *Captains' Letters* in the Record Office. For Bligh, Adams, etc., *see* Belcher's *Mutineers of the Bounty ;* Sir T. Barrow, *Mutiny of the Bounty,* 1831 ; *Notes and Queries,* 1856, 1871, 1872 ; Marshall's *Royal Naval Biography ;* and articles in the

Dictionary of National Biography. For Bruce, *cf.* his *Travels* (1790) ; Playfair's *Travels* in footsteps of Bruce (1877) and the *Travels* of Lord Valentia and of Salt, Bruce's chief critics. For Flinders, his *Voyage to Terra Australis* (1814) and his *Observations on the Coasts of Van Diemen's Land*, etc. (1801). For Park, his *Travels* in the *Journal of a Mission to the Interior of Africa* (1815) and Pinkerton's *Collection of Voyages*, vol. xvi. On the history of colonisation in general, C. P. Lucas, *Historical Geography of the British Colonies ;* Egerton, *Origin and Growth of English Colonies.*

Church History, 1715-1815.—Atterbury, *Correspondence* and Memoir by Nichols ; Coxe, *Walpole Parl. Hist.*, vii., viii., xxviii., xxix. ; Secker, *Works*, esp. vol. v. ; Leland, *View of the Principal Deistical Writers ;* Lathbury, *History of the Nonjurors ;* Overton, *The Nonjurors ; Life and Works* of Archdeacon Blackburne ; *Lives* of Law, by Overton ; Waterland, by Van Mildert ; Warburton, by Hurd ; Wesley, by Tyerman ; Simeon, by Carus ; Wilberforce, *History of the American Church ;* Overton, *The English Church in the Eighteenth Century ;* and the excellent summary in Perry, *Church History*, iii., especially the notes and illustrations.

Philosophy.—Bowring, *Life of Bentham* (in his ed. of Bentham's works), shows Bentham's political influence ; but much of it was indirect : *cf.* Bain, *Life of James Mill ;* Leslie Stephen, *English Thought in the Eighteenth Century.*

Science, Medicine, and *Art*, as in c. xviii. ; *Agriculture* as in c. xvii. ; *Manufactures* as in c. xx. ; *Social Life*, as in c. xix., with the addition of A. H. Norway, History of the *Post Office Packet Service ;* and W. Macritchie, *A Diary of a Tour through Great Britain.*

Economic History.—The Journal of the House of Commons and Reports of Parliamentary Committees and Commissions—*e.g.* those on the *Wool Trade* in 1803, 1804, and 1806 ; on the *Cotton Trade* in 1808 and 1809 ; on *Finance* and *Currency* in 1797 and 1811. Cunningham, *Growth of English Industry and Commerce ;* Leone Levi, *History of British Commerce ;* Tooke, *History of Prices ;* Jacob, *Enquiry into the Production and Consumption of the Precious Metals ;* Dowell, *History of Taxation ;* Aschrott, *English Poor-Law System ;* Adam Smith, *Wealth of Nations ;* Malthus, *Essay on the Principle of Population ;* Eden, *State of the Poor ;* Nicholls, *History of the English Poor-Law ;* McLeod, *Theory and Practice of Banking ;* Macpherson, *Annals of Commerce ;* Porter, *Progress of the Nation ;* Marx, *Das Kapital* (contains much valuable fact extracted from Blue Books, etc.) ; Walker, *Money ;* the works of Ricardo ; Bagehot, *Economic Studies ;* Price, *History of Political Economy in England ;* Arthur, *Young's Autobiography.*

Prisons and Prison Reform.—John Howard, *State of Prisons in England and Wales*, 4th ed. (1792) ; Pringle, *Jayl Fever* (*sic*) (1750). Among Acts of Parliament, Popham's Act to abolish gaol fees, 16 Geo. III. c. 43, substituting imprisonment for transportation ; 19 Geo. III. c. 74, establishing Penitentiary Houses, are noteworthy, as also the proceedings of the Select Committee on Police and Convict Establishments, 1798, and the Report of the Parliamentary Committee on Penitentiary Houses, 1811. *See* also Jeremy Bentham, *The Panopticon, or the Inspection House* (Bentham's Works, ed. Bowring, vol. iv.) ; Eden, *Principles of Penal Law ;* Heath on *Secundary Punishment*, in the App. to Parliamentary Reports, 1837 ; Lecky, vol. vi. ; Neild, *State of Prisons*, 1812.

Scotland, 1742-1815.—*General :* Chambers, *Jacobite Rebellion* (1745-6) (with Bishop Forbes' MSS., 1834, now published by Scottish Historical Society in the *Lyon in Mourning*) ; Chevalier Johnston, *Memoirs of the Rebellion* (1745-6) ; Omond, *Lord Advocates* and *Arniston Memoirs* (Dundas family). *Economic Condition.—Lowlands :* Histories of Edinburgh, by Maitland (1753), and Arnot (1788) ; Cleland, *Annals of Glasgow* (1816) ; Kames, *Gentleman Farmer* (1788) ; Wight, *Present State of Agriculture* (1778-84) ; *Statistical Account* (1791-99) ; *County Reports to the Board of Agriculture*, 7 vols. (1797-1818) ; Robertson, *Rural Recollections* (1765-1829). *Highlands :* Buchanan, *Condition of the Hebrides* (1780) ; Walker, *Economic Condition* (1808) ; Selkirk, *Observations on the Highlands* (1805) ; Loch, *Sutherland Improvements* (1820) ; Sellar, *Sutherland Evictions in* 1812-1814 (1883) ; *Report of the Crofter Commission* (1884) ; Histories by Stewart (1825), Skene (1837), Browne (1849-53) ; Logan, *Scottish Gael*

(1831). *Orkney and Shetland:* Tudor, *History* (1883), the latest and most complete. *Topography, etc. :* John McCulloch, *Highlands and Western Isles* (1824). *Travels : e.g.* Pococke (1760), Gray (1764 : Tovey, *Gray and his Friends*, 1890), Pennant (1769-72), Johnson and Boswell (1773), Francis Douglas (1782), Newte (1791), Gilpin (1792), Heron (1792), Lettice (1794), St. Fond (Paris, 1794), Stoddart (1799), Hon. Mrs. Murray (1799-1802), Alexander Campbell (1802), Dorothy Wordsworth (1803), Hogg, the Ettrick Shepherd (1803). *Social Life.—Memoirs* by Alexander Carlyle of Inveresk (1721-1805); Ramsay of Ochtertyre (1736-1814); Isaac Forsyth, bookseller in Elgin (1768-1859); Somerville of Jedburgh (1741-1814); William Forsyth, merchant in Cromarty (1722-99). *Reminiscences* of Philo-Scotus (1785-1821); Mrs. Grant of Laggan's *Memoirs and Correspondence* (1844) (a delightful picture of Highland Life); Donald Sage, *Memorabilia Domestica* (1889); Henry Cockburn (1779-1854), *Memorials, Journal, Circuit Journeys;* Mrs. Fletcher, *Autobiography* (1875). *Lives*—of Kames, by Lord Woodhouselee; Dr. Erskine, by Moncrieff; John Home, by Henry Mackenzie; Adam Smith, by Dugald Stewart; Jeffrey, by Cockburn; Burns, by Currie; Henry Erskine, by Fergusson; Lockhart's *Scott. Manners.*—Topham, *Letters from Edinburgh* (1776); David Allan, *Illustrations to the Gentle Shepherd* (1788); *Poems* of Ferguson and Burns; Jackson, *History of the Scottish Stage* (1793); Smollett, *Humphrey Clinker; Peter's Letters to his Kinsfolk;* and among modern books—Daniel Wilson, *Memorials of Old Edinburgh* (1848); Robert Chambers, *Traditions of Old Edinburgh;* Gregor, *Folk Lore of the North-east of Scotland* (1881); Alexander, *Northern Rural Life* (1877); Graham, *Social Life of Scotland in the Eighteenth Century.*

Ireland, 1714-1800.—Lecky, *History of England in the Eighteenth Century;* Froude, *English in Ireland in the Eighteenth Century;* Plowden, *History of Ireland;* Two *Centuries of Irish History,* ed. Bryce; Dunbar Ingram, *Two Chapters of Irish History;* Rt. Hon. J. T. Ball, *Historical Review of Legislative Systems in Ireland;* Swift, *Works;* Musgrave, *History of the Irish Rebellion;* Barry O'Brien, *Autobiography of Wolfe Tone;* J. T. Gilbert, *Memoirs and Correspondence of Lord Charlemont; Correspondence* of Castlereagh, and of Cornwallis; *Lives* and *Speeches* of Grattan, Flood, Plunket, and Curran; Burke's *Works;* Barrington, *Rise and Fall of the Irish Nation;* Madden, *History of the United Irishmen;* Moore, *Life of Lord Edward Fitzgerald; Autobiography* of Hamilton Rowan; Reid, *History of the Presbyterian Church in Ireland;* Swift McNeill, *English Interference with Irish Industries,* and *How the Union was Carried; Correspondence between Pitt and Rutland;* Hutchinson, *Commercial Restraints on Ireland.*

Photo: W. Lawrence, Dublin.
VINEGAR HILL, ENNISCORTHY.

CHAPTER XX.

ENGLAND'S STRUGGLE FOR EXISTENCE. 1802–1815.

ADDINGTON had succeeded Pitt as Prime Minister in 1801 and formed a cabinet of complete mediocrity which governed England till 1804. During the early portion of this administration England won great successes by land and by sea The victories of Alexandria (March 21st), and Copenhagen (April 2nd, 1801), accelerated the negotiations for peace, while the accession of Alexander I. to the Russian throne led to the conclusion of a treaty between England and Russia in June of the same year. The French having failed to carry out an attempt to invade England agreed to come to terms, and in October the preliminaries of peace were signed. England yielded all her conquests except Ceylon, Trinidad, British Guiana, and Tobago. Before the preliminary treaty had been ratified, Bonaparte had by his intrigues established French influence in Holland, Switzerland, and Italy, thus justifying the fears of Grenville and others that the First Consul had no intention of relinquishing his aggressive schemes. The English nation was, however, weary of war. Pitt was confident that Bonaparte would recognise the advantages of peace, and it was felt that England, having made almost uncalled-for concessions, would convince Europe that her motives had been disinterested. On March 27th, 1802, the peace of Amiens was signed. Before, however, the year was over it became apparent that the peace would be but a truce. Bonaparte's aggressions never ceased; he annexed Elba and a large part of North Italy in the autumn of 1802, occupied Switzerland, and adopted a policy towards England which, while in its commercial aspect anticipating the famous Berlin Decrees (p. 708), was calculated to bring on a fresh European war. He demanded the suppression of the English journals by which he had been attacked, he required the expulsion of all French

ARTHUR HASSALL. Political History.

Addington's Ministry.

The Peace of Amiens

emigrants and the removal from England of the Bourbon princes, and his agents endeavoured to stir up the Irish to rebellion.

Bonaparte was determined to secure Malta, which the English Government fortunately had not as yet transferred to the Knights of St. John. At the beginning of 1803 even

War Breaks out Afresh.

Addington recognised that war was imminent, and acted with some show of vigour. Lord Whitworth, our ambassador in Paris, was withdrawn, and on May 18th war was declared. A great struggle was now begun against the power of the First Consul. The French Revolution, in its earlier stages, had sympathised with the efforts of all nations desiring national liberty, and as the result of the revolutionary movement many small dynasties had been swept away, and Europe had experienced a sudden though salutary awakening. With the rise of Bonaparte the principles of the revolution were set aside and a period of aggression and conquest began which threatened to establish the French predominance in Europe. Against the danger of this domination Europe slowly rose, the struggles against Bonaparte became national, and " before the uprising of nations he gradually succumbed." Emmett's rebellion in 1803, the product of French agents working on the economic discontent of Ireland, increased Addington's difficulties. His Government was incompetent to deal with the critical state of affairs, the king's health was failing, a strong ministry was required, and at length on April 26th, 1804, Addington resigned, and Pitt, after endeavouring to secure

Pitt's Second Ministry, 1804-1806.

the services of Fox and Grenville, was forced in consequence of the latter's hostility to form a Tory Ministry after the king's own heart, composed of such men as Harrowby, Eldon, Portland, Castlereagh, Hawkesbury, Melville, and Camden, while Canning, Huskisson, and Perceval occupied subordinate positions. The ministry, formed on a narrow Tory basis, was weak, and Pitt found himself, with a small majority in the Commons, compelled to prosecute the war against Bonaparte.

In December, 1804, the First Consul became Emperor, and at once planned an invasion of England. Elaborate preparations for defence were made, the Additional Force Bill was passed, the fleet was largely increased. Danger from France, however, by no means lessened Pitt's difficulties in Parliament. In

December, 1804, Lord Harrowby, the Foreign Minister, was
compelled by an accident to resign, and Addington, taking the
title of Lord Sidmouth, joined the ministry.   About the same
time the Opposition attacked the able and successful administration of the navy by Lord Melville (p. 739).   By a majority of
one the House of Commons, on April 8th, 1805, censured the
minister, who at once resigned, his example being in July

BRITANNIA BETWEEN DEATH AND THE DOCTORS.
(*From a caricature by James Gillray.*)

followed by Sidmouth, between whom and Pitt relations had
become very strained.   Lord Melville was formally impeached,
but the House of Lords (June 12th, 1806) acquitted him.

　　While Pitt was pursued by difficulties in Parliament, his **Pitt's**
foreign policy had at first met with success.   Nelson and Calder **Foreign Policy**
had saved England from all danger of invasion, while the
formation of the Third Coalition between England, Russia,
and Austria in 1805 had shown Napoleon the necessity of
attacking the Hapsburgs.   On October 20th he surrounded and
captured an Austrian army under Mack at Ulm, and, on
December 2nd, " the Battle of the Three Emperors " took place
at Austerlitz, the French winning a complete victory.   Though
successful on land, France had suffered a serious disaster at sea.

243

On October 21st Nelson had won the battle of Trafalgar, losing his life early in the action. The sea passed under the command of the English, Napoleon's last fleet was destroyed, and England's trade was practically secure.

"All the
Talents."
1806.

On January 23rd, 1806, Pitt died, the news of Austerlitz and the dissolution of the coalition having seriously affected his already declining health. All hope of any successful opposition to France had for the time disappeared, and the ensuing two years saw the development of gigantic schemes of conquest and annexation on the part of Napoleon. The death of Pitt was followed by the break-up of the Cabinet, and the formation under Grenville of the Ministry of All the Talents, which included Fox as Secretary of State for Foreign Affairs, Howick First Lord of the Admiralty, Sidmouth Privy Seal, Petty Chancellor of the Exchequer, Spencer and Windham Secretaries for the Home and War Departments, Fitzwilliam President of the Council, and Lord Moira Master-General of the Ordnance. The slave trade was at once abolished, the Abolition Bill being passed on March 25th, 1807, and negotiations with the French were opened which demonstrated clearly the impossibility of trusting Napoleon. In September, 1806, Fox died, and was succeeded as Foreign Secretary by Howick. The ministry had realised the necessity of carrying on the war with vigour; in October, 1806, the battles of Jena and Auerstadt had overthrown Prussia, and on November 21st Napoleon had issued his famous

LAST PAGE OF NELSON'S DIARY.

(Royal United Service Institution, by permission of W. E. Eyre Matcham, Esq.)

THE DEATH OF NELSON.

(After the painting by A. W. Devis at Greenwich Hospital.)

Phot.: A. Rischgitz.

The Berlin Decrees. Berlin Decrees. By these he declared that the whole of the British Isles were in a state of blockade, that France and all her dependent countries were forbidden to correspond or trade with them, that all English merchandise and all private property of Englishmen was confiscated, and all British subjects were prisoners of war. On January 7th, 1807, the Grenville Ministry replied by issuing the first of a series of Orders in Council forbidding vessels to trade between any ports in the possession of France or of her allies. A commercial war thus began which continued till 1815. "The French soldiers were turned into coastguardsmen to shut out Great Britain from her markets; the British ships became revenue cutters to prohibit the trade of France." The Decrees and Orders eventually roused a bitter feeling in Prussia against Napoleon, and in the United States against England. Before, however, any further measures could be taken against France, and before the Bill for the abolition of

Fall of the Ministry of All the Talents. the slave trade finally became law, the Grenville Ministry had fallen. The question of the Catholic claims had again been revived in the form of an Army and Navy Service Bill. In Ireland Roman Catholics, since 1793, had been allowed to hold any rank in the Irish army up to that of colonel, but after the Union they still continued unable to hold their rank when in England. In proposing to remove this anomaly ministers determined that the whole army and navy should be thrown open to Roman Catholics as well as to Nonconformists. The king, whose fears had been roused by Lord Sidmouth, and who relied on the Duke of Portland's offer to form a ministry, decided that he would not accept anything beyond the completion of the Act of 1793, and declared that he only meant to assimilate the law in England and Ireland. Though the ministry agreed to drop the Bill the king demanded a pledge that the subject of Catholic emancipation should not be brought forward again. The ministers naturally refused to give such a pledge, and on March 18th, 1807, were dismissed. George III. had again triumphed. In 1770 he had placed Lord North at the head of affairs, in 1784 he had secured the services of William Pitt, and now in 1807 he had finally discomfited the Whigs, who were not again in office till the time of the great Reform Bill. That George was supported by public opinion in his opposition to the Whig families is undoubted, that on each occasion his personal wishes were aided by underhand intrigues is equally true. On April 27th Parliament was dissolved, the constituencies supported the king, and the new ministry found itself in possession of a considerable majority.

The new anti-Catholic Administration was headed by the Duke of Portland, under whom served Eldon, the Chancellor, Perceval Chancellor of the Exchequer, Canning Foreign Secretary, Castlereagh War and Colonial Secretary, Hawkesbury — afterwards Lord Liverpool — Home Secretary. The ministry continued with vigour the warlike policy which Grenville had found it necessary to pursue during the last days of his ministry. A second Order in Council was issued in November, 1807, granting reprisals " against the goods, ships, and inhabitants of Tuscany, Naples, Dalmatia and the Ionian Islands," and by the third and fourth various plans of evasion were forbidden, such as the sale of a ship by a belligerent to a neutral. These retaliatory measures were rendered necessary by Napoleon's extension of the Continental system to the Mediterranean and by his deliberate attempt to annihilate English trade. *The Portland Ministry, 1807.*

Having overthrown the Russians at Eylau on February 7th, he had on July 7th made with Alexander the Treaty of Tilsit, which was in itself a menace to the independence of Europe. To this arrangement between the Russian and French Emperors, Canning replied by seizing the Danish fleet on September 8th, while Russia attempted to force Sweden, England's ally, to join the Continental system. English forces had already defeated the French at the battle of Maida, had retaken Cape Colony from the Dutch, and had attacked Buenos Ayres, a Spanish colony (pp. 732, 738). But the importance of these small expeditions paled before the famous and successful opposition of England to Napoleon's attempt to subjugate the Spanish Peninsula. He had determined to make one of his relations King of Spain, to appropriate Portugal, and to close its ports against England. *Treaty of Tilsit.*

In June, 1808, his brother Joseph was placed on the Spanish throne, Junot having already, in November, 1807, occupied Lisbon on the flight of the Portuguese royal family to Brazil. An English expedition landed in Portugal on August 1st, 1808, and Wellesley won the battle of Vimiera on August 21st, but on August 30th Sir Hew Dalrymple made the Convention of Cintra *England and Portugal.*

SATIRE ON THE BRITISH SEIZURE OF THE DANISH FLEET, 1807.

(From a caricature by James Gillray.)

with the French. Great indignation was experienced in England at this convention, and Sir John Moore, to whom was given the command of the British army in Portugal, advanced to Salamanca. Hearing of the approach of Napoleon he retreated, and on January 16th, 1809, fought the battle of Corunna. His death, following the Convention of Cintra, for a time discouraged the English ministry, and it was not till Wellesley was given the command in April, 1809, that the Peninsular War may be said to have begun.

During the year 1809 the Ministry was assaulted by the

OFFICER'S SASH AND PRAYER-BOOK USED AT THE BURIAL OF SIR JOHN MOORE.
(*Royal United Service Institution.*)

Opposition and was not at one with itself. Attacks were made on the general purity of the Administration, and especially on the Duke of York, the Commander-in-Chief, on Castlereagh, and on Perceval. The Walcheren expedition, which was itself right in principle, proved a disastrous failure (p. 734). One result of this disaster was a duel between Castlereagh and Canning on September 9th, followed by the resignation of both, and the reconstruction of the Ministry. In October Perceval became Prime Minister, Lord Wellesley Minister for Foreign Affairs, and Lord Liverpool took the War Office, with Lord Palmerston as Under Secretary. During these months of continual agitation at home Arthur Wellesley was winning victories in Portugal. He had forced the French armies to retire and had marched towards Madrid. In July he had won the battle of Talavera, and

Perceval Prime Minister.

Peninsular War

had it not been for the weak war administration in England he might have gained some conspicuous advantages. As it was he devoted himself to the defence of Portugal and fortified the lines of Torres Vedras. Massena having failed to dislodge him, was beaten off at the battle of Busaco on September 29th, 1810. The year 1811 found him (after Talavera he had been raised to the peerage as Viscount Wellington) still acting on the defensive. He fought the battles of Fuentes d'Onoro and Albuera in May, while the French, having completed the conquest of the east of Spain, were threatening to make a vigorous attack on Portugal.

WATERLOO: FRAGMENT OF THE GATE
OF HOUGOMONT.
(Royal United Service Institution.)

But events in central and north-eastern Europe came to the aid of the English. Though the Austrian opposition to Napoleon in 1809 had failed, and the peace of Vienna (October 14th, 1809) had cut short the Austrian territories, it had become evident that a national opposition to the French was growing. The power of the people all over Europe was gradually but surely coming into collision with the despotic tendencies of the French Emperor.

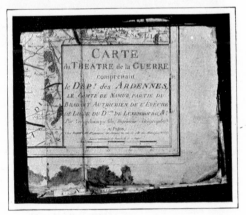

WATERLOO: A RELIC OF GENERAL PICTON
(Royal United Service Institution.)

At the close of 1811, too, the relations between Napoleon and Alexander had become strained, and both monarchs prepared for war. In 1812 the famous Moscow expedition took place, with the result that the north of Germany rose. Prussia and Russia formed an alliance which was later joined by Austria, and the war of Liberation began. In contributing to the fall of Napoleon the operations of Wellington in Portugal played a considerable part. In November, 1810, George III.'s

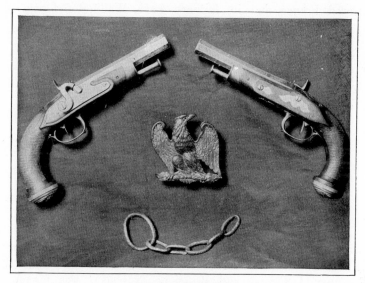

WATERLOO RELICS.
(Royal United Service Institution.)

illness had necessitated the appointment of the Prince of Wales as Regent, and in 1811 a Regency Bill was passed restricting the power of the prince.

The Perceval Ministry was continued, but in February, 1812, Wellesley retired from office, and in May Perceval was assassinated by a man named Bellingham. Lord Liverpool became Prime Minister, with Castlereagh as Foreign Secretary, the other ministers remaining in office. Wellington was heartily supported, and a war with America caused by the Orders in Council, ended after a series of struggles on land and on sea —in which success and failure were pretty evenly balanced

Lord Liverpool Prime Minister.

—in the Convention of Ghent, signed on December 24th, 1814.

Welling-ton's Victories.   In 1812, Wellington, having taken Ciudad Rodrigo and Badajos, won Salamanca and entered Madrid on August 12th. Forced to retreat to Portugal by the overwhelming French forces, he again advanced in 1813, won the battle of Vittoria on June 21st, and the battle of the Pyrenées, Soult in the following January evacuating Bayonne. In October Napoleon, having lost the battle of Leipzig, had fallen back across the Rhine. The allies entered France, and in January, 1814, Wellington forced the

BRASS CANNON CAPTURED AT MALTA, 1800.
(Tower of London.)

Over-throw of Napoleon.   passage of the Bidassoa, defeated Soult at Orthez in February, and at Toulouse in April. After a brilliant campaign against the Russians, Austrians, and Prussians, Napoleon was forced to abdicate, and early in April the war came to a conclusion. Louis XVIII. was restored, and at the Congress of Vienna Europe was reconstructed. During the Congress Napoleon escaped from Elba in March, 1815, and it was not till June 18th that the battle of Waterloo overthrew his hopes and led to the second restoration of Louis XVIII. on terms arranged under the influence of England. In the settlement at Vienna of the various problems which had arisen during the struggle against Napoleon, Lord Castlereagh and the Duke of Wellington exercised considerable influence. England secured Malta, the Ionian Islands, Heligoland, the Cape of Good Hope, Mauritius, Ceylon, Trinidad, and Tobago. The Austrian Netherlands and Holland were united under the Prince of Orange, Norway and Sweden were placed

under one king, Russia received a large share of Poland, while
Prussia was given a portion of Saxony, Austria secured Venice
and its possessions, and the Republic of Genoa was handed over
to the King of Sardinia. After much negotiation the English
representatives succeeded in inducing France, Spain, Portugal,
and the Netherlands to abolish the slave trade.

Settlement after
Waterloo.

The completion of the settlement of Europe, though in many
ways unsatisfactory, came as a great relief to England. The
nation had been raised to a position of the highest importance
in Europe, but required a period of peace in order that full
attention might be devoted to the satisfactory solution of the
many pressing problems which had arisen during the war.

IMMEDIATELY after the peace of Amiens, England, eager to
disarm, had reduced her army almost to vanishing point, and
consequently on the resumption of hostilities with France she
found herself in a position of the greatest danger. To repel
Napoleon's threatened invasion of her soil, she could only place
40,000 regulars in the field. By dint of incredible exertions the
ministers in the course of a few months succeeded in raising an
army, formidable at least in point of numbers. The returns for
1804 show that in Great Britain there were serving 75,000 regular
infantry, 12,000 regular cavalry, 80,000 militia, and 343,000
yeomanry and volunteers. These last were enrolled for local,
not for general purposes of defence; and it was asserted that
they absorbed so large a number of the classes who should have
served in the regular army or in the militia, that the difficulties
of recruiting for these, the first and second lines of defence, were
greatly increased. The wits of the day indeed said that the
Ministry had "not only not provided an army, but rendered it
impossible that an army should be provided." Whether the
existence of the volunteers did or did not diminish the numbers
of the recruits for the line and the militia, it is certain that the
effort of keeping the army up to its full strength during the war
was enormous, though after 1808 only about 22,000 men were
annually required to make good the deficiency caused by death,
desertion, and discharge. As if in anticipation of the system
that now connects the militia with the regular army, Pitt
affiliated to each line regiment a militia corps, which regularly

G. LE M.
GRETTON.
The Army

Garrison
of Great
Britain,
1804.

supplied their linked battalions with "food for powder," and thus to a large extent facilitated recruiting. During the twelve years between 1803 and 1814, out of some 270,000 men who joined the army, no less than 113,000 were volunteers from the ranks of the militia. But this was not enough to make good the annual waste; the army was unpopular chiefly because men had to enlist for unlimited service—or in other words, to become soldiers for the rest of their lives. Although Government actually sanctioned the enlistment of boys under sixteen, to the extent of 10 per cent. of the strength of the regiments, and although, according to Dupin, "the hulks were drained and the prisons emptied more than once to supply the want of soldiers," recruits became so hard to obtain that in 1807 each man cost in bounty and levy money nearly £40. In that year a system of limited engagement (short service) was introduced; men undertook to serve from seven to twelve years with the colours, with power to renew their engagement from time to time, and thus ultimately to earn a pension for their old age. The immediate effect of this concession to public opinion was to produce so many more recruits for the regular army that their market price fell from £40 to £30.

A ROYAL IRISH FUSILIER, 1793.
(*J. Cannon, " Historical Records of the 87th Regiment.*")

Irish Troops.   Until the middle of the last century the ranks of the army were almost exclusively filled by Englishmen and Lowland Scots. During the seven years' war Chatham threw open the career of arms to the Highlanders, who eagerly embraced it; but it was not until 1800 that Irishmen were "admitted into the army without forfeiting their creed or nationality."[1]   Then they

[1] Major-Gen. Sir W. F. Butler, "Plea for the Peasant" [in his "Far Out"]. p. 299.

CITIZEN SOLDIERS.

Surrey Yeomanry and London and Westminster Light Horse.

(*Thomas Rowlandson, "Loyal Volunteers of London." 1798.*)

joyfully swarmed into the army, literally by tens of thousands :
and during the first fourteen years of the nineteenth century
Ireland sent forth 100,000 of her sons to fight in the battles of
the United Kingdom.

Foreign
Troops.

In all our eighteenth century wars England had largely
recruited her forces with foreigners, of whom we formed
battalions, which became an integral part of our army.   During
the Napoleonic war we enrolled a large quantity of continentals;
in 1809 there were 37,000 in our service; in 1812 the number
had risen to 45,000; and in 1813, out of some 261,000 regulars
in our service, about 54,000, or more than 20 per cent., were of
foreign nationality.   Many of these were Germans, thoroughly
reliable troops ; there were also corps of French Royalists, Swiss,
Greeks, Maltese, Sicilians, Corsicans and Calabrians.   Some of
these battalions were composed of good materials, but others
were most undesirable accessions to the British army, and were
a source of danger rather than of strength to the generals under
whom they served.[1]

The
Militia
Ballot.

Service in the militia is by the law of England compulsory
on every adult male ; and although the general practice has
been to trust to volunteers for maintaining our home service
army up to proper strength, there have been times when its
ranks have been filled by conscripts and not by volunteers.
In the Seven Years' War Chatham kept the militia up to their
strength by means of the ballot ; and during our great war with
France the ballot was rigorously enforced from 1792 to 1811 ;
in other words, the militia was raised by conscription whenever
the supply of voluntary recruits became inadequate.   In 1808,
with the intention of supplementing the regular militia, who
were liable to do duty in any part of the United Kingdom, a new
force, termed " local militia," was raised by ballot, not for general
service, but for the defence of their own districts only.   Curiously
enough, a well-to-do man who was drawn by ballot to serve in
the local militia was not allowed to buy a substitute, though in the
regular militia this privilege was allowed to the monied classes.
To the abuses which gathered round this system of purchasing
substitutes is due the suspension of the ballot.   The national
feeling revolted at such incidents as were recorded in the

[1] See the account of the mutiny at Malta in Bunbury, "Passages in the
Great War with France," p. 310.

MILITARY EXERCISES: "PRIME AND LOAD."
(*Thomas Rowlandson, "Loyal Volunteers of London," 1798.*)

Annual Register of 1810, when at Plymouth a substitute was paid £60 for his services; when another was hired on condition of receiving four shillings a day during the continuance of the war, and a third sold himself by weight for 7s. 3d. per pound! After 1811 the militia was recruited by free men obtained by " beat of drum," and no longer by conscripts forced to serve against their will.

The Militia.
During the whole of the great war the militia rendered invaluable service to the country.   Not only did the " Constitutional Force " supply nearly half the recruits for the army, but it also relieved large numbers of line regiments from garrison duty in the United Kingdom, and thus set them free for foreign service.   After an embodiment of several years the militia battalions were in no way inferior to those of the line ; and in 1814 a large brigade, exclusively composed of militia, was sent to reinforce Wellington in France, but it arrived too late to take part in the concluding operations of the war.

Distribution of the Army.
During the Napoleonic wars England maintained an immense army scattered all over the face of the globe.   Thus, in 1809, six years before the struggle with France ended, nearly 700,000 soldiers were serving under the British flag.   As garrison of the United Kingdom, there were in round numbers 108,000 regular cavalry and infantry, and 65,000 regular militia ; 200,000 local militia, and 190,000 volunteers.   Abroad were 110,000 more regular troops, distributed as follows : In the Mediterranean were 22,000 ; and in the West Indies nearly as many.   In India, including the East India Company's 4,000 Europeans, 24,000 white men gave solidity to the native troops in our employ.   In North America there were 8,000 redcoats ; 4,000 garrisoned Ceylon ; 1,300 fighting men were absorbed in guarding convicts in New South Wales.   In Madeira 900 were stationed; and the Cape of Good Hope, the half-way house to India, required the protection of nearly 6,000 bayonets. Detachments of troops at sea, the regiment of artillery and the corps of engineers together, represented about 18,000 more ; while fighting against the French in Portugal was a little army of 22,000 strong.

This generation, accustomed to the wise care bestowed upon the wants and comforts of the private soldier, can scarcely credit the neglect with which the British Government treated their troops in the Peninsula. Though Wellington did his best for the men under his command, even his remarkable powers of organisation could not atone for the apathy with which the ministry regarded the war in Spain. Reinforcements of men the War Office did indeed send him; but small supplies of stores and little money ever reached him, though millions were annually shipped from England to the Continent to bribe the powers to fight their own battles against Napoleon. More than once his men did not receive their pay for six months together; they marched barefooted and in rags; during four campaigns they were unprovided with tents. In health they were often short of food; in sickness they were badly tended, for the hospitals were so ill-equipped, the doctors so few in number, that two hundred dying men were left with one solitary hospital mate to dress their wounds and minister to their wants. Against this state of things Wellington struggled hard, and as far as the range of his personal influence extended, with success. But officers, even under the duke's own eyes, were callous to the sufferings of the rank and file, and must often have escaped scot-free, though condign punishment occasionally overtook them.

FRENCH IMPERIAL EAGLE CAPTURED AT BAROSSA, 1811. (*J. Cannon, "Records of the 87th Regiment."*)

Thus Wellington one evening at dinner was told that at a British post, several miles distant, there were a considerable number of sick soldiers lying in the open, without shelter and exposed to the weather. That night the duke rode to the village, inspected the sick, and then roused the officers from the comfortable houses in which they had taken up their quarters. To his inquiry why the sick were thus left neglected, the commanding officer coolly replied that there was no accommodation for them in the place! The duke himself went round to all the houses occupied by these unworthy officers, and settled the numbers of the sick who were to be billeted in each dwelling; he then gave specific orders that the invalids were to be at once moved into the houses, and to remain where he

244

had placed them.   So sulkily were these orders received that Wellington next night paid a surprise visit to the village, and found that the invalids had been again turned out into the streets !   The sick were reinstated; the offending officers were placed under arrest, and marched to headquarters, where they were promptly tried and cashiered for disobedience to orders.

Officers and Men.   Much might have been done by the regimental officers to mitigate the hardships of the rank and file, by looking after them and protecting them against the consequences of the carelessness ingrained in the British soldier; but except in the Guards and in Craufurd's Light Division, and in a few of the best line regiments, it was not the fashion for the commissioned ranks to interest themselves about the men under their immediate command.   In fact, it is hardly too much to say that one of Wellington's greatest difficulties was to induce his officers to do their duty towards the men.   Thus in September, 1812, in a general order, Wellington "entreats" all officers to obey the important orders which he had recently issued respecting the daily inspection of the men's ammunition.   A few weeks later, in a circular letter, he says that in the retreat from Burgos the officers had from the first lost all command over their men, hence excesses, outrages and inexcusable losses, of which the true cause was the habitual neglect of duty by regimental officers.   Yet badly as they often were treated, the men never failed to fight well.   They possessed a stern courage, and a priceless inability to recognise when they were beaten ; but if their soldierly virtues were magnificent, their shortcomings during the first years of the war were grievous.   They were drunken, marauding, and undisciplined, and when under the influence of great excitement liable to fits of savage cruelty which rendered them even more dangerous to friends than foes.

Military Morals.   But in justice to the men it must be said that many of their superiors set them a very bad example, not only in Spain, but in all parts of the world.   The reports of the courts-martial show how low a standard at this time prevailed among many of our regimental officers.   Some were cashiered for drunkenness on guard, on parade, or on duty ; others for de-faulting with Government money.   Some, again, were dismissed the service for striking their superior officers ; a colonel was cashiered for beating a sergeant in the public streets; and a captain for drinking in a barrack room with his men, and abetting them in the commission of an act of outrageous cruelty upon a woman. It must also be remembered that in the Peninsula many of the soldiers were deprived of all the restraining influences of religion. There were a few Protestant chaplains; but not one single priest was attached to the army to minister to the spiritual wants of the Roman Catholics, who formed fully half the strength of Wellington's expedition.

In every army discipline must be stern and punishment **Flogging.** severe, but at the beginning of the nineteenth century severity in the English service had degenerated into mere brutality. Except in the comparatively rare cases where death was awarded, the stock punishment for every description of military offence, great or small, was flogging, inflicted with a degree of reckless cruelty which this generation can hardly comprehend. Courts-martial used to sentence soldiers to 1,500 lashes, until, in 1807, the commander-in-chief ordered that for the future 1,000 lashes should be the greatest number inflicted. In some battalions flogging was so prevalent that it was estimated that half the men had been tied up to the "triangles" for punishment. In one unfortunate regiment quartered in India the average number of lashes inflicted monthly was 17,000. On some occasions the drummers, who acted as flagellators, were ordered to count five slowly between each stroke, in order that the torture might be prolonged; and surgeons stood by the triangles to revive the miserable wretches when they fainted under the cat, and thus render it possible for them to receive the full number of lashes to which they had been sentenced. Terrible as was the flogging in the regular army, it is said to have been even worse in the militia, where the officers, less experienced in the management of men, awarded it upon the slightest occasion. Gradually public opinion demanded some mitigation of these horrors, and in 1812 a fresh order from the Horse Guards limited the powers of regimental courts-martial to 300 lashes; but even before the promulgation of this order there had been a movement for reform among the more enlightened regimental officers themselves. Among the troops quartered in the Mediterranean a few bold and humane commanding officers had ventured to depart from precedent and from the strict letter of the regulations; instead of flogging men for slight military offences, they awarded solitary confinement with hard labour (the modern "cells"), with very satisfactory results. But these new ideas gained ground but slowly, and all through the great war order in the British Army was principally maintained by the lash, though whenever an outbreak of marauding took place Wellington ruthlessly hanged the culprits upon the trees along the roads. It is not surprising, therefore, that men recruited from the lowest classes, contaminated by compulsory association with criminals and habitually kept under an iron discipline, on occasions such as the final storming of Badajos should have cast restraint to the winds and committed most horrible excesses.

Tactics. When the French Revolution plunged Europe into universal war, the system of tactics prevalent throughout the monarchical armies of the Continent was that of Frederick the Great (p. 24). The great Prussian's linear movements were, however based on the assumption that the soldiers who executed them were thoroughly drilled and disciplined, and were therefore inapplicable to the young levies of the French revolutionary armies, whose officers accordingly reverted to a modification of the attack in column, which Frederick had discarded for the attack in line. Instead, however, of moving in the huge unwieldy masses which had found favour in the middle of the century, the French recruits were formed into small handy columns, 400 to 500 strong, which advanced against the enemy preceded by a swarm of skirmishers, whose function it was to cover the movements of the column by a rapid and well-directed musketry fire.

Decline of the French Army These shallow columns moved with the interval between them necessary to enable them to deploy, *i.e.* to change their formation from column to line. Thus, if themselves attacked, they could rapidly deploy, and from a continuous three-deep line pour their volleys into the advancing foe; if the enemy stood on the defensive, they remained in column and charged him with the bayonet. This formation has been aptly described as bearing to Frederick's line the resemblance which a flexible chain bears to a bar of iron; it required comparatively little steadiness in drill, and left much to the remarkable courage, intelligence, and self-control of the individual soldiers who served under the Republican flag; and therefore it answered admirably as long as the high standard of the French rank and file was maintained. But when Napoleon assumed the purple, one of his bids for popularity was to substitute conscription for the universal military service enforced by the Republic. The well-to-do classes, now allowed to purchase substitutes from among the uneducated masses, availed themselves of this privilege in numbers which every year increased; and thus the intellectual element was gradually eliminated from the ranks of the Imperial army. As time went on, the Republican veterans began to die off; and to meet the ceaseless and terrible drain which campaigns in every part of Europe made upon the nation, half-grown lads were sent into the field before their nerves could stand the strain to which their sturdy predecessors were accustomed. The quality of the regimental officers also deteriorated, for even originally there were comparatively few men competent to command battalions fighting in small and isolated columns; and as they were promoted or killed off, their successors often proved unable to follow in their footsteps. From these varied causes it was soon found that the Imperial armies could not fight in the shallow formations of the Republic; and, therefore, to give the recruits confidence, and to bring the battalion officers more directly under the eyes of the generals, the columns gradually were made more massive, and consequently more unwieldy. The climax was reached at Waterloo, where the columns launched against the British line were twenty-four ranks deep.

Napoleon's artillery tactics consisted in massing his guns and concentrating their fire upon the particular part of the enemy's position which he proposed to attack, so as to breach the line and demoralise and crush its defenders by his projectiles before his columns assailed them with the bayonet. In cavalry work, his advance guard of light horse moved forty, fifty, or even a hundred miles in front of his main body, whose front and flanks they screened with a chain of moving outposts along every road; thus they obtained information about the enemy, and prevented his reconnoitring parties from approaching the main body of their own army. Wellington could never emulate Napoleon's daring employment of his horsemen, for the niggardly policy of the British government kept him ill supplied both with cavalry

Napoleon's Methods.

and with artillery.   In the Peninsula he usually depended on his staff officers for information about the enemy.   They hung on the flanks of the French columns, just out of gunshot, and coolly took notes on all they saw, confident that the great speed of the blood horses which they rode would always secure them against capture.   The duke never appears to have appreciated the effect of the concentrated fire of a great mass of artillery; but the essential difference between his tactics and those of Napoleon was in the handling of infantry.   The emperor always attacked in column, while the duke invariably attacked in line, and used the column solely as a manœuvring and not as a fighting formation.   Whether in attack or defence, British foot soldiers in a thin two-deep line could always be trusted to fight against hostile infantry in any formation; and their steadiness, both on the defensive and in a counter attack, is well described by Marshal Bugeaud, a distinguished French officer, in the following words :—

The British Line.

"The English generally occupied well-chosen defensive positions, having a certain command, and they showed only a portion of their force.   The usual artillery action first took place.   Soon, in great haste, without studying the position, without taking time to examine if there were means to make a flank attack, we marched straight on, taking the bull by the horns.   About 1,000 yards from the English line the men became excited, spoke to one another, and hurried their march; the column began to be a little confused.

"The English remained quite silent, with ordered arms, and from their steadiness appeared to be a long red wall.   This steadiness invariably produced an effect on the young soldiers.

"Very soon we got nearer, shouting 'Vive l'Empereur, en avant! à la bayonette!'   Shakos were raised on the muzzles of the muskets; the column began to double, the ranks got into confusion, the agitation produced a tumult; shots were fired as we advanced.

"The English line remained still, silent and immovable, with ordered arms, even when we were only 300 paces distant, and it appeared to ignore the storm about to break.

"The contrast was striking: in our inmost thoughts, each felt that the enemy was a long time in firing, and that this fire, reserved for so long, would be very unpleasant when it did come.   Our ardour cooled.   The moral power of steadiness, which nothing shakes (even if it be only in appearance), over disorder which stupefies itself with noise, overcame our minds.   At this moment of intense excitement, the English wall shouldered arms, an indescribable feeling rooted many of our men to the ground, they began to fire. The enemy's steady concentrated volleys swept our ranks; decimated we turned round seeking to recover our equilibrium; then three deafening cheers broke the silence of our opponents; at the third they were on us, pushing our disorganised flight. But to our great surprise, they did not push their advantage beyond a hundred yards, retiring calmly to their lines to await a second attack."

In the opinion of General Marbot, who served with distinc- **Musketry.** tion on the staff of Massena and of Lannes in Spain, one of the principal causes of the French defeats in the Peninsula was the steady shooting of the British infantry. He describes them as the best shots in Europe, the only troops who were properly taught the use of their fire-arms. Yet, even allowing for the inferiority of the weapon then in use, the standard of marksmanship does not seem to have been high : in 1804 it was said of a crack corps, "that they were such excellent shots that they were sure to hit the target at 150 yards !" The riflemen seem to have been allowed sixty rounds of ball cartridge for their yearly instruction in shooting ; the light infantry had ten less ; and the line and militia were considered adequately trained for battle when they had fired thirty rounds a year ! From a quarter-master in the Rifle Brigade we learn that he established a great reputation for shooting as a recruit ; out of the first ten rounds he fired, all hit the target, and two reached the bullseye ! The targets were six feet high by two feet wide, the bullseye was eight inches round, the distance only fifty yards ; but the performance was considered so good that it won him much praise, and a tip of sixpence from his captain ![1]

During the Peninsular War there were considerable changes **Dress.** in uniform. Tight-fitting coatees with miniature tails, tight trousers, and short gaiters like the modern spat came into fashion, and displaced the loose coat, breeches and long buttoned gaiters, more practical though less showy, which had been so long the uniform of the British line. On active service the officers gradually substituted cloth caps for the regulation cocked hats, which were so huge that the ends almost touched the shoulders. But if they retrenched in the size of their hats, they revenged themselves by wearing coats so long that the skirts almost swept the ground. Their sashes were worn round the waist, not over the left shoulder, as in the present day ; and their hair was allowed to attain a length shocking to the ideas of a generation who have been taught by the commander-in-chief that "in the field no man's hair should be half an inch in

[1] Surtees, "Twenty-five Years in the Rifle Brigade," p. 42.

length." One glorious innovation there was: in 1808 pigtails
were finally done away with, to the intense joy of the soldiers
throughout the army. One regiment, already embarked for
foreign service when the welcome order came, gave three cheers
as they flung the pigtails into Portsmouth harbour; another
buried them with mock solemnity; while a third made a bonfire
of these relics of a barbarous and senseless fashion.

The Private's Load.   If, when permission was given to discard pigtails, some improvement had been made in the distribution of the burden
carried by the troops in marching order, much misery and many

PIGTAILS IN THE ARMY AND NAVY.
(From a print by W. M. Craig, in the Royal United Service Institution.)

lives would have been saved on active service. The load in
itself, " enough to impede the free motions of a donkey," was so
awkwardly placed that the body was cramped, the head forced
forward, the action of the heart impeded; in fact, to use the
expression of an indignant private, " the man was half beaten
before he came to the scratch." [1]

[1] Rifleman Harris, a regimental shoemaker in the Rifle Brigade, in his
" Recollections " (ed. Curling, p. 26), thus describes the burden laid upon the
backs of the men in the Peninsula. " Besides my well-filled kit, there was the
great-coat rolled on the top, my blanket and camp kettle, my haversack stuffed
full of leather for repairing the men's shoes, together with a hammer and other
tools, ship's biscuits and beef for three days, my canteen filled with water, my
hatchet and rifle, and 80 rounds of cartridge in my pouch." Only the rifle regiments were armed with rifles: the rest of the army carried the smooth-bore
musket, popularly known as Brown Bess.

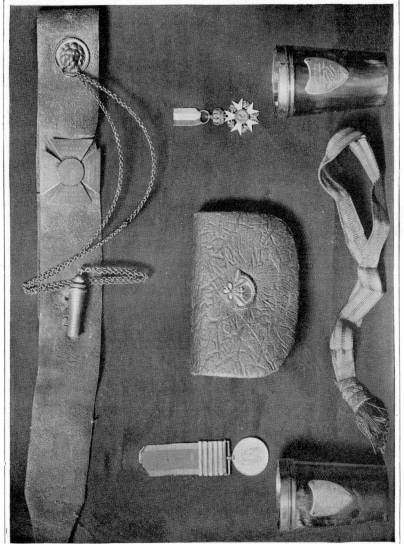

RELICS OF THE PENINSULAR WAR.

(Royal United Service Institution.)

Minor Military Expeditions, 1802-1815.

So well known are Wellington's victories that it is unnecessary to touch upon them here; indeed, so much has the attention of Englishmen been directed to our splendid achievements in the Peninsular and the Waterloo campaigns, that many of our minor expeditions had been almost forgotten. Yet in the history of many of these enterprises there is much that is instructive, though often mortifying to our national pride. It is true that our attacks upon the enemies' colonies were usually successful, and added Cape Colony and Mauritius, Guiana and St. Lucia to the British Empire. It is also true that Canada was successfully defended against the United States during the war of 1812-14, though not without reverses to our arms. But in Europe, those of our campaigns which were not conducted by Wellington, when not absolutely disastrous, were at any rate singularly barren of result. Even before Trafalgar the Navy was strong enough to convoy safely fleets of transports containing British soldiers to any point on the shores of the Mediterranean or the North Sea; yet at high-water mark the limits of our ascendancy were reached. Against the dull stupidity of the Government in military matters the army could not contend. The ministry and their military advisers seemed alike incapable of planning a successful land operation in Europe, of explaining to their generals the objects of the expedition upon which they were despatched, and of providing for the needs of the expeditionary force. Often for months together the officers commanding abroad were left without instructions from the War Office, and when despatches did arrive, they were frequently so worded as to be virtually unintelligible.

Naples and Sicily, 1805.

In 1805 England sent an expedition of 7,000 men to Naples, nominally to co-operate with the Neapolitans and their Russian allies in expelling the French from Italy; but really with secret orders to occupy Sicily and prevent its falling into the hands of Napoleon. The combined army of English, Russians and Neapolitans were placed under the command of Lacy, an Irishman of high rank in the service of the Czar, a curious specimen of the generals whom the Continental powers frequently pitted against Napoleon and his young and vigorous marshals. This veteran of nearly eighty winters used to astonish the members of the council of war which were held at Naples by calmly producing and donning a nightcap, in

which he used peacefully to sleep while his subordinates
transacted the business before them. But even in his extreme
old age Lacy retained the fire of his race, for, to use his own
expression, " he was always for fighting." [1] But fighting there
was none in this campaign. Relieved from all anxiety in their
rear by the news of the victory of Austerlitz, the French troops
in the north of Italy advanced against the allies in overwhelming
numbers. The Russians embarked their troops for the Ionian
Isles, the English for Sicily, where with the permission of its
sovereign, the King of Naples, we maintained until 1813 a
large garrison, chiefly quartered along the Straits of Messina.
It is perhaps as well that there was no powder burned in
Southern Italy in 1805, for the British general had made the
discovery, on his way from England, that the supply of
ammunition and flints at Malta, his base of operations, was
dangerously low. Certainly in 1805 expeditions to foreign
countries were curiously ill-supplied, for if our own troops
were short of ammunition, the Russians were left unprovided
with money, and when they came to embark at Naples, it
was found that they had no provisions for their voyage to
Corfu, no money, and no credit with the local merchants.
Bunbury says, " they could not have escaped had not the
English general run the risk of supplying them with biscuit,
and lending them £25,000."

During the next year occurred the one redeeming episode **Battle of Maida.**
in our proceedings in the Mediterranean, the victory of Maida.
General Stuart, the British commander, decided to make a
sudden raid upon the French, who in large numbers occupied
the province of Calabria, the toe of Italy. With a secrecy and
a promptitude not too common in our military history, about
6,000 men were embarked at Messina and landed in the Gulf
of St. Eufemia, near the village of Maida, from which the battle
takes its name. Next day (2nd July) Stuart, after leaving a
detachment to protect his retreat, advanced against the French,
whom he encountered on the plain of Maida, under the command
of their well-known general, Reynier. His corps outnumbered
Stuart's by about 1,000, and possessed 300 cavalry, an arm with
which the British force was totally unprovided, so that the odds
were distinctly in favour of the French.

[1] Bunbury, " Passages in the Great War with France," p. 218.

Both sides advanced to the attack, and a fierce fight took place, in which the deadly volleys of the British infantry and the alacrity with which they advanced to cross bayonets with Napoleon's veterans, were alike surprising to the French.   At the crisis of the battle, Reynier's right was turned; and the French wavered and broke before the British, whose prowess on land they had so long affected to despise.   Owing to his want of cavalry Stuart was unable to pursue the French, so his troops returned to the beach, where later in the day occurred an incident amusing in itself and showing how strongly the sense of discipline was already developed among

THE BATTLE OF MAIDA, 1806.
(From a contemporary view.)

our men.   A brigade was bathing in the sea when a staff officer galloped in from the front to give warning that the French cavalry were coming down upon them.   In a moment the bathers, "rushing out of the sea, throwing their belts over their shoulders, grasped their muskets, and drew up in line without attempting to assume an article of clothing! The alarm was utterly groundless; a great dust and an imperfect view of a herd of scampering buffaloes" had deceived the eyes of the young staff officer.

Our success was not vigorously followed up; in a few days the troops were withdrawn, and the material results of the victory were small.   But the moral effect was immense, for it restored the waning confidence of England in the valour of her soldiery, and roused the aggressive spirit which found its ultimate expression in Wellington's expedition to the Peninsula.

As a base of operations Sicily seems to have been of
singularly little use to us, for though several expeditions
sailed from her ports, none had any real influence upon the
struggle with Napoleon. The garrison did indeed dispossess
the French troops who occupied the Ionian Isles; but when
they attacked the Turks in Egypt, they were heavily repulsed,
while their demonstrations against the French army in the
South of Italy were feeble in the extreme. Our troops in
Sicily provided the force with which Lord William Bentinck
in 1813 landed on the north-east coast of Spain, hoping to
create a diversion in favour of Wellington by attacking the
French in Catalonia—a well-intentioned, but indifferently
executed project. Next year Bentinck won easy laurels at
the head of an Anglo-Italian expedition by wresting Genoa
from the feeble French force which garrisoned it.

But if our operations in the Mediterranean were futile, at **The Walcheren
Expedi-
tion.**
any rate they were not gigantic failures such as the Walcheren
expedition, in which numbers of men were sent to rot, inactive,
in the fever-stricken islands of the Scheldt. The ever-increasing
strength and importance of Antwerp as a French naval station
had long caused uneasiness in England; and in 1809 a noble
armament was despatched to the Scheldt with instructions to
destroy the arsenals and dockyards of Antwerp and of
Flushing. In July thirty-seven ships of the line, twenty-three
frigates, thirty-three sloops, eighty-two gunboats, and transports
containing 39,000 troops sailed for the Batavian Archipelago;
and from all the French accounts it seems clear that had an
immediate attack been made on Antwerp, the city must have
surrendered, so reduced at that moment were the numbers of
its garrison. Unhappily, Court favour had conferred the
command of the army upon Lord Chatham, a respectable
nonentity, "who neither inherited the energy of his father nor
shared the capacity of his brother, William Pitt." From
stupidity or obstinacy, he wholly misinterpreted his orders;
and instead of seizing Antwerp with a rush, he played into
the hands of the French by wasting invaluable time in laying
siege to Flushing. So slow was he in his movements that six
days after this fortress had fallen the army had only advanced
thirty miles towards their goal. During these delays the French
had made Antwerp virtually impregnable; and the Walcheren

fever had fastened on our army. The entries in an official
diary of the campaign show how rapidly this disease, a virulent
form of fever and ague, spread among the troops. On August
22nd, "sickness began to show itself," and "greatly increased
during the next twenty-four hours." On the 25th 3,000 men
were down; next day "it continued to an alarming degree";
on the 27th, "it increases every hour"; and on the 28th it
reached "alarming proportions, nearly 4,000 men on the sick
list."

At the end of August Chatham summoned a council of
war to consider the position of affairs; and it was decided to
forego all projects against Antwerp, to leave a garrison of
15,000 men in the island of Walcheren, and to send the
remainder of the army back to England immediately. Before
this resolution could be fully carried into effect the fever had
claimed many more victims. On the 8th September the sick of
the whole army, including those already sent back to England,
amounted to 10,948; while two days later, in the island of
Walcheren alone, 7,300 wretched men were ill, "shaking to
such an extent they could hardly walk." James, the naval
historian, asserts that early in 1810 there were more than
11,000 men in England still sick from the fever.

An intelligent private relates that three weeks after his
battalion landed in Walcheren there were only three or four
men of his company left on their legs; the rest, "reduced in
strength to infants, lay groaning in rows in a barn among the
heaps of lumpy black bread which they were unable to eat."
The surgeons were puzzled and overworked; two of them had
to attend five hundred patients until they were reinforced
by doctors from the fleet, which was entirely free from the
disease. As soon as possible the sick were huddled together
on crowded transports and sent home, dosed on the voyage
with an infusion of bark which was carried about the ship in
pails and given to the men in tumblers. In the hospitals in
England the Walcheren men died rapidly; one who was
fortunate enough to recover was in a ward containing eleven
beds, "and from my bed in the corner where I lay I saw this
ward refilled ten times, the former patients being all carried
out to the grave." It was found impossible to maintain a
garrison in this fever-stricken island; and before Christmas

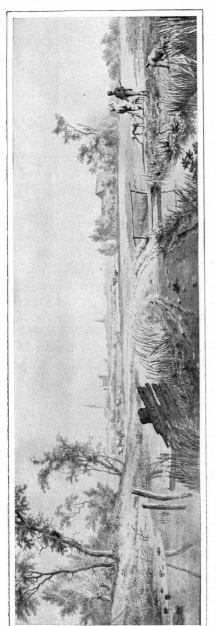
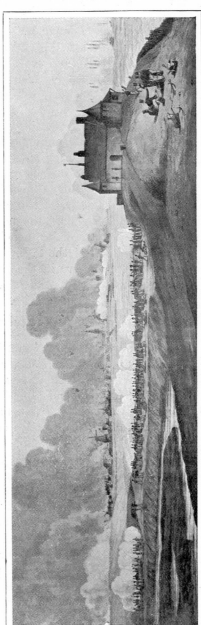

VIEWS IN THE ISLAND OF WALCHEREN. (*Middelburg Museum.*)

the troops finally evacuated it. In this miserable campaign 7,000 men were lost, killed by the climate, not by the enemy, and nearly half the survivors returned to England with constitutions ruined for life.

Moore's Retreat through Spain.

The year 1809 was certainly a chequered and memorable one for the army; in the autumn the Walcheren disaster, in the summer Wellington's victory at Talavera, in January Moore's retreat through Spain, and his brilliant action at Corunna. In this celebrated retreat the troops suffered terribly from cold, hunger and fatigue; discipline often disappeared, but valour never; and the soldiers whom resolute commanders like Craufurd flogged for insubordination while the enemy was almost within sight of the triangles, never failed to do their duty on the battle field, though their backs were still bleeding from the effects of the lash.

Soldiers' Families.

A curious feature in the British armies of this period was the large number of soldiers' wives and families who followed the troops on foreign service. In Moore's campaign numbers fell into the hands of the French; Marbot indeed asserts that in one granary no less "than 1,000 or 1,200 English women and children, nearly all beautiful," were found, too exhausted to keep up with the army, and therefore abandoned to the tender mercies of the enemy. Others succeeded in reaching the coast, and rejoined their friends after strange adventures.[1]

Craufurd and Buenos Ayres.

In the commissioned ranks also, men were wont to take their wives and children on active service. When in 1806 Craufurd was appointed to the command of a small division intended to attack the Spaniards at Chili, he had great difficulty in inducing his married officers to leave their families behind them in England. The details of this expedition show the extraordinary slowness with which our oversea campaigns were then conducted. Although the 5,000 troops under Craufurd's command had been embarked at the end of July, it was not until the middle of November that they were ordered to sail from Falmouth. Their first port was St. Jago, one of the Cape de Verde islands, where they spent four weeks waiting for orders; then the word was given to steer for Cape Colony, where they arrived in the middle of March, 1807. With a truly national ignorance of geography, the fleet dropped anchor in

---

[1] Well described in "Recollections of Rifleman Harris."

False Bay, " from whence, on discovering that a place where neither bread nor water could be procured was not immediately adapted for refitting an expedition," they proceeded to Cape Town itself. Here Craufurd received orders to hasten, not to Chili, but to the River Plate; and by the middle of June, after nearly eleven months at sea, the weary troops joyfully landed near Monte Video. Here they found a considerable force, sent from England to rescue 1,400 British soldiers from the Spanish colonists, into whose hands they had fallen in 1806. Early in that year Admiral Sir Home Popham, who had convoyed Baird's successful expedition to Cape Colony, became infatuated with the idea of organising the conquest of the Spanish settlements on the River Plate. He persuaded Baird to lend him 1,500 men, and without any orders from home, he sailed across the Atlantic, and landed these troops near the city of Buenos Ayres. At first Beresford, who commanded them, carried all before him; but before long the Spaniards turned the tables so completely upon him, that he was compelled to surrender with all his men.

245

VIEW OF THE CITY OF ST. PHILIP, MONTE VIDEO, 1807.

(From a drawing by Lieut. G. Robinson, Royal Marines.)

Soon after the arrival of Craufurd's reinforcement our army commenced its march on Buenos Ayres (July, 1807); but unhappily the general in command was Whitelocke, a creature whose disgraceful incapacity and timidity (to use no stronger word) ruined the expedition. After several marches across plains swarming with Spanish horsemen, who used their lassos upon all stragglers with fatal effect, the troops arrived before

THE POPULAR VIEW OF WHITELOCKE'S DESERTS.
(*By George Cruikshank.*)

Buenos Ayres; and the Spaniards themselves have since admitted that had we at once pushed straight on, the town would have surrendered. But Whitelocke hesitated so long that the inhabitants had ample time to place their capital in a state of defence. The houses were flat-roofed with strong parapets running round them; the windows were few, and heavily barred; the mahogany doors were of immense thickness. Every man, woman, or child who could press a trigger was stationed at a loophole; each house became a fortress; trenches were dug across the streets and batteries planted in commanding positions. For some inexplicable reason Whitelocke ordered the flints to be removed from the muskets; and expected his men to engage in street fighting armed with

pikes only and not with firearms! The attacking parties were
sent into the town in small detachments, without cohesion,
without orders, without reinforcements, without tools to breach
the doors of the houses from which the inhabitants rained
bullets upon them. Naturally the attack was a failure. Of
the officers, seventy were killed or wounded and 120 were
taken prisoners; 1,000 men were killed or wounded and 1,500
were taken prisoners; 1,500 muskets and at least three colours
fell into the hands of the Spaniards. Instead of renewing the
attack next day, as he could easily have done, Whitelocke
agreed to retire altogether from the River Plate on the
Spaniards releasing their English prisoners. The troops, raging
at their defeat, were shipped home to England, where on his
arrival Whitelocke was tried by court-martial and cashiered
for his misconduct in South America.

After such a long series of blunders and failures, is it surprising that Wellington's achievements in the Peninsula fairly
intoxicated the British nation with success? It is scarcely too
much to say that as during the eighteenth century England
produced only three great captains, Marlborough, Wolfe
and Clive, so in our long struggle with France the name of
Wellington stands alone among our generals as that of a
born leader of men.

Effects of Wellington's Victories.

WHEN the war with France recommenced, in 1803, Lord St.
Vincent, who, during the four years ending in 1799 had held the
Mediterranean command, was First Lord of the Admiralty. In
the Mediterranean he had distinguished himself as one of the
best organisers and disciplinarians of his time, and he had
brought up to an extraordinary pitch of efficiency the fleet
with which Nelson subsequently astonished the world; but his
reign at the Admiralty was not a success. He devoted himself
in an inopportune moment to dockyard reform, and to the
making of a hundred petty economies; and there can be no
doubt that his policy had the effect of rendering the hard work
which confronted Nelson even more difficult than it would
otherwise have been. Nor was St. Vincent's successor at Whitehall a more suitable man for the moment. Henry, Viscount
Melville, may have been honest, but his transactions were at
least so questionable as to procure his impeachment; and,

W. LAIRD CLOWES. The Navy.

although he was acquitted on all the ten articles exhibited against him, he left Westminster Hall a discredited politician. If England's captains had not at that crisis in her fortunes been better and stronger men than her administrators, things would indeed have gone hardly with her.

Improvements. The general condition of the Navy during the Napoleonic War remained very much what it had been during the War of the French Revolution; but several improvements were made from time to time. In 1806, for example, increased rates of pay and pensions were granted; and in 1809 some considerable encouragements were offered to the Royal Marines. And in

THE EARLIEST MORTAR APPARATUS.
(*G. W. Manby, "Essay on the Preservation of Shipwrecked Persons,"* 1812.)

1809, also, the Royal Naval Asylum became a fixed establishment, much to the advantage of the orphans and other children of the men of the service.

Life-Saving Apparatus The improvements made in the *matériel* were more striking. The lifeboat invented by Mr. Henry Greathead, of South Shields, having been perfected, came into common use around our shores. The inventor received from the Society of Arts a gold medal and fifty guineas, from Parliament £1,200, and other rewards from the Trinity House and from Lloyd's; but it must be feared that his merits and memory have never been done full justice to. Captain John Shanks's invention of the sliding keel is another one that deserves notice. During the whole war vessels fitted with these keels were constantly employed, the effect of the device being to make shallow-draught craft sail faster, steer more easily, tack and wear more quickly, ride more comfortably at anchor, and take the ground with less risk. An invention which was in some sort

H.M.S. *VICTORY.*

the complement of Greathead's was the life-saving apparatus of Captain G. W. Manby, R.N. This was the prototype of the modern rocket apparatus, and it consisted of a projectile, which, being attached to a line, was thrown from a mortar in such a manner as to carry the line across a wreck lying within a moderate distance of the point of discharge. Peril from water was scarcely, however, in those days of wooden ships, more pressing than peril from fire; and to cope with this, Lieutenant Jekyll, R.N., in 1811, perfected a method of transferring the common hand-pump then used in ships into a powerful fire-engine, which would throw a column of water over a 20-gun ship's top-gallant yard. It was worked on board the *Royal William*, by seven men, and found to throw a stream 76 ft. vertically and 108 ft. diagonally ; but far better results were attained when the water of three pumps was united in a receiver with a single discharging pipe. Thereupon, it was fitted in the *Venerable* and *Tigre*, and all other

LINE OF BATTLE SHIP OF THE EARLY NINETEENTH CENTURY.
(*From a model, by permission of Mrs. Edenborough.   Victoria and Albert Museum.*)

ships of war were ordered to be supplied with it as they should come into port for repair.

Naval Strength.   The total vote for the Navy in 1803 was £10,211,378, and the number of seamen and marines maintained in the latter months of that year was 100,000. In the last year of the war the supplies amounted to £19,032,700, and the maximum number of seamen and marines maintained to 90,000. But in some of the intervening years a far larger number of men had been employed. In 1812, for example, it had been 145,000. Between 1803 and 1815, moreover, the number of officers naturally grew enormously. The admirals on the active list increased from 45 to 70; the vice-admirals, from 36 to 73; the rear-admirals, from 51 to 76; the post-captains, from 668 to 824; the commanders, from 413 to 762; the lieutenants, from 2,480 to 3,211; and the masters, from 529 to 666. The increase of *matériel* was proportionate. At the beginning of 1803, the number of ships of the line was 172, with a tonnage of 299,350; at the beginning of 1815, the number of ships of the line was 214, and the tonnage 389,961. But the increase in ships of other classes was even greater. The number of frigates grew from 184 to 245; and whereas in 1803 the total number of cruising ships of all classes was but 546, with a tonnage of 516,978, in 1815 it was 792, with a tonnage of 716,805. The number was at its highest in 1813, when it stood at 919, with a tonnage of 797,204; and in that year there were in addition 90 troopships, store-ships, surveying vessels, etc., bringing the gross number of ships of the Navy to 1,009, with a tonnage of 869,954. In the twelve years we added to the Navy, by capture from our various enemies, 33 ships of the line and 68 frigates, besides smaller craft to an enormous number; and of vessels which we did not sub-sequently adopt into the service, we captured or destroyed 36 of the line and 70 frigates.

THE Church at the beginning of the nineteenth century had felt the full benefit of the Evangelical movement. It was no longer considered immoral, or even unfashionable, to be enthusiastic. The "Spiritual Quixote," that curious expression of a cynicism which aped orthodoxy, had made way for the serious and earnest appeals of writers profoundly influenced by Christian zeal, such as William Wilberforce and Hannah More. It is, indeed, on the lives of eminent laymen rather than in the published utterances of the clergy that the influence of the Church may best be traced. Closer to the heart of Dr. Johnson than even his Toryism was his sincere and pious churchmanship. Hannah More links the age of the "great lexicographer" to that of moderns like Macaulay and Freeman; and in her Church feeling she united principles which were active in both periods. Personal action, popular ballads, theological essays, even that odious weapon the didactic novel, were

W. H.
HUTTON.
The
Church.

The Laity.

freely employed by Hannah More in defence of Christian faith during her long and devoted life. And it was as a churchwoman *par excellence* that she wrote. Of the Establishment she thought like Pope of the government of the universe, or the Duke of Wellington of the unreformed British Constitution :—

> "Nor do I think our Church wants mending;
> But I *do* think it wants attending."

HANNAH MORE IN 1786.
(After the painting by John Opie.)

And the name of Hannah More was a household word throughout England. The position of William Wilberforce was even more striking. A politician from his youth, he was the intimate friend of William Pitt and the influential adviser of many of the leading statesmen. But he was famous still more throughout the world as the enthusiastic and untiring advocate of the abolition of slavery, and as the one statesman of the day who placed religion before every other consideration. As the founder and supporter of many religious societies, as a philanthropist of unquestionable sincerity, and as a religious writer of wide popularity—his "Practical View" is certainly the best synopsis of the religious condition of society at the close of the eighteenth century—he furnished the best example of the practical effects of Evangelical teaching within the Church. The laity of the beginning of the nineteenth century had been educated under the influence of the Methodist revival, and the results were visible among

Photo: Walker & Cockerell.

UNFINISHED SKETCH OF WILLIAM WILBERFORCE, BY SIR THOMAS LAWRENCE, P.R.A.

(National Portrait Gallery.)

many who could by no means be considered Evangelical. Southey, Wordsworth, and Coleridge, in very different ways, were profoundly touched by church feeling, and it came to them unquestionably through an atmosphere charged with Evangelicalism. Scott, on the other hand, was religiously one of the most powerful influences in the foundation of a new movement of sympathy with medievalism and historic continuity.

The Church, again, had now shaken itself free from irre-

**The
Church
and
Politics.**

sponsible attachment to any political party. There were again
Tory bishops as well as Whig bishops. If the Evangelical party
threw itself strongly into the new Conservatism which arose
as a protest against the Revolution, there was still room
for sound Whiggery among the parochial clergy. Dr. Parr
was a worshipper of Charles James Fox, and he even dared

DEAN CYRIL JACKSON.
(*By permission of the Dean and Governing Body, Christ Church, Oxford.*)

to say, " I hope, sir, you think that our Church established
would not be the worse for a little republicanism."

**The
Bishops.**

The strength then of Church feeling in the country lay in
the support of conscientious and eminent laymen. It would
be impossible, in face of abundant testimony to the high
character and power of many of the bishops, to condemn the
episcopate as unworthy of its position. But the scandals in
the exercise of Government patronage were by no means
abolished, and there was not only a fine stock of " Greek-play

bishops," but also a number of followers of Hoadly (p. 549), to the " deadly leaven " of whose Latitudinarianism Bishop Wilberforce was wont to attribute the worst features of the episcopal character which the century produced. And it is unquestionable that a lack of moral fervour was still characteristic of the pulpit teaching. It was admitted and deplored by clerical critics themselves.[1]

The condition of churchmanship at the Universities affords an excellent example of the general tone. The great Dean of Christ Church, Cyril Jackson, was said to be much more than a bishop—he was a bishop-maker, for the Government consulted him on all appointments. He was hardly a great churchman. His successor was chiefly conspicuous for delaying his appearance at daily service till just before the Prayer of St. Chrysostom. It was an atmosphere, thought Thomas Jefferson Hogg, of "cold unedifying discourses, evidences, probabilities, credibilities, and the whole farrago of frigid rationalism." Such were the surroundings against which Shelley revolted and amid which the clergy whom Jane Austen immortalised were trained.

FROM about the beginning of the nineteenth century the accumulation of scientific discoveries goes on at an accelerated rate. New general theories also are established which raise the more recent sciences to a higher level. To the present short period of twelve years are to be assigned the promulgation of the atomic theory in chemistry, and in optics the renewal of the undulatory theory in such a form as made its acceptance only a question of time. The mechanical theory of heat was prepared for by experimental work that effectually overthrew the doctrine of a material caloric. Botanical classification was systematised anew ; and in the physiology of the nervous system a discovery was made that comes nearer in importance to Harvey's discovery of the circulation of the blood than anything that had been done for physiology in the interval.

In astronomy important work was done by Sir William

THOMAS WHITTAKER.
Science and Philosophy.

[1] See especially " A Secular Essay," 1802, by Rev. J. Brewster, Vicar of Stockton-on-Tees, pp. 169–170.

Astro-
nomy :
Herschel.

Uranus.

Herschel (1738–1822), who, though born at Hanover, lived most of his life in England.   With him must be associated his sister, Caroline Herschel (1750–1848), who not only aided his astronomical observations, but herself discovered several comets, and detected many of the nebulæ included in her brother's catalogue.   Herschel's most memorable discovery is that of the planet Uranus, which he made with one of his own improved reflecting telescopes in 1781.   During the succeeding years mathematicians were occupied in trying to calculate its orbit.   The result was that no supposition satisfied the observations except that of its planetary character.   On this supposition, its motions were found completely conformable to the Newtonian astronomy.   This was the first new planet to be added to the ancient list of seven.   Herschel continued his observations on Uranus, and discovered some of its satellites.   Among his later observations, those which he made on double stars were of special importance as adding to the proofs of the law of gravitation.   In a series of papers addressed to the Royal Society from 1784 to 1818, he succeeded in determining the position of the sun among the stars.

Chemistry :
The New
Departure.

Dalton's
Atomic
Theory.

A new form had now been given to chemical science by Lavoisier, who, taking up the discoveries of Priestley and Cavendish, had applied them to overthrow the doctrine of phlogiston, and had gone on to the construction of an immensely improved theory.   Lavoisier's first memoir on the subject of his new theory appeared in 1775.   In his "Traité Elémentaire de Chimie" (1789) he had drawn up a provisional list of chemical elements according to his system.   The next great advance in chemical theory was made by John Dalton (1766–1844), who first communicated his ideas to his friend Dr. Thomson in 1804.   For a considerable part of his life, Dalton was a teacher of mathematics at Manchester.   Before turning his attention to chemistry, he had done important work in physics.   The first germs of his atomic theory are found in a paper "On the Constitution of Mixed Gases," read before the Manchester Literary and Philosophical Society in 1801.   Having been struck with the applicability of the ancient atomic hypothesis in physics, he went on to apply it to chemistry, where he was able to give it such a form that the most general laws made out by experiment were immediately deducible from it.   In the period preceding

Dalton, the ideas of an "equivalency" between different weights of the different chemical elements, and of their combination in " definite proportions," had been approaching distinct formulation. Dalton, having at last formulated the laws of equivalency and of definite proportions with complete precision, showed further how they could be explained by supposing matter to

SIR WILLIAM HERSCHEL, BY H. W. PICKERSGILL, R.A.
(*St. John's College, Cambridge.*)

consist of atoms, that is, particles not perhaps strictly indivisible, yet never actually divided in any chemical process. The atoms or ultimate particles of the elements, possess definite weights, invariable for each element. Of these weights the ratios can be denoted by numbers. When elements unite with one another to form a compound, what takes place is union of the atoms in groups identical as to the number and character of their constituent atoms. These molecules or groups of atoms form the ultimate units of the compound so long as it remains chemically the same. Chemical decomposition involves re-distribution of the atoms. From this conception, both the equivalency of a certain quantity of one element to a certain quantity of another, and the definite proportions of the quantities of the elements in a compound, necessarily follow. Dalton's law of " multiple proportions " follows from the power, which he supposes in the atom of an element, to combine with one, two, or more atoms of other elements.

Dalton's first convert, Dr. Thomson, made the theory known in the third edition of his " System of Chemistry " (1807). Dalton himself gave his first statement of it to the public in his " New System of Chemical Philosophy" (Vol I., 1808). As with all the great scientific theories, parts of Dalton's chemical theory had been more or less vaguely anticipated by others ; but no one before him had applied it to systematise all the previously disconnected generalisations of chemistry according to a single conception. The new system rapidly made its way among chemists, and ever since it has been the foundation of the whole science.

Electrical Science and Chemistry. While Dalton was making his great advance in chemical theory, an enlarged range was being given to experimental chemistry by electrical discoveries. In 1790 Galvani had observed the action of the limbs of a dissected frog when touched by pieces of two different metals. This observation added a new branch to electrical science. In 1800, Volta had completed the invention of his electric pile, which was a device for multiplying the action of the new kind of electricity by repeating the arrangement of two metals in contact with a fluid capable of acting upon them chemically. In the same year Nicholson and Carlisle found that water was decomposed by the pile of Volta. This discovery was the starting-point of the electro-chemical researches of Sir Humphry Davy (1778–1829). Davy began his experiments in 1800. In 1807 he succeeded in decomposing caustic potash into oxygen and the metal potassium. The decomposition of soda and of the alkaline earths followed. In a paper read before the Royal Society in 1806, Davy had put forward the conclusion that electro-chemical combinations and decompositions are referable to the law of electric attractions and repulsions, and had maintained that " chemical and electrical

EMINENT MEN OF SCIENCE, 1807-8.

(*National Portrait Gallery.*)

attractions are produced by the same cause, acting in the one case on the particles, in the other on the masses." His most notable experimental results thus came after the development of his theoretical views. In connection with these results he continued to elaborate his electro-chemical theory, which ascribes a positively electric character to some elements, and a negatively electric character to others. This was afterwards carried further by Faraday.

Theory of Heat.   Davy's researches on heat were of special importance as preparing for the mechanical theory. In a paper published in 1798 he sought to disprove the doctrine of a material caloric by showing the generation of heat through friction to an extent quite inexplicable on the received hypothesis. Researches on heat tending in the same direction had an important part among the varied investigations of Benjamin Thompson (1753-1814), better known as Count Rumford.

Count Rumford.   The names of Rumford and Davy are closely connected, not only by the similar direction and results of their researches on heat, but also by their common association with the Royal Institution. In 1799 the Royal Institution was projected by Count Rumford and Sir Joseph Banks; in 1800 it received its charter of incorporation, and Rumford himself selected Davy as the first lecturer there.

New laws of radiant heat were established by Sir John Leslie (1766–1832), in his "Experimental Inquiry into the Nature and Propagation of Heat" (1804). Leslie here inclines to reject the "calorific and frigorific fluid," and suggests that some theory of vibration is probably the true one. In 1805 he succeeded Playfair in the chair of mathematics at Edinburgh. There was some unsuccessful theological opposition to his appointment, on the ground that he had maintained a view of cause and effect identical with that of Hume. This opposition gave occasion to the defence of Hume's doctrine of causation by Thomas Brown (p. 755).

Wollaston.   Noteworthy discoveries both in chemistry and physics were made by William Hyde Wollaston (1766-1828), a great-grandson of the ethical writer, William Wollaston (p. 58). In particular, Wollaston discovered a number of new metals; invented the reflecting goniometer and the camera lucida; noticed the dark lines in the solar spectrum; and, by his process for the manufacture of platinum, was the first to make platinum crucibles available in the laboratory. He was one of the first to take up and advocate the atomic theory in chemistry. He had himself been on the verge of stating Dalton's law of multiple proportions; but, along with his accuracy in experimental work, there went a speculative caution which kept him back from making new generalisations of his own.

It is, of course, impossible even to mention all the investigations of importance in this period; but Dr. Wells's "Essay on Dew" (1814) is notable as a classical illustration of the inductive method. Wells, by varied experiments, showed that the deposition of dew is fully explained if we suppose the bodies on which it is deposited to be first cooled down by radiation to a temperature at which the aqueous vapour in the air cannot all be retained in the gaseous state.

Wells on Dew.

The greatest name among the physicists of this period is Thomas Young (1773–1829). Young was a man of many powers and acquirements. He practised as a physician, and made important physiological researches on blood-pressure. He was a colleague of Davy at the Royal Institution. From 1802 he was foreign secretary to the Royal Society. As early as 1814 he had made considerable progress in the decipherment of Egyptian hieroglyphics, on which he published a work in 1823. His distinctive achievement, however, was to put the undulatory theory of optics on a firm basis of experiment and calculation. The theory that light is a vibratory motion of an ethereal medium filling all space had already been advocated by Hooke and Huyghens, but in an imperfect form; and the authority of Newton had caused the scientific world generally to accept the emission theory, according to which light consists of particles projected from luminous objects. Newton, it is to be remarked, had not altogether dispensed with the notion of an ether. And while Huyghens succeeded in explaining some phenomena better than Newton had done, his theory failed to explain others through assuming the vibrations of the luminiferous ether to be longitudinal—that is, in the direction of the ray—like the aërial vibrations which produce sound. Young was led to substitute the assumption of transverse for that of longitudinal vibrations, and was thus able to explain the many curious phenomena of diffraction, interference, polarisation, and

Young and Optics.

double refraction, which had received no satisfying explanation either from the Newtonian theory of emission or from the older form of the undulatory theory. More than this, Young was able to predict phenomena hitherto unobserved. That was exactly what had not happened in the case of the emission theory. For every new phenomenon the theory of emission had had to be complicated by a new hypothesis.

Young's optical investigations were not well received at first. His Bakerian lecture " On the Theory of Light and Colours " was attacked by Brougham in the *Edinburgh Review* (1803) as a dangerous relaxation of sound Baconian and Newtonian methods. Nor did scientific men take up his views with much more favour. In France, some years later than Young, Fresnel put forward the undulatory theory almost independently, and developed it with a more accomplished employment of mathematics. Though opposed at first by some of the older mathematicians, Fresnel's theory had able supporters, and at length gained the victory. Not till Young's theory came thus reinforced by the coincidence of Fresnel's, and by the acceptance of this in France, did it at last gain general acceptance in England.

Botany.

Our present period is marked by a great advance in what is known as the " natural system " of botanical classification. This advance was the work of Robert Brown (1773–1858), whose " Prodromus Floræ Novæ Hollandiæ et Insulæ Van Diemen " (Vol. I.) was published in 1810. In 1801 Brown had taken the post of naturalist to the expedition fitted out under Captain Flinders (p. 545) for survey of the coasts of New Holland. In 1805 he brought home nearly four thousand species of plants. Many of these being new, it was necessary to modify the " natural system " to make it capable of receiving them. The natural system itself Brown had adopted from the two Jussieus, whose classification was itself an advance on the " artificial system " of Linnæus. This artificial classification, when it was introduced about the middle of the eighteenth century, was an immense reform of previous systems; for the earlier views, though they prefigured the modern notion of a natural classification, were not at the time capable of being worked out so as to make plants easily recognisable. The end of easy recognition was secured by the Linnæan classification, and the terminology, and nomenclature of Linnæus have become a permanent possession ; but a natural system, as Linnæus himself saw, was still a desideratum.   By Brown the natural system was placed on a permanent basis.   Still later, in the days of Darwin, the imperfectly understood aims of such a system—which had remained rather an affair of the naturalist's instinct than of logical definition—have been made intelligible by the idea of genetic connection.

The other great biological advance of the period was in animal physiology, and is due to Sir Charles Bell (1774–1842). In 1811 Bell published "A New Idea of the Anatomy of the Brain."   Here he announced his discovery that certain portions of the cerebro-spinal nervous system—ultimately, different fibres —have the function of conveying impressions of sense to the brain, and of conveying motor impulses from the brain.   This specialisation of functions was unknown to Willis, whose "Anatome Cerebri" (1664) is the basis of the anatomical enumeration of the nerves still recognised.   Willis and all succeeding anatomists down to Bell's time had supposed that the same portions of nervous substance perform sensory and motor functions indifferently.   In reality, as Bell showed, most of the cranial nerves are either purely sensory or purely motor. The posterior roots of the spinal nerves conduct only sensory impressions from the periphery ; the anterior roots conduct only motor impulses to the periphery.   To form the spinal nerves the primitive fibres of the roots unite in a single nervous cord, and then again separate to supply the muscles and the skin. Thus, although the particular arrangements of nerve-fibres in the nerves are not uniform, the antithesis of motor and sensory fibres is fundamental throughout.   Another work of Sir C. Bell, the "Anatomy of Expression" (1804), is important for the stimulus it gave to the study of the relations between feeling and muscular movement, and remains a scientific classic.

Animal Physiology. Sir Charles Bell.

To this period may be assigned Dugald Stewart (1753–1828) and Thomas Brown (1778–1820), both of whom are of greater interest in psychology than in philosophy proper.   Both emerge from the school of Reid.   Stewart, though in his psychology he laid more stress on association, remained attached to his master's doctrine, and helped to diffuse it by his eloquent expositions.   In Brown, on the other hand, though he did not

Philosophy : Stewart and Brown.

entirely break with Reid's doctrine of perception, there is observed a decided tendency to go beyond it, and a preparation for the doctrines of later English Associationism.

Brown's pamphlet on Hume's theory of causation (1804) had become in the third edition (1818) a treatise entitled "Inquiry into the Relation of Cause and Effect." Brown regards this relation as consisting in nothing but antecedence and sequence; at the same time he rejects Hume's scepticism, and admits an intuitive belief in the permanence and universality of the causal connection. His general psychology is contained in his "Lectures on the Philosophy of the Human Mind" (four vols.), published after his death. In 1851 this treatise had reached its nineteenth edition in England. Brown rejects the doctrine of "mental faculties" revived by Reid from the scholastic tradition, and treats psychology as phenomenal science dealing with states of consciousness and having analysis for its instrument. His theory of extension is especially valuable. Here he was enabled to make advances by his analysis of touch into touch proper and "muscular sense." Brown tries to show how muscular sensations successive in time become grouped so as to give origin to the perception of positions as co-existing in space. This process he explains by laws of association, or, as he preferred to call it, "suggestion." He distinguished between "external" and "internal" affections of mind; and, for the latter, between "simple" and "relative" suggestion. To simple suggestion he referred memory and the like; to relative suggestion, acts of judgment, comparison, and so forth. His analysis of voluntary reminiscence and constructive imagination is ranked by later representatives of English psychology, along with what he did for the theory of perception, as an original contribution to the development of the general principle of association.

D'ARCY POWER. Medicine and Public Health. THE opening years of the nineteenth century were years of gloom and anxiety for the more far-seeing members of the medical profession in England. The brilliant men who had done so much for the advancement of medicine, surgery, and pathology during the earlier years of the reign of George III. were dead. William Hunter went to his rest in 1783, Percivall Pott died an old man in 1788, John Hunter (perhaps the greatest of the

band) exactly ten years later.   Matthew Baillie, indeed, continued to advance the work which his illustrious uncles had
left unfinished, but he, Brodie, and perhaps Abernethy, are the
only names which stand out above the general mediocrity of
their contemporaries.

The College of Physicians and the Apothecaries' Society

DR. THOMAS BROWN.
(After the painting by George Watson, P.R.S.A.)

maintained the even tenor of their way, but the College of **The Pro-**
Surgeons had again fallen into bad hands, in spite of the **fession.**
attempt made to reorganise it when its charter was granted in
1800.   At this time it was unnecessary for one who desired to
practise as a doctor to pass any examination.   The majority of
those who practised in the large towns took care to become
members of the College of Physicians, of the College of Surgeons,
or of the Apothecaries' Society, for it gave them a position
which they could not otherwise attain.   The membership of the

College of Physicians was practically restricted to the graduates
of the older Universities.   The membership of the College of
Surgeons and of the Society of Apothecaries was obtained by
apprenticeship and by the passing of examinations.   The number
of unlicensed practitioners and of Scotch graduates made the
competition unduly keen for those who had gone to the
expense of a better education.   The apothecaries in particular
suffered severely.   They were paid for the medicines which
they supplied to their patients and not for their advice.   A tax
was put upon glass in 1812, and the price of bottles was thereby
increased.   This tax proved the breaking strain to the apothecaries, for it reduced to a vanishing point the profits upon
the draughts which they were accustomed to supply to their
patients in packets of a dozen at a time.   A meeting was held,
July 3rd, 1812, and in the following year representations were
made as to the necessity then existing for placing the
apothecary, the surgeon-apothecary, and the practitioner in
midwifery under the direction of a proper controlling body.
A Society of Associated Apothecaries and Surgeon-Apothecaries
was accordingly formed, with Dr. Mann Burrows as its moving
spirit.   An attempt was also made to establish an examining
body independent of all the existing corporations, but the
opposition of the two Colleges and of the Apothecaries' Society
defeated the project.   Much correspondence ensued between the
Associated Apothecaries and the licensing bodies, and eventually
the Society of Apothecaries agreed to introduce a new Bill into
Parliament in a form approved by the College of Physicians,
the College of Surgeons standing wholly aloof.   The Bill passed
the Legislature on January 15th, 1815, and it established the
legal practice of medicine and surgery substantially upon its
present basis.

The Practice of Medicine.   Vaccination made steady progress amongst the more cultured
classes in England, whilst the enthusiasm of Ring and others
enabled a large number of poor persons to be vaccinated
gratuitously.   The number of deaths from smallpox in London
diminished rapidly.   In 1804 only 622 died of this disease, and
in 1811 only 751 died of the smallpox at a time when the total
number of deaths in the metropolis was a little more than
17,000.   These numbers compare favourably with the average of
1,200 to 2,000 deaths which had occurred during the period

1761–1800. It is doubtful whether or not the whole of this decrease, or even its major part, was not due to a natural decline in the course which marks the course of every endemic disease after a period of unusual activity. A Parliamentary Committee was appointed in 1802 to consider the merits of vaccination and Jenner's claim to priority as the discoverer of the method. It reported favourably, and the House of Commons immediately voted that a sum not exceeding £10,000 should be "granted to his Majesty, to be paid as a remuneration to Dr. Edward Jenner for promulgating the discovery of the vaccine inoculation, by which mode that terrible disease the smallpox was prevented." A further sum of £20,000 was voted in a similar manner on July 29th, 1807; and on June 8th, 1808, a National Vaccine Establishment was formed. It has now become a part of the Local Government Board, and has kept up an uninterrupted supply of lymph for the purposes of vaccination throughout the country.

Dr. Creighton, in his " History of Epidemics in Britain," says there were several fatal epidemics of measles in the seventeenth and eighteenth centuries. These epidemics were isolated, and it was not until the end of the eighteenth century that measles, whooping-cough, and scarlet fever began to assume their present deadly attitude towards infants and children. The deaths from whooping-cough rose steadily during the eighteenth century from zero in 1704 and 1705 to a maximum of 573 in the year 1780. This disease, however, was not a new one, and the increase was due in part to a better system of classification and in part to a more accurate nomenclature. Convulsions are a frequent cause of death in whooping-cough, and as the item convulsions diminishes in the returns whooping-cough, the real cause of death, increases.

The beginning of the nineteenth century, too, appears to have been marked by several epidemics of scarlet fever, one of which was preceded by a remarkable epidemic of an apparently analogous disease which is said to have killed off "myriads" of cats. It was not until later in the century, however, that the full force of the disease in its most fatal forms was felt in England. Dysentery, on the other hand, began to decrease in intensity, and almost ceased to be epidemic. It had been very prevalent during the eighteenth century and was especially fatal during the years 1758–62 and 1780–82. There was also a remarkable decline in the number of deaths from typhus and other continued fevers in England during the years 1803–1816. This decline was synchronous with the great increase of prosperity due to the rise in wages which resulted from the war expenditure of these years.

The organisation of the army medical service in 1799 is known to us through the regulations of the Army Medical Board, issued to regimental surgeons in September of that year. There were no intermediate grades at this time between the members of the Medical Board and the Inspector-General, who were usually civilians, and the regimental surgeons. The surgeons were nominated to their regiments after passing an examination, at first carried out by the Surgeons' Company, but afterwards by a special board constituted for the purpose. They possessed considerable authority, and were in some matters independent of their commanding officers. They were allowed to deduct four shillings a week from the pay of each sick soldier for the purpose of providing a hospital dietary, " with every reasonable comfort and indulgence that can be afforded." It is specially enjoined that the finest wheaten bread and fresh meat were to be given to the sick. Wine and malt liquors, however (spirits are not specified), were provided at the expense of the Government. They were to be administered personally by the surgeon or his assistant, but when this was impossible they were to be mixed with the medicine or with the food of the patient, so as to make them less palatable. Hospital beds were to be provided for four per cent. of the strength. A nurse was also to be provided. She was to receive a shilling a day, to prepare slops and comforts for the sick, to wash for them, and occasionally to assist in administering their medicines and in cooking their rations.

REGINALD HUGHES. Painting and Engraving. SPACE does not enable us to refer, except in the briefest and most perfunctory manner, to the successors and followers of Lawrence, who came to the front in what we may term the Napoleonic Era, such as Harlow—best known by his stagey "Trial of Queen Catherine "—John Jackson, Thomas Phillips, William Owen, and Martin Archer Shee. With the exception of Harlow most of their best work was done subsequently, and like

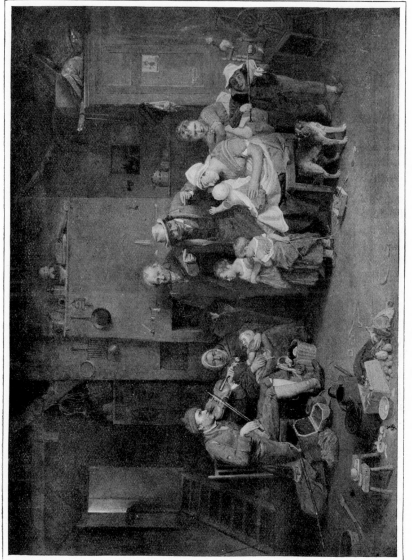

THE BLIND FIDDLER, BY SIR DAVID WILKIE, R.A.

(*National Gallery.*)

Watson Gordon, Howard, Hilton, Etty, and Haydon, they really belong to a later day.

From the chronological point of view, the same is true of David Wilkie, but as most of the works which form the foundation of the school of English genre were painted in the period under review, he demands notice here. He was the son of a Scotch minister, born in 1785, at Cults, in Fifeshire, and his bent—even as a child—towards art was so marked, that despite the prejudice natural to a Presbyterian family, his father despatched him at fourteen to the Trustees Academy at Edinburgh. It was then under the direction of the insipid historical painter, John Graham, R.A., who as a teacher had this merit—that he kept Wilkie at work on the human figure. Though Wilkie worked steadily at large figure subjects he was conscious that his talents lay in another direction. At eighteen he returned to Cults and found his subject in the annual fair that took place in the neighbouring village of Pitlassie. In colour and workmanship it is not much like his maturer work, but it is vigorously conceived. Wilkie was then only nineteen, but he was bent on going to London, which a successful sale of the " Fair " for £25 enabled him to do. At twenty we find him settled in London and a student at the Academy, and before his twenty-first birthday he had painted the " Village Politicians," and had written to his father, " I have the vanity to hope that Scotland will one day be proud of David Wilkie." In the succeeding years he painted " The Blind Fiddler," " The Letter of Introduction," " The Village Festival," and " Blindman's Buff." In May, 1812, he had done sufficient to warrant an exhibition "of his own pictures." He was made an Associate at the earliest age allowed by the rules, and in 1811 became a full Academician.

A fine feeling for colour, though even in his earlier time inclining to heaviness, distinguishes all his works; but the finesse, the spirit, the movement, of his groups is unequalled. Later, after his long second tour on the Continent, during which he visited Paris, Munich, Rome, and Madrid, he changed his methods and subjects, greatly for the worse. He had been much impressed by what he had seen, particularly in Spain, and came back "determined to try a bolder and more effective style." It was in this manner that he painted his later historical subjects, but he was quite out of his depth, and these, and among them the famous " Preaching of John Knox," are disappointing. It was after his journey that he became so reckless in the use of asphaltum, which, if it gave a rich quality at first, made for blackness in the end. If in his latter works his influence both in method and manner was evil, in those of his earlier days it was excellent. Above all Wilkie deserves to be remembered as the pioneer who added a new field to be tilled by English artists. It was in truth a new kind of art, and one which Englishmen could practise with success, that was ushered in by Wilkie. He taught his countrymen how a story of humble contemporary life, not a satire nor a sermon, might be told on canvas so as to be interesting and yet remain a work of art. He showed them, too, that this was as possible in the England of the Regency as it had formerly been in Republican Holland.

Slow as was the progress of landscape art in English studios, the appreciation of landscape by the public outside was still slower. Wilson died in the utmost penury because no one would buy the genuine gold of his skies, or his pinchbeck Italian scenery. Gainsborough's landscapes fared no better, though they were, in spite of all defects, full of the most vivid impressions of the country, inspired by the truest feeling for its natural beauty. The conquest of public opinion by the landscape painter had to wait for the admirable prose of Constable, and for the marvellous poetry of Turner. But in the interval between the defeat of Wilson and Gainsborough, and Constable's and Turner's victory, a generation of artists lived and worked, not entirely without result. Some of these turned chiefly towards the Dutch masters, some towards Wilson, some towards Gainsborough, and at least one towards Nature herself. Later Land-
scape.

First among them comes George Morland. He was born in 1763 in London, the son of an artist, who, as an engraver and pastellist, had some reputation. He was another of the interminable series of infant prodigies, and at ten exhibited drawings at the Academy. He was regularly trained by his father, who, out of regard to his morals, refused to allow him to go to the Academy School to consort with the students. As regards artistic training the plan was a success. He learned to draw well, and his bits of colour are always well placed Morland.

and effective.   But as regards young Morland's morals it was
an abject failure.   From a very early age he gave himself
up to idleness and drink, painting only for the means of
debauchery.   This was his uniform course through life, and
his marriage with the sister of his friend, Ward, the animal
painter, which occurred when he was twenty-three, did not
materially improve matters.   He was continually in debt.
Sometimes he was locked up and allowed to paint himself
back to liberty ; at other times he would evade the writs of
indignant creditors by taking to a nomad life in the country,
sleeping in barns and low taverns, or camping out with the
gipsies.   To great facility of execution he joined a keen observation and a retentive memory, and this enabled the painter
to utilise the experiences of the fugitive debtor.   His death
in a sponging house, at the age of forty-two, appropriately
closed a consistently vicious career.   It lent, however, a fictitious
sort of glamour to his name, and added to the vogue enjoyed
by his pictures.   They are chiefly pastoral subjects, and he
shows much affinity with Gainsborough, particularly in his
treatment of foliage.   His drinking scenes are numerous ; and
so are his barns with rough country horses at the manger, his
wayside inns with travellers resting, his night poachers, and
his gipsy encampments.   Realist in spirit, he had many artificial tricks, and constantly repeats an artificial chord of colour.
He was a thorough artist, however, and even in his most
commonplace subjects he manages to interest the eye, and his
colour is occasionally exquisite.   Unlike most of the men of
his day, Ibbetson and Sir George Beaumont for instance, whose
work is that of an attenuated Wilson, Morland is always himself.   It was reserved for this drunkard to show his countrymen
how readily the idyllic life of an English countryside lends
itself to the needs of the artist.   His art was in no sense
great, but it was art, intelligible and enjoyable, and he taught
the public to admire it.

Nasmyth and Callcott.   Probably the taste for realistic landscape created by Morland
made the way easy for Patrick Nasmyth.   He was the son of
a Scottish landscape painter, who in turn had been a pupil
of the honest if uninspired Ramsay, and he came to London
in 1805, two years after Morland's death.   Scotchman though
he was, he had a keener eye for the simple pastoral beauty of

THE INSIDE OF A STABLE, BY GEORGE MORLAND.

(*National Gallery.*)

the South of England, its rich pasture and pleasant lanes.
His manner has great affinity to the Dutchmen, and particularly to Wynants, whom he resembles, both in clearness and
simplicity of colour and subject.   His somewhat tight and hard
manner of painting is in striking contrast to Morland's; but
it had in it the same elements of popularity: it was pretty
and intelligible.   The same may be said of Nasmyth's contemporary Callcott, afterwards Sir Augustus; who from choir-
boy to Royal Academician had a career of typically respectable
success.   But the taste for landscape had now definitely set
in, and Callcott's pastures with cattle and river, and occasionally coast scenes, are pleasant enough, and, indeed, he sometimes paints a sunny tide-way with rare felicitousness.   He
studied under Hoppner, obtained the dignity of Associate in
1806, and that of Academician in 1810.   His early success
makes it natural to mention him here; but he struck out no
new path, and had little or no influence on the art of his
country.

"Old
Crome."
There is one landscape artist, however, who, if fate had
been kinder, might have had the glory of founding modern
landscape.   This was John Crome, of Norwich, who was born
in 1768, and was largely the anticipator of Constable, though
hardly of Turner.   Other painters have had to breast the blows
of circumstance, some with much, some with very little, adven-
titious aid; but John Crome had no aid from any source whatever.   He was the son of an artisan, a weaver, and his home
was in a second-rate provincial town where there was no art
school or museum.   He was brought up almost without any
schooling, and from the age of eleven, or thereabouts, earned
his own living—first as an apothecary's errand boy, and then
as a house-painter's apprentice.   Sign-painting for public-houses
seems to have formed part of his master's calling, and thus he
acquired in some sort the rudiments of his art.   But the only
serious education he received came from himself, and consisted in the conscientious copying of the Dutch and Flemish
landscapes of a Mr. Hervey, of Catton.   Anyhow, it served its
purpose so well that he ventured to set up as a drawing-
master.   He gained a large *clientèle*, but did not give up
his practice in sign-boards, and this and his drawing lessons
kept the family.   But from the first he made landscape

sketches, and these are full of individuality, and show a distinct advance. Gainsborough, with his infallible instinct for landscape, had painted tree masses with perfect feeling; but Crome, more accurate in drawing, and with a stronger grip of a kind—though not the most pleasing kind—of natural beauty, painted the trees themselves, and painted them in the spirit in which Reynolds painted men. In Crome's works, too, we find perhaps, the earliest example of the modern feeling for the impressiveness of everyday scenes. Crome, though clearly at times affected by Wilson's pictures, does not need to go to the Campagna to get the feeling of loneliness and isolation. The flat country of Norfolk, with its little rising and falling of the ground that does duty for hills and valleys, serves his purpose as well as the wilderness or the Himalayas. A perfect example of this power is the "Mousehold Heath near Norwich," now in the National Gallery—a work, says a French critic, "of such simplicity that only a master could have given it grandeur. It represents a long slope of pale verdure, which, from a foreground of weeds and heather, mounts quickly towards the sky. Big golden clouds float over the rounded top of the hills. There is nothing more. Yet with this little, Crome has given the perfect similitude of solitude and stillness. In this little fold of earth, which not a breath of wind ruffles, not a sound disturbs, one might think oneself as far from the busy town as anywhere in the world. It is the desert, and the majesty of the desert." Crome's art is the art of the centre; but just because its environment was unfavourable, its influence was small. Though a friend of Beechey's, he never exhibited at the Academy until 1806, when he was over forty. During the fifteen years which elapsed between that day and his death, little more than a dozen of his pictures were seen in London. But in 1803 he gathered the artists of Norwich together into a society, which, though not fated to exercise a great influence, or to become a permanent factor in our art-life, yet has more right to be termed a school than anything that England had for half a century.

To this school belonged John Sell Cotman, himself a Norwich man, though trained in London, who, besides painting numerous sea-pieces in oils, was distinguished as a water-colourist and as an etcher. Some of his etchings, many of

The Norwich School.

which are architectural, are of fine quality.   To the same
school belonged James Stark, Crome's pupil, whose manner,
though a little dry, lacking the largeness of his master, is

A TOWN IN HOLLAND, BY J S. COTMAN.
(*By permission of Sir W. Cuthbert Quilter, M.P.*)

simple and true to Nature.   Crome's other famous pupil was
George Vincent, who was of more versatile temperament.   His
most famous work is a noble view of Greenwich Hospital as
seen from the river, which is crowded with shipping and full
of sunlight.   But perhaps the pupil who came nearest to

Crome in sentiment was Robert Ladbrooke, who married a sister of Crome's wife. His woodland scenes and views in the neighbourhood of Norwich, while thoroughly naturalistic, frequently attain the grave, impressive beauty of Crome himself. The sons of both artists followed in their fathers' steps; but, with the exception of John Bernay Crome, who became famous for his moonlight scenes, never achieved more than a local reputation. The Norwich Society was not long-lived. Their last exhibition was in 1818; and with the death of John Crome in 1821, the Norwich School ceases to be a distinguishable entity.

We postpone all considerations of the career of the two men to whom we have before referred as the two greatest painters of English landscape—Constable, the great master of its eloquent prose, and Turner, the great landscape poet. We are constrained to do this because, though both were born and educated within the period under review, the work which fixes their prominence was executed later. The country-bred John Constable (1776–1837), to whom landscape owes its final emancipation from convention, was not only slow in making himself felt by his contemporaries, but even in realising wherein his true strength lay. Indeed, it was not till 1802 that he became fixed in his design to become " a natural painter," and never more " to seek the truth at second hand." But in 1813 he was still painting portrait heads at fifteen guineas (though it must be owned this was done for the sake of a living), and his large landscape of " The Lock," of 1814, was so unsuccessful that in later years he got it back, and gave the owner a totally new version in exchange. Still, though the time from 1802 to 1815 was not idly spent by Constable, it was the seed-time rather than the harvest. Constable's genius, which was destined to revolutionise the landscape art of Europe, had yet to wait not only for general homage but for general recognition. *[Constable's Early Work.]*

Turner, who was born in April, 1775, in Maiden Lane, London, a year before Constable, and who did not die till 1851, had not to complain that his contemporaries did not recognise his talent. At twenty-four he was an Associate, and three years later (in 1803) an Academician. We have something to say elsewhere of his early mastery of water-colour work. In water colour, in oils, and as an etcher, his skill of execution was *[Turner's Early Work.]*

247

equally amazing. His " Liber Studiorum " is the most exquisite collection of engraved landscapes that exists; and it is note-worthy that some of the etchings done by his own hand actually surpass the original studies. Nevertheless, finished artist as he was in many different fields, during the period under review, and, indeed, up to his Continental journey of 1819, he is in the imitative stage. The oil-paintings of the earlier period have been called the works of a student, and, prodigious as they are, the dictum is true of them in the sense that they repeat the manner, first of one master and then of another. At first it is Wilson and the Dutch marine painters; then it is Poussin and Claude, and occasionally it is Morland that is imitated. But though the imitations frequently surpass the original in every noble quality of art, there can be no question but that they are imitations. Turner—the world's wonder, the master of every enchantment of streaming light and radiant cloud perspective, Turner painting in the manner of Turner, the Turner of " The Fighting *Téméraire*," and the " Childe Harold Pilgrimage," and the " Polyphemus Deriding Ulysses "—belongs to the period of the long peace, not to the era of warfare that ended in 1815.

Miniature Painting. The art of the miniaturist, the earliest fruit of the English talent for portraiture, reached, as we have seen, its most flourishing epoch in the times of the Stuarts. Samuel Cooper, the contemporary of Pepys, whose delicate heads are unsurpassed by later or earlier workers, represents the fourth generation from the Elizabethan Nicholas Hilliard. Flatman and Alexander Browne, Boit and Lens and Goupy carried on the succession into the eighteenth century. George II. and Caroline of Anspach patronised the miniature painters and enamellists of their day. Michael Moser, the first keeper of the Royal Academy, and Nathaniel Hone and Meyer, who were contemporaries of the great portrait painters, were all Academicians of the first installation. Ozias Humphrey and Collins, Meyer's pupil, Samuel Shelley and James Nixon, equally deserved and obtained patronage, both for portraits and small historical subjects. The most famous of the miniaturists of the century was, however, **Cosway.** Richard Cosway, born in 1740. He was like Sir Joshua, a West-countryman, the son of a schoolmaster, and, like him, a pupil of Hudson. He was celebrated not only for his heads, but for small full-lengths, the figure deftly sketched and the face finished with the utmost care. An extraordinary though slightly monotonous sweetness of expression, a universal grace, and very taking colour, make his work easily recognisable. No painter has possessed the gift of flattery more perfectly, nor used it with greater hardihood. It is said that he drew all the beauties of the day and all that wished to be beauties, and always gave satisfaction. At thirty he was elected an Associate, and in the following year an Academician. His wife was also a miniaturist, and the pair, owing to the eccentric vanity and talent of the husband, and the beauty and flightiness of the wife, became more than the fashion. In the midst of his gay career Cosway became a Swedenborgian, and, according to his assertion, held interviews with more than one person of the Trinity, and had sittings from the Virgin Mary. His wife abandoned him in 1804, and after a luxurious life in the Paris of the Empire

THE DUCHESS OF DEVONSHIRE.
(After Richard Cosway.)

became superior of a religious house at Lyons. He lived to be over eighty, and left behind him a vast body of most attractive work.

Cosway's most famous imitator was Henry Edridge, who was **Edridge.** also distinguished as a mezzotint engraver and as a landscape painter and architectural draughtsman. After this the art declined, though fine works of this class, both on ivory and paper, were executed by Alfred Chalon, and in enamel by Henry Bone, who was appointed Royal Enamellist by George III., an honour which was confirmed to him by the two succeeding sovereigns.

Not the least important of the artistic developments of the eighteenth century was that which occurred towards the end of its third quarter in connection with book illustration and

Engraving. engraving. Works like Alderman Boydell's " Shakespeare" had, as we have seen, found employment for famous and fashionable artists such as Romney and West, Northcote and Opie. But besides the greater names, among which that of Angelica Kauffmann must be counted, mention might be made of a host of the lesser artists. Such were Mortimer (the youth who took away a prize from Romney), Wheatley, justly celebrated for the prettiness of his rustic genre, Hamilton and Cipriani, Smirke and Richard Westall. Amongst this crowd were two men of such peculiar and individual talent that they cannot be passed over. These were William Blake and Thomas Stothard. Both were (in effect) Londoners, and almost of the same age, the former being born in 1757, the latter in **Stothard.** 1755. Stothard, like Lawrence, was the son of an innkeeper. His chief training came from his being apprenticed to a pattern draughtsman for silk fabrics. It was a peculiar school, but in it he learned the value of line and balance in composition. His manner of treating masses in low relief, and the grace of his composition, as we see them in his famous design for the Wellington Shield, are highly suggestive of the uses of this training. He had a passionate love for the art of the illustrator, and quickly found work from the publishers. He illustrated all the poets (in Bell's famous edition) from Homer downwards, though anything less heroic than Stothard's pencil can scarcely be conceived. Pathos he reached occasionally, but tragedy never ; graceful mirth too, now and then, but glee and broad humour were beyond him. ." It seems," says Mr. Ruskin, " as if he could not conceive wickedness and coarseness or baseness. Everyone of his figures looks as if it had been copied from some creature who had never harboured an unkind thought or permitted itself an ignoble action. With this intense love of purity is joined a love of mere physical smoothness and soft-ness, so that he lived in a universe of soft grass and stainless fountains, of tender trees and stones at which no foot could stumble." It is true that nothing could be more pitiable than every endeavour by Stothard to express facts beyond his own sphere ; but within it he was a master. He was a most prolific worker, too, his designs having been estimated at four thousand, and this is probably an under-estimate. He was curiously with-out any of the *mauvaise honte* of the artist ; nothing came

SHAKESPEARE'S CHARACTERS, BY THOMAS STOTHARD.
(*Victoria and Albert Museum.*)

THE CANTERBURY PILGRIMS, BY THOMAS STOTHARD.
(*National Gallery.*)

THE GHOST OF A FLEA.

(From the original drawing by William Blake.
By permission of the Messrs. Linnell.)

amiss to him. Pocket-books, keepsakes, fashion books, children's books; anything and everything he touched with the same simple and effeminate grace. His merit was greatly appreciated by the Academicians, and he was elected a member of their body in 1794. He painted in oils, too, though these are probably among his feeblest productions. Stothard has been often compared to Fra Angelico, and Turner declared that he was the Giotto of England!

While Stothard is the type of all that is calm, simple, graceful, and happy, even to ineffectiveness and mono-

Blake

tony, Blake is the wildest figure in the history of English art and letters. He was apprenticed to the younger Basire, an engraver of repute, but while earning his bread by engraving during the day—some of Stothard's blameless inventions were executed by him —he employed his nights in mysterious and visionary compositions. In these he was poet and prophet, illustrator and engraver, all in one. His work of all kinds is surprising in its inequality. In some fragments of his verse — for instance, like the lines to

THE SPIRITUAL FORM OF PITT GUIDING
BEHEMOTH, BY WILLIAM BLAKE.

(National Gallery.)

" The Evening Star "—there are passages of such perfection as are not to be matched by any poet of the eighteenth century. On the other hand, much of it is unintelligible, some of it absolutely absurd. So, too, of his drawing; part is graceful, brilliant, and effective; part incoherent and violent, and even grotesque. His methods, too, were equally various. Thus his " Songs of Experience " were executed in a most extraordinary manner, which he explained as the result of a direct revelation from his brother Robert, in a vision of the night.

He used all kinds of pigments without oil, including metallic gold and silver, and with singular success. His skill in this kind of iridescent colouring is marvellous, to be only partially gauged by the singular figure in the National Gallery, " The Spiritual form of Pitt guiding Behemoth." This was a companion to a figure of Nelson engaged in similar avocations, and is not too intelligible. But Blake was not content with allegories of so comparatively simple a character. From the heights of Heaven to the abyss

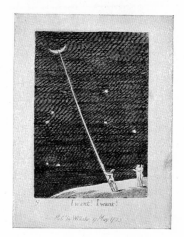

I WANT! I WANT!

(*" The Gates of Paradise," by William Blake.*)

of Hell, and from the souls of heroes and virgins, the personification of thunder, of God the Father, and Death plucking down the sun, to the Canterbury pilgrims and the ghost of a flea—nothing was too great or too small for his voracious imagination to feed upon. It is not surprising that with such a temperament he was always seeing visions. Not only in Westminster Abbey did ghosts of great men rise and walk with him, but in the unromantic roads of Peckham Rye he saw trees " full of angels," and at Fulham he was present at a fairy's funeral. A madman, but a truly inspired madman, is the verdict of posterity on Blake. That he should have found scant encouragement in the era of the French Revolution, and in the England of the Regency, is not to be wondered at. He died in great poverty, having lived true to the faith of his youth, that his business was not " to gather gold but to make glorious shapes expressing godlike notions." His influence was less than nothing with his contemporaries, but it was unquestionably felt by one considerable painter whose death is still recent and who, like Blake, was a great poet.

YOUTHFUL SPORTS.—I.
(*T. Bewick, " Natural History of Quadrupeds."*)

Another intensely individual artist, almost exactly contemporary with Blake and Stothard, remains to be noticed, and, though he worked in a much humbler sphere, he contributed greatly to the progress of English art. This

Bewick. was Thomas Bewick, born in 1753 at Newcastle-on-Tyne. If he did not rediscover, he reintroduced the art of wood engraving in England. His book of quadrupeds, and his history of British birds, show a really extraordinary gift. A profound knowledge of natural history, of animal gesture and expression, was coupled with a unique faculty for interpreting the texture of fur and feather, and a quaint but genuine humour. It is noticeable, too, that his landscape settings are realistic, and sometimes of singular elegance. He was helped in many of these last by his brother, and one Robert Johnson, both of whom were among his pupils. To Bewick belongs

YOUTHFUL SPORTS.—II.
(*T. Bewick, " Natural History of Quadrupeds."*)

the merit of having founded the school of wood-engravers, which has persisted to the present day, and given scope to so much and such varied talent.

Bewick was, as we have indicated, a humorist in his quiet

way, but he lived in an age when something more virile, con- **Humor-**
crete, and topical was generally demanded. There was still a **ists.**
market for satire of the Hogarthian type, even though it
contained hardly any of the Hogarthian flavour. But Hogarth's
imitators—some of whom, like Sandby, were of his enemies, and
others, like Collett, of his friends—were, on the whole, a feeble
folk. The imitation is obvious ; but one has only to compare
the people, say in such a work as de Loutherbourg's "At Spring
Gardens," to see every coarseness and exaggeration of Hogarth
—the brutal mouth, the dwarfed figure, the big head, coarsened
and exaggerated, and without the justification offered by his
unparalleled ingenuity.

But the troubles that preceded, and the wars that followed,
the French Revolutionary movement seem to have first awakened,
and then favoured the growth, of a new form of pictorial satire.
Politics became all-absorbing, and the populace were as excited
as their betters. Sayer, Bunbury, Woodward, Boyne, and a long
list of less known men, thus found not only inspiration but a
ready sale for their works. The great development, or revival,
in satirical art is, however, chiefly associated with the names of
two men, James Gillray and Thomas Rowlandson. The first of **Gillray**
these, Gillray, was the son of a trooper who had fought at
Fontenoy. Like Bewick, he was a North-countryman, and, like
Hogarth, he was apprenticed to a metal-chaser. He, too, is said
to have been an infant prodigy, and to have drawn and etched a
plate at the age of twelve. The first work certainly is his, however, dated in 1779, when he was twenty-four. He entered the
Academy in that year, and thenceforth, through the long period
of the struggle with France, he poured out a series of squibs,
pasquinades, and satirical invectives which for vigour and
brutality have never been surpassed. An excellent and expres-
sive draughtsman, with a considerable gift of arrangement and
composition, and, as a satirist, hitting always as hard as he could,
he seems to have taken his motto from one of the Frenchmen
whom he hated so cordially—" *L'audace, et l'audace, et toujours
l'audace.*" His virulent attacks on France, the French Revolution, and the English sympathisers with France, were naturally
popular with the king and queen, and the Gillray drawings
were supplied regularly at Windsor. A typical example of this
sort is " The State Dinner to Dumouriez at St. James's." It

represents the victorious general as the most horrible type of *sans culotte*, flourishing a dagger, and waited on by the Opposition chiefs, Tooke and Fox and Sheridan. Among the *plats* are a royal crown and a bishop's mitre, while the head waiter, Charles James Fox, is putting on table a calf's head that bears the familiar features of William Pitt. Gillray's caricatures of Napoleon and his family, Napoleon baking gingerbread kings, or as Gulliver sailing his boat in the presence of the Brobdingnagians George and Charlotte, Josephine as a fishwoman, and similar indecencies, equally commended themselves to the royal taste. Nor does it seem that the old king and queen were much shocked by " The Anti-Saccharites " (p. 505)—the royal couple teaching the sulky princesses the advantages of drinking tea without sugar, the king repeating " Delicious! delicious ! "—or with the brutal realism of the " Affability," where the king is bawling into the ear of a stone-deaf and frightened peasant. His most audacious drawing is the famous " Sin, Death, and the Devil," the queen (whom he always makes a gap-toothed hag) interfering between Pitt and Thurlow. This was an insult not to be forgiven, but the loss of Court favour did not seem to matter to Gillray. Mrs. Humphreys's shop window in St. James's Street, where his pictures were sold, and which is represented in " Very Slippy Weather," continued to be besieged. Repulsive as he often is, nothing can be more spirited than Gillray at his best, and many of his drawings look as if they had been evolved under the stress of genuine passion. He did not long survive the fall of Napoleon, the target of his most venomous satire, and his last years were clouded by imbecility.

Rowland-
son.

The pictorial satire of Thomas Rowlandson was wider in its scope, less violent, but also less vigorous than Gillray's. Indeed, his best works have little relation to caricature. The pair of confidential young ladies on a sofa, for example, in the favourite drawing called " Harmony," have an elegance that is akin to Gainsborough's art, and the suggestion of kinship is further strengthened by his brilliant drawing of their elaborately dressed hair. He came of a middle-class stock, and at sixteen entered the Academy. He, however, soon quitted London for Paris, where his aunt lived. There he received an excellent training, and he returned to England a complete master of his trade. In London he began seriously enough: had a studio in

CUCKFIELD, SUSSEX.

("*The Tour to Brighthelmstone*," by T. Rowlandson.)

Wardour Street, and sent portraits and figure subjects to the Academy. But later on he gave himself up to the playful and humorous delineation which made his name. His sketching at all times is brilliant and decisive; he is a master of outline; his figures are full of movement and frequently of grace. Add to this that he was the most prolific artist of them all. Less engrossed with politics, or with the *chronique scandaleuse* of the most scandalous period, than his contemporaries, his drawings are a mine of wealth to the student of manners. Racing, hunting, coaching, the barracks, the counting-house, the colleges of Oxford, the theatre, the coffee-house, the fencing-room, dogfights, fairs, levées, the cries of London, hunt dinners—all the humours of the town and country came with equal ease to him. His satire is, as a rule, of a gentle character, and only occasionally he deals a swashing blow at some imposture, as in the famous death-bed, where he shows the sufferer surrounded by a roomful of friends and physicians, and of all present only one is compassionate, and that is Death. He was, too, particularly happy in those "travel-pictures" of which Hogarth was the pioneer. The most important of these are the "Tour to the Wreck of the *Royal George*," in 1782; "The Tour to Brighthelmstone," in 1789; and the "Tour to North and South Wales," which dates from 1800. Among the drawings interspersed among the letterpress (provided by his friend Wigstead) there is one, "The Young Ladies of Lymington in a Strong Wind," that inevitably reminds one of John Leech. He died in 1827, after a protracted illness.

Isaac Cruikshank

Among the many rivals of Gillray and Rowlandson, Isaac Cruikshank deserves special mention, not only for his own work, but as being the father of the long-lived and popular George. The elder Cruikshank devoted himself almost entirely to politics; but satire was probably not his *forte*—rather a serious and not ungraceful realism. If one compares such drawings as "A General Fast, Lambeth," with such works as its companion, "Spitalfields," the contrast is striking. The realistic group of the wife of the starving weaver and her children is elegant. The caricature of the guzzling Archbishop is childish. He died about 1811, leaving behind him two sons, Robert and George. Both were artists, but it was on the younger that the father's mantle conspicuously fell. The father died of alcoholism, and in this doubtless lies the explanation of the almost fanatical passion with which, to the last hour of his long and busy life, his son George fought against the liquor traffic. Within two years of his father's death, he was at work drawing. His " Court of Love," of which the Regent and Lady Hertford are the tutelaries, bears date 1st November, 1812. The young satirist, barely turned eighteen, has already commenced his crusade against drunkenness, and his freedom, not only in the words he puts into the mouths of his personages but in the representation of the characters, is prodigious. The picture of the favourite, drunk, seated on the knee of the Regent, with her husband standing by, is startling, even in an age of licence. But George Cruikshank, although he began thus early, and though in spirit he recalls the era of the Restoration, as a worker belongs to the later nineteenth century, not to the Napoleonic era.

The eighteenth century, and particularly the latter half of it, was prolific in almost all branches of art. Besides the great portrait and landscape painters in oils and the great designers and illustrators, many Englishmen attained fame and fortune as pastellists. Their work, it is true, mostly strikes us now as careful, hard, and somewhat uninteresting as art, but its wonderful permanence makes it extremely valuable as history. Francis Knapton, who died in 1788, at the age of ninety, may be considered the founder of the school, and William Hoare, the teacher of Lawrence and Francis Cotes and his pupil, John Russell, were his most distinguished followers. Engraving, too, in all its branches, including mezzotint and etching, made great strides at this time. Before the reign of George III. most of the engravers of note, like Hollar and Simon, had been foreigners, though here and there a few English names occur. But a whole group of Englishmen and naturalised foreigners now come to the front. Such were Vivarès and Woollett, famous for their skill in rendering foliage, Bartolozzi, Sir Robert Strange, Fittler, Sharp, and Sandby—this last an Academician, who reproduced his own pictures in aquatint. More than a hundred mezzotint engravers are said to have found employment in reproducing the works of Sir Joshua alone.

English water-colour painting in the eighteenth century may be, not improperly, regarded as a fresh art, and in its final results, if not in its immediate harvest, it is the most important of all

George Cruik- shank's Early Work.

Pastellists.

Engravers.

Rise of English Water- Colour.

the new departures of the period. Of course, water colours were old, older than oils, nor was water-colour painting on paper an entirely new thing. The Dutch painters had produced finished water-colour drawings a century before, and the miniaturists had worked successfully with the same materials in the days before ivory came into use. But the difference between such work and that of Turner's ripened skill is a difference not of degree only but of kind. This gives unusual point to the fact that the practice of our early water colourists was derived neither from Dutchmen like Ostade and Dusart, nor from Englishmen like Cooper and Flatman. It clearly grew out of the stained, washed, or tinted drawings of the architectural draughtsmen. These men, the humble helpers of the anti-quarian and the annalist, yet worked directly from Nature, and so set down their immediate impressions, unconscious of the charm that such directness and immediateness possesses. From this class, too, the artists sent out by the Government on scientific cruises were naturally chosen, and thus Captain Cook, on his last voyage in 1776, took John Webber on his ship, while William Alexander accompanied Lord Macartney's mission. Some of the Chinese sketches of the last-named artist are, indeed, fully coloured; but this was in 1792. Paul Sandby (Vol. III., p. 75), whom George III. employed as a draw-ing master, was born in 1725, so that he truly belongs to the primitive time; but he hardly got beyond the tinted work of the topographer. He has been called the father of water-colour art, but the title more properly belongs to John Cozens, his junior by twenty-seven years. John was the son of Alexander **Cozens.** Cozens, also an artist, who was said to be the natural son of Peter the Great, and was born in Italy. Though he hardly did more than suggest the colour, he was an artist in the highest sense, and certainly the first painter in water-colour who was penetrated with the sentiment of the landscapist. Indeed, Constable said of him in a moment of expansion that he was the greatest genius that ever touched landscape. He seems to have invented, or at least to have known, a good many of the modern devices, such as washing and abrasion of the surface, and the like. He is best known by his Italian views, painted for Alderman Beckford. Once, and once only, he exhibited at the Royal Academy, and his work drew from

Turner a declaration that he had learnt more from it than from any other picture. This was called " A Landscape, with Hannibal on his March in the Alps, Showing to his Army the Fertile Plains of Italy "—a thoroughly Turnerian subject which, unfortunately, has now disappeared. The contemporaries of Cozens, William Payne, a neighbour of Sir Joshua's at Plympton, and John Smith (known as Warwick Smith), introduced further refinements into the practice of water colour. The former had a great name as a teacher, and Gainsborough said of the latter that he was the first water-colourist " who carried his imitation through."

A still further advance was made by Thomas Girtin, a **Girtin.** Londoner, who, though he died in 1802, cut off at the early age of twenty-nine, is much more modern in feeling, displays much greater breadth, spending himself more on mass than outline, and on depth and richness rather than precision of colour. He was a pupil of Dayes, a water-colourist of the old school, for a short time; but his best training seems to have consisted in copying the works of earlier men, such as the Rookers, Hearne, and Cozens, and sketching from Dr. Munro's windows. This took place at the doctor's rooms in the Adelphi, where Girtin had for a fellow-student another Londoner: none other than Joseph Mallord William Turner. This wonderful **Turner's** man there began the study which occupied his life: the perfect **Water-** rendering of light. His earliest step in this direction was to **Colour.** paint the shadows of their true tint—first at some sacrifice of the lights, but gradually with fuller knowledge came perfect mastery over lighted surfaces as well. It is noteworthy that Turner, the water-colourist, from the beginning to the end of his career, forbore from gaining his effect by the use of body-colour in his pictures (though he employed it freely for memoranda), declaring that its use would ruin water-colour art, and destroy its beauty and individuality.

It is always difficult to fix a date for the maturity of a movement, but accepting 1800 as the date at which Turner had completely mastered his system, we may fix that as the year in which the water-colour art of England attained to manhood.

Behind the actual pioneers and the immense and original talent of Turner stood a considerable group of artists in water colours, partly their contemporaries in age, partly men whose

The Water-Colour Society,

meridian belongs to a subsequent generation.   Discontented with the small, ill-lighted room which the Royal Academy allotted to their works, a section of these *frondeurs* seceded, and in November, 1804, established "The Water-Colour Society."   The leading spirits in this affair—Hills, Pyne, Shelley, Wells, John Varley, Glover, and W. S. Gilpin—were not quite the first in their profession, and of course Turner

HULKS ON THE THAMES, BY DAVID COX.
(*Victoria and Albert Museum.*)

was not among them, as he had been already elected an Academician.   The Society was limited to twenty-four, and the right of exhibition was confined to members.   At first great success attended their exhibition; but their exclusiveness created jealousy among outsiders, with the result that the year 1808 saw the establishment of a rival association. For the time, however, water colour had gone out of fashion. The new association rapidly died of inanition, and the older society found itself in such straits that after a few years a dissolution was agreed to.   Not all the members, however, accepted extinction; and a group of a dozen or more, including Barret, Glover, Copley Fielding, and, after a short interval, David Cox and Linnell, started a new exhibition.

But the fates were adverse to this also, notwithstanding the high rank of the artists. The year's show was a failure, and the next year's exhibition never took place. This, which, in matter of popularity, probably marks the low tide of water colour, occurred in 1815. Nevertheless, the art was already too firmly established to be seriously affected by the temporary breakdown of the machinery of exhibition. One has only to recall who were at work at the date in question, to be convinced of this. Of the older school, the frugal George Barret and the prolific John Varley were still in their prime. The suggestive architectural draughtsman, Samuel Prout, just elected to the society, was then thirty-two, and almost of the same age were Peter de Wint and David Cox, the greatest of them all. Fielding, the master of deep misty distances, was twenty-eight, and William Henry Hunt, to whom no subject came amiss, was three years younger. Obviously our most distinctively national branch of art had not only reached a flourishing stage, but was never in less danger of failing than in 1815.

Among the sculptors practising in England in the first half **Sculpture.** of the eighteenth century, though a few English names, like that of Francis Bird, occur, there is only one artist of real distinction —the Frenchman, Louis Roubillac of Lyons (p. 118). But when, in 1768, the Academy was founded, Roubillac had been dead for two years, Rysbrach and Scheemakers, his would-be rivals, had fallen into obscurity, and the only sculptors elected original members were, it would appear, Joseph Wilton and Agostino Carlini. Of the latter we know little, except that he executed some tolerable busts, and was the first keeper at the Royal Academy. The second keeper was Wilton, who, though **Wilton.** warped by the taste of the time, was an accomplished and independent artist, a good anatomist, and a skilful worker in marble. He had studied under the French sculptor Pigalle, and had resided several years in Italy, and his work seems to reflect a divided aim. He may fairly be gauged by his monument to Wolfe, which himself and his contemporaries regarded as a masterpiece, but which strikes us now as somewhat heavy and confused, exhibiting an unfortunate mixture of figures in relief and in the round. But the opening of the Schools of the Academy, and the fact that the first two keepers were

248

Bacon.

sculptors, gave an undoubted impetus to the art of the modeller. The names of three of the pupils, Nollekens, Banks, and Bacon, sufficiently corroborate this view.

Bacon, who was born in 1740, five years the junior of Banks

MONUMENT TO WOLFE, BY JOSEPH WILTON.
(Westminster Abbey.)

and three years younger than Nollekens, came to the Academy from the Chelsea china works, and afterwards modelled groups, figures, and animals for the manufacturers of a kind of pottery called lithodipra. He was a wonderful prize-winner, and out of sixteen public monuments for which he competed he was success-ful fifteen times. His works are plentiful at Westminster, his

most famous work being Chatham's monument, and his most
attractive that of Brigadier Hope. Banks had been apprenticed **Banks.**
to a wood-carver, and had studied for a year in the St. Martin's
Academy, so that his advantages in point of training were considerable. He was, however, an inferior artist. He attempted
many strange subjects, "Armed Neutrality" for one, which he
designed for the Empress Catherine, and "The Frenzied
Achilles," which never found a purchaser. His gigantic
cenotaph to Sir Eyre Coote, with the palm-tree in the centre,
is one of the eyesores in Westminster Abbey. He had, however,
a certain gift of graceful pathos, and it is said that Queen
Charlotte burst into tears at the sight of his monument to
Penelope Boothby. He possessed a genuine admiration, not
to say yearning, for the antique, but was apt, doubtless, to
mistake memory for inspiration. Joseph Nollekens was an **Nollekens**
artist of a much more masculine character. He, like Chantrey,
had a real gift for portraiture, but, in effect, for portraiture alone.
His busts are exceedingly actual, if occasionally mannered, and it
is by their vigorous realism that he is remembered. He died in
1819 at the age of eighty-one, but he had long abandoned the
practice of his profession.

The one English sculptor of the century to whom the title of **Flaxman.**
genius may properly be given was John Flaxman. He was born
in 1755 at York, and was the son of a cast-maker employed by
Roubillac. John was too sickly a child to go to an ordinary
school, so that his childhood was passed in his father's work-
shop, drawing or modelling, or trying to teach himself Latin,
and getting by heart classic fables. At twelve his medallion
won a prize at the Society of Arts, and at fifteen he became
a student at the Royal Academy and carried off the silver
medal. At twenty he was engaged by Wedgwood's firm to
model classical groups and portrait medallions for their ware.
For this he showed more than ordinary aptitude. His skill
in dealing with reliefs on a small scale is really phenomenal;
but working under such restrictions as to size undoubtedly
had a cramping influence on his talent. Even after his seven
years' stay in Italy, which commenced when he was thirty-two,
he never quite threw it off—never grew to be quite at home with
life-size representation. His most paying work in Italy was his
designs for Homer and Dante, which are not only ingenious, but

full of a classical feeling that is almost Greek.   He produced few
busts and statues, and his emblematic groups and public monuments do not exhibit his talent at its best.   His numerous

THE ARCHANGEL MICHAEL CONTENDING WITH SATAN, BY
JOHN FLAXMAN.
(University College, London.)

memorial reliefs, of which many cathedrals and churches
contain examples, better display his genuine, if limited, gift.
Most of them consist of symbolic groups embodying some
simple idea, as sorrow, resignation, comfort.   In his hands
such themes, though treated in the classical spirit, are neither

cold nor conventional, and he manages to combine a certain touch of real human pathos with the grace which never deserts him. Almost alone of English sculptors, he has the secret of uniting the rhythmic flow of antique composition with the unaffected pose and gesture of actual life. His talent can, however, be gauged best of all by the collections of his drawings, sketches, and studies in London and Cambridge. Romney was one of his earliest backers; Blake and Stothard were the friends of his adolescence. In 1800 he was elected a full Academician, and appointed Professor of Sculpture in the Academy in 1810. His lectures are valuable and of mark in many ways, and not the least in this—that they show how a passionate classicist can do justice to Gothic art.

IT is a common and perhaps a convenient practice to date the reaction against eighteenth century classicism in English poetry from the period 1798-1800. For in the former of those two years appeared the first edition of the " Lyrical Ballads," while the latter witnessed the publication of the second edition of that almost too celebrated volume, accompanied by that certainly too famous preface in which Wordsworth laid down what he conceived to be the true principles of poetic composition. Yet, whether we look at the Reaction from its Romantic or its Naturalist side; whether we regard it as preparing the way for a bolder, franker, more picturesque treatment of human action and passion, or as leading poets to seek a closer contact with nature and a simpler and sincerer form of poetic language, neither of these two dates is accurate. Coleridge, whom we regard as the representative of the movement in the former aspect, made no converts to Romanticism by his example as displayed in the " Lyrical Ballads," nor certainly, either by force of example in the text or of precept in the preface, did Wordsworth succeed in convincing the world that he had rediscovered the true but forgotten speech of the Muse. The justification, however—and it is perhaps a sufficient one for treating the " Lyrical Ballads " as epoch-making—is that both poets had clearly conceived the movement in its twofold character, and did deliberately purpose its initiation when the plan of the volume shaped itself in their minds. Coleridge's

H. D. TRAILL. Literature. The Reaction against Classicism.

account of the matter is at any rate distinct to this effect. In a well-known passage of the "Biographia Literaria," he says :—

"The thought suggested itself (to which of us I do not recollect) that a series of poems might be composed of two sets. In the one the incidents and the agents were to be in part, at least, supernatural; and the excellence aimed at was to consist in the interesting of the affections by the dramatic truth of such emotions as could naturally accompany such situations, supposing them real. . . . For the second class subjects were to be chosen from ordinary life; the character and incidents were to be such as will be found in every village and its vicinity where there is a meditative and feeling mind to seek after them, or to notice them when they present themselves."

With the omission of the accidental ingredient of the supernatural (obviously only one of many ways of removing "incidents" and "agents" from the sphere of every-day life: which removal alone is of the *essence* of the definition) the second sentence in the above quotation defines the "romantic" by genus and differentia. Generically it differs from realistic forms of poetry by deliberately dealing with incidents which, from supernatural or other causes, are of stronger interest than those of ordinary life, and with character heightened accordingly; specifically it is distinguished from the merely fantastic by its dramatic truth. The last sentence of course contains Wordsworth's theory of the subject matter of poetry, which he was afterwards to supplement in the Preface to the "Lyrical Ballads" with his theory of its language.

The result of the experiment is well known. Coleridge contributed but two pieces to the joint-stock production, and Wordsworth the remainder—a disproportion so great that "my compositions," says the former poet, "instead of balancing the others, appeared rather an interpolation of heterogeneous matter." His chief contribution, moreover, the immortal "Ancient Mariner," belongs rather to the school of allegorical fantasy than to that of romance, its plot and incidents having hardly enough coherence to give it that 'human interest" at which the poet admitted himself to have aimed; while the fragment of "Christabel," his true romantic masterpiece, and the real parent seed of the Romance poetry, was destined by a chance unprecedented in literature to fructify *in manuscript* through its inspiration of another poet who read it in that form years before it appeared in print. As to the famous poetic theory enunciated by Words-worth two years later, he did not even at the time secure the adhesion of his colleague, by whom, moreover, in the "Biographia Literaria," published seventeen years afterwards, it was with many expressions of affectionate esteem and ad-miration for its author irreparably demolished.

The theory itself and the criticism—one of the acutest and most closely reasoned pieces of critical analysis in the language —may here be briefly set forth. Wordsworth's positions were mainly these two : (1) that "the language of poetry is identical with that of prose" (by which he meant not merely that poets may, and must, make large use of ordinary prose language, but that *any* and every substantive, adjective, verb, phrase, or sen-tence which is of legitimate use in prose is equally suited to poetry) ; and (2) that, for a number of reasons, of which Coleridge successively demon-strates the futility, the language

Photo: Walker & Cockerell.
SAMUEL TAYLOR COLERIDGE, BY PETER VANDYKE.
(National Portrait Gallery.)

of rustic life is better suited than any other to serve this twofold purpose. In other words, Poetry and Prose, accord-ing to this theory, speak but one tongue, and that the tongue of the peasant. This is in effect the counterpart and supplement of the famous discovery of Monsieur Jour-dain. Indeed, the country bumpkin had even greater cause for complacency than the worthy *bourgeois:* since, however agreeable it may have been to the latter to discover that "for more than forty years" he had been without knowing it "talking prose," it should have been a source of still higher gratification to the former to learn that poetry had been the unsuspected language of his whole life.

Even to the "plain man," however, unassisted by any critical acumen or special study of the subject, the theory

[margin note: Words-worth's Theory of Poetry.]

His
Practice.

must have suggested one obvious question : If prose does not essentially differ from poetry, why be at the trouble of writing poetry instead of prose ?   Wordsworth, to do him justice, antici- pates this inquiry in his preface, and his answer is exquisitely characteristic of his humourless attitude of mind. " Why," he asks, " am I to be condemned if to such description "—that is, to the description of rustic things and persons, expressed in what he holds to be the true poetic tongue—" I have endeavoured to superadd the charm which by the consent of all nations is acknowledged to exist in metrical language ? "   One thinks of the lines—

> " In distant countries I have been—
> And yet I have not often seen
> A healthy man, a man full grown,
> Weep in the public roads alone ; "

and, comparing it with Coleridge's somewhat malicious but perfectly accurate and much more rustically worded paraphrase, " I have been in a many parts far and near, and I don't know that I ever before saw a man crying by himself in the public road—a grown man, I mean, that was neither sick nor hurt,' etc. etc., we ask ourselves with amazement where in the name and " by the consent of all nations" the superadded " charm of metrical language " comes in.   Even if it could be traced, it would not afford the slightest support to Wordsworth's theory as to the simple rustic diction being the natural language of poetry ; because Coleridge's paraphrase, and not Wordsworth's original, is, as the former points out, the *natural* way in which a peasant would express himself, and it differs in mere vocabulary, as *e.g.* in its synonyms for "distant countries," "weep," etc., from the poet's own language.

It is of course evident that in desiring any "superadded charm " at all, Wordsworth gives away his theory with both hands.   Once admit that prose language requires, or even only may require, to have something artificially added to it, in order to invest it with the peculiar charm of poetry, and the Wordsworthian position is surrendered.   It follows from this admission that the proper language of poetry is not, and cannot be, either the ordinary talk of this or that class of society as such, or any other arbitrarily selected and dogmat- ically defined form of expression ; but that it is, and must ever be, solely that mode of speech which, whether as regards the choice of words, or their arrangement, or both, is best calculated to heighten the pleasure which the reader derives from the literary embodiment of the writer's idea. Whether

Photo : Walker & Cockerell.
WILLIAM WORDSWORTH, BY ROBERT HANCOCK.
(*National Portrait Gallery.*)

the words so chosen and so arranged do or do not heighten this pleasure is a question not of poetic law, but of æsthetic fact ; and it is one to which no man's poetry supplies a greater variety of answers than does Wordsworth's. When he says to the leech gatherer : "But where is it you live and what is it you do ?" he certainly does not succeed in heightening whatever pleasure we should derive from having the question put in plain prose. When, on the other hand, he compares the leech gatherer's motionless figure at the tarn-side to a cloud

      "That heareth not the loud winds when they call,
        But moveth altogether if it move at all,"

he as certainly does succeed.

It is unnecessary to follow Coleridge through his elaborate
and overwhelming exposure of this singular delusion. For that
exposure almost any one of his arguments would singly have
sufficed. But his strongest points are: (1) that even if the
vocabulary of poetry were identical with that of prose,
the variation in the syntactic order of the words under the
exigencies of rhyme would create a vital difference between the
two forms of speech ; and (2) that Wordsworth's own practice
stultified his precepts, seeing that he only rises into poetry
when he allows himself to use poetic language, while, whenever
he deliberately denies himself the use of that language, he sinks
into the flattest and baldest prose.

Wordsworth's example, however, redeemed his theories,
and Coleridge had no theories to redeem. The latter's influence was therefore the earlier in its operation, while that of
the former has been perhaps the greater in the long run. Yet,
by a somewhat ironical fate, it has turned out that Coleridge,
who concerned himself rather with the matter than the
mechanism of poetry, has taken rank as one of the greatest
English masters of poetic form, while Wordsworth, who believed
himself to be the inventor of a new, or at any rate the restorer
of the true, language of poetry, owes his place in our literature
to a force and depth of poetic feeling which even his many
defects of form have proved unable to outweigh. The match-
less music of the one singer has enriched the note, as the
inspired vision of the other has enlarged the outlook, of all
English poetry since their day.

To conceive of them, however, as the immediate founders of
a "school" in the sense in which, or in any analogous sense to
that in which, a Greek philosopher or an "old master" commonly receives that title, would be a mistake. There was no
Lake School in this sense, as was long since pointed out by an
eminent writer whose name in the early days of the century
was often united with those of the men by whom the school
was supposed to have been formed. Wordsworth, as it
happened, had a natural connection with the Lake country by
birth and marriage, and he by force of the literary sympathy
between them attracted Coleridge, who in turn, through the tie
of matrimonial affinity, drew Southey thither also. By such
accidents of personal or family connections was the Lake

colony originally gathered; but contemporary criticism, un-
aware or incurious of the real facts, imagined them to have been
brought together by common views on the subject of literature,
especially with regard to the true function of poetry and the
true theory of poetic diction. Thus misled, people went on, con-

Photo: J. Chaffin & Sons, Taunton.

COLERIDGE'S COTTAGE, NETHER STOWEY, SOMERSET.

tinues De Quincey, "to find in their writings all the common
characteristics which their blunder had presumed, and they
incorporated the whole community under the name of the
Lake School. Yet Wordsworth and Southey never had one
principle in common; their hostility was ever flagrant."

Nevertheless, the accident of their common place of abode
was, on the whole, not otherwise than fortunate. If the
mistaken impression produced by it did occasional injustice
to individuals, it tended indirectly and ultimately to popularise
a knowledge of the new poetry and to stimulate curiosity as

to the personalities and genius of the men by whom it was being produced. Such familiar expressions as the "Lake School," "the Lakists," "the Lake poetry," did undoubtedly direct public attention to questions of poetic matter and manner upon which it was very desirable to concentrate it. But, strictly speaking, the so-called school never at any time contained more than the two masters, Wordsworth and Coleridge; for Southey, though an admirable prose-writer, was a poet of far inferior calibre to either, and his poems, once highly considered, have now found their proper level of respectable rhetorical verse; while Lamb, De Quincey, and others, whose names were often associated with the school in the controversies of the day, belonged to it less as adherents of its principles than as admirers of its two great masters.

"Christ-abel."

Moreover, for all doctrinal purposes, either of precept or practice, its two great masters were too quickly reduced to one. Coleridge's "Christabel" wrought its influence even before publication, and though not wide, yet a most potent and memorable influence it was; but the poem itself was not published till 1816, and produced little impression upon the critical, and still less upon the general, public even then. Further, it must be remembered that but a few years after the composition of this poem (that is to say, about 1802–3) Coleridge's poetical powers fell, under the combined influence of ill-health and opium, into almost complete abeyance. He had ripened much more quickly than Wordsworth, but his time of blossoming and fruitage was lamentably short. The elder poet, on the other hand, continued steadily at work for a long series of years. It cannot be said that it was an uninterrupted period of growth with him, or not, at any rate, on all sides of his genius; for sense of style and power of self-criticism were faculties which Wordsworth never acquired. The "Excursion"

The "Excursion."

—his greatest, in the sense of his longest, poem—falls within the period with which we are dealing. It was written in 1814, and may, therefore, be taken to represent the full maturity of the poet's genius; nor is it wanting in passages which do that genius justice. Yet in no poem is Wordsworth's inequality more conspicuous; in none do we so suddenly or so often descend from the empyrean of poetry to the flats of prose; in scarcely

any do we find a more constant necessity of reminding ourselves that the mechanical weaver of these commonplaces was
also the inspired builder of the great "Ode on the Intimations
of Immortality."

It was, as is well known, the unfinished poem of "Christabel,"   Scott's
read by him only in manuscript, which gave its first impulse to   Poems.

Photo: Green Bros., Grasmere.

WORDSWORTH'S HOME, DOVE COTTAGE, GRASMERE.

the romantic poetry of Walter Scott.   He had hitherto been
known as the author only of some metrical translations from
the German and a few short original pieces in verse, though his
true feeling for romance had been shown as collector and
editor of the Scottish Border Ballads.   But in 1805, a casual
recitation of "Christabel," heard a year or two before, having
"fixed," says Lockhart, "the music of that noble poem in his
memory," he was fired with the idea of "throwing the story of
Gilpin Horner into somewhat of a similar cadence," and the
result was the "Lay of the Last Minstrel."   "Marmion" followed
in 1808; the "Lady of the Lake" in 1810; and thenceforth
Scott continued to publish a romantic poem almost yearly, until
the series closed with the "Lord of the Isles" in 1815.   Their

success was great and well deserved ; for though Scott had
neither Coleridge's extraordinary musical faculty, nor his dreamy
tenderness of sentiment, nor his gift of mystical imagination,
there is a spirit and fire in his narrative verse, and a certain
masterly breadth in his treatment of nature—as witness the
noble opening to the " Lady of the Lake," " The stag at eve had
drunk his fill," etc.—which must irresistibly challenge all those
who scruple at bestowing the name of poetry on these splendid
rhymed romances to enlarge their definitions.   Scott's ardour of
inspiration had no doubt begun to abate somewhat in 1815,
after ten years of active poetic production ; but, as is well
known, it was the belief, not wholly unfounded, that the earlier
romantic poems of Byron threatened to supplant his own in
popular favour which caused him, to his own greater glory and
to the imperishable gain of our literature, to exchange poetry
for prose.

**Byron's
Early
Poems.**

But the poet who had thus driven him from the field, though
destined indeed to surpass him in achievement, had certainly not
yet done so ; and it is proof rather of a fickleness of affection
than of a quickness of appreciation on the part of the public
that they should have abandoned the genuine dramatic stuff
of " Marmion " and " The Lay " for the stage heroics of the
" Corsair " and the " Giaour."   For it must be remembered that
it was solely on these brilliant but artificial romances that in the
year 1815 the fame of Byron as a serious poet principally rested.
The two earlier and vastly inferior cantos of " Childe Harold "
had indeed appeared ; but they gave little, if any, promise of
their two splendid successors.   It was not till the period treated
of in the next volume that Byron stepped into that place in our
poetic literature which, after a short interval of disputed title,
the judgment of posterity has now irrevocably confirmed to him.

**Shelley's
Early
Work.**

The case of Shelley, our account of whom must also be
deferred to a later stage of this work, is somewhat different.
Though he was five years younger than Byron and much more
than five years later in attaining fame, his genius came far more
rapidly to maturity, and at an age when the future author of
" Don Juan " and the third and fourth cantos of " Childe
Harold " was still content with the crudity and commonplace of
the " Hours of Idleness," the future author of the " Prometheus
Unbound " and the " Cenci " had already produced " Queen

Mab." The faults and immaturities of this singular poem are indeed conspicuous enough. Ridiculed in so far as it was not ignored at the time of its appearance, it has in later times and in some quarters been absurdly overpraised; but, with all its defects and excesses of youth, an impartial criticism can hardly hesitate to pronounce it the most striking and powerful work of imagination, and by far the richest in promise, that has ever sprung from the brain of a poet who had not yet passed his twentieth year. There is at least no denying that in its finer passages we get much more of the real Shelley than we get of the real Byron before 1816, when the elder poet had already attained the age of twenty.

Among the other and (as we must now perhaps style them, though they would certainly have resented such a designation in their own day) minor poets of this period, the names of Campbell and Moore must not pass without a word of mention. The first of them indeed, if we were to confine our attention to those shorter pieces to which he himself attached the least value, might perhaps make good his claim to a more honourable title. The two battle pieces and the one patriotic ballad of Thomas Campbell—"Ye Mariners of England," "Hohenlinden," and the lines composed in celebration of the naval victory of Copenhagen —still take rank among the most stirring specimens of the Tyrtæan lyric in our language. They are read and admired in their entirety when of the "Pleasures of Hope"—that smooth and elegant verse exercise in the manner of Goldsmith which so curiously lifted Campbell into youthful fame at a period (1799) when Goldsmith's manner might have been thought to have become hopelessly obsolete—but a few isolated lines survive in memory. After an abstention of nearly ten years from poetic utterances *de longue haleine,* he was in 1809 attracted by the new movement to the field of romance, and the result was "Gertrude of Wyoming," a poem which, though well received, was far from repeating his earlier success. Campbell, in fact, has lived, and will live, by his least ambitious efforts, sharing in that respect the limited and qualified immortality of Moore. Thomas Moore (1779–1852) who, in the earlier years of the present period had acquired a certain vogue by the publication of a volume of elegant but somewhat indecorous amatory poems, entered in 1807 into an arrangement with a music publisher to supply

Campbell
and Moore.

words to a collection of the native melodies of Ireland. No such distinguished success was ever before, or has ever since, been achieved in the not very distinguished art of "writing up to" music. The "Irish Melodies," it is true, show many marks of their conventional origin; they are in a certain sense artificial

THOMAS CAMPBELL, BY SIR T.
LAWRENCE, P.R.A.
(National Portrait Gallery.)

products, altogether wanting in the freshness and *naïveté*, the epic force and simplicity of the genuine folksong; but they were the work of a man in whom the melancholy charm of his country and of his country's music inspired a feeling so genuine and, indeed, so intense as continually to lift, if it could not consistently maintain, his expression above the level of the commonplace. It is the lack of this emotional sincerity which leaves his more ambitious efforts comparatively cold and lifeless, and has consigned "Lalla Rookh" to an oblivion which the "Irish Melodies" and a few other lyrics of Moore's have escaped.

Prose,
1802-15.

Considering the remarkable amount and varied character of its literary activity, the short period with which we are dealing is somewhat singularly wanting in specimens of the greater prose. It is necessary to limit this remark to the product itself as distinct from its producers, because between 1802 and 1815 there were men living and writing who were afterwards to leave a lasting mark upon our prose literature. But they had either not yet reached their maturity, or had hitherto failed to find their real strength. Scott was engaged throughout nearly the whole period in cultivating the muse of metrical romance, and only published "Waverley" in 1815, the year of its close. De Quincey divided the period between Bohemianising in London and lion-hunting at the Lakes. Hazlitt, although a contributor to

the periodical press in 1812, had not yet exhibited those powers
as a critic in which few, if any, of his contemporaries or successors have approached him.   Charles Lamb had desisted from
those early and not very fortunate attempts at verse to which
he had been impelled by his friendship with and admiration for
Coleridge; and after an equally short and still less successful
courtship of the dramatic muse, had published only those earlier
prose pieces which, while they revealed to the world the
admirably sensitive and sympathetic critic of Elizabethan
poetry, only partially displayed the quaint and delightful genius
of the essayist who, under the name of " Elia," was to make an
imperishable addition to the prose classics of the language.

Only one prose writer of the first order was producing works **Southey's**
of a corresponding rank.   It was during these years that **Prose.**
Southey expanded a review-article into the shortest but greatest
of his biographies, the "Life of Nelson," a work which, with
others by the same author, may fairly be taken as fixing the
standard of early nineteenth-century prose.   It does this all the
more effectively from the very fact that Southey, unlike the
two greatest prose writers of the previous generation, was not
impelled by any overmastering force of individuality to indi-
vidualise his style.   Writers in whom this force is strong no
doubt accomplish the greater things, and leave behind them the
more splendid monuments of themselves.   But for that very
reason they are less representative of their era, and their works
less accurately indicate the particular stage of development
reached by the literary language of their nation at the period in
which they write.   Southey's biographies mark the beginnings,
and fix the character, of nineteenth-century prose.   Less formal
in structure and less rhetorical in vocabulary than the prose of
the preceding era, it has gained in simplicity and directness, in
artistic compression and reserve.   Southey's prose had none of
the qualities which impress us in the prose of Gibbon, or which
enchant and almost intoxicate us in that of Burke ; but we feel,
all the same, that neither Burke nor Gibbon could have turned
their instrument of language to the purposes of a short biography
with such mastery as Southey in the " Life of Nelson " displays
in the use of his.   Above all, we feel that a race of beings among
whom mortal will always be more common than immortal writers
have been supplied with an incomparably more useful model for
    249

imitation in the prose of Southey than in that of Gibbon or of Burke.

The Liter-ature of Criticism.

If, however, the biographical masterpieces of this eminent writer constitute the only notable additions to our prose literature during this period, its first decennium was marked by two events of lasting importance to our general literary history. For it witnessed what may be fairly called the organisation of criticism as a distinct branch of English letters. Great individual critics, often men of dominating force of intellect and character, had of course flourished before. Dryden in the seventeenth century and Johnson in the eighteenth are notable examples. But they took criticism, so to speak, "in their stride"; they were poets, scholars, historians, moralists essentially, and in the first place; critics only in the second place, and by accident. Above all, the weight which their criticism carried was solely that of their own names. Where those names were not signed or not known, there was no means of replacing the consequent loss of individual influence by any form of corporate authority. It "said nothing," for instance, to anybody that such and such a paper on this or that new book or literary subject had appeared in the "World" or the "Connoisseur." Literary criticism had not yet organised itself, as political and social criticism had long since learned to do. It had never yet provided itself with any authoritative medium of expression in the periodical press—never yet found a voice to which people would listen, because, even though the tone could not always be identified, it was known to proceed from one or other of a band of collaborators all more or less accomplished as writers, and all men of acknowledged competence as critics.

The "Edin-burgh Review."

Criticism, however, was to find such a voice in the very year with which this period commences. In 1802, the *Edinburgh Review* was projected by a small coterie of literary men, united by a general sympathy in the matter of letters and by a common Whiggery in politics. They were all men of distinct, if unequal, ability, most of them men of considerable information, and at least one of them, Brougham, a man of "omniscience." Scott lent the services of his pen to its earlier numbers; Sydney Smith contributed wit in abundance; the future Chancellor wrote untiringly and with extraordinary speed on every conceivable subject; Francis Jeffrey, the first editor,

was in many respects heaven-born to the craft; and thus in a
few years' time the new literary periodical had become a power
in the land. An ill-judged and ungenerous attack in 1809 on
the Spanish patriots then endeavouring to make head against
the encroachments of Napoleon disgusted and alienated its Tory
subscribers, and the result was a secession and the establish-

Photo: Walker & Cockerell.

ROBERT SOUTHEY, BY HENRY EDRIDGE, A.R.A.

(*National Portrait Gallery.*)

ment of its rival the *Quarterly.* The new review, which commanded the good-will and active literary assistance of Scott from
the first, and soon afterwards enlisted powerful recruits such as
Southey, Lockhart, and others, stepped at once into a position of
at least equality with the older periodical; and for more than a
generation the two reviews together may be said to have played
the part of "commissioners to execute" that office of "Lord
High Censor of Literature," which had been filled in earlier
periods with so much authority by individual men of letters,

but which since the death of Johnson had practically ceased to exist.

Jeffrey and his Colleagues. They were of course not more infallible than other Boards of Commissioners known to past or even, it may be, to present history; and it was their misfortune that among the mistakes committed by them were one or two of a monumental character, which have come down to posterity in inseparable association with the names of the men whose genius they failed to recognise. For this they have suffered—as perhaps a still earlier critic may have suffered before them for a similar offence —an excessive penalty. Zoïlus, for all we know, may have been a very competent judge of poetry: it was through his ill-luck in attacking an immortal that he has immortalised himself in the opposite character. He survives under the undesirable nickname of " Homeromastix " because it was upon the " Iliad " and on the " Odyssey " that he pronounced his sentence of " This will never do." Happily for the critic who slighted Wordsworth, and for the critic who failed to recognise Keats, these failures do not constitute their whole record. They have many other and sounder judgments to refer us to, and it is unfair, though it has been too common, to dwell upon these memorable blunders. Jeffrey, after all, was a critic of no mean ability, as many an acute and impartial appreciation of contemporary literature under his hand exists to prove; and he was seconded, as was Gifford in the *Quarterly,* by a staff of writers whose services in upholding sound literary standards and in exposing the pretensions of literary impostors far outweighed any errors of critical judgment which have ever been brought home to them. That their verdicts were now and then biased by the keen political partisanship which prevailed during the early years of the century, and invaded regions into which

Photo: Walker & Cockerell.
FRANCIS, LORD JEFFREY, BY PATRICK PARK.
(National Portrait Gallery.)

politics should never have been allowed to intrude, is undeniable ;
but this is only to say that the men sometimes failed to rise to
the level of their method. To the method itself it is no reproach,
and it does not therefore detract from the merits and the claims
of the men by whom it was introduced. The fact remains that
the two great literary periodicals which were founded in the
early years of the present century were the first to provide for

WILLIAM GIFFORD, BY JOHN HOPPNER, R.A.
(National Portrait Gallery.)

the systematic and efficient performance of a work of the
highest importance to the interests of English literature ; that
the chief contributors to them did undoubtedly constitute in a
genuine sense of the words a " college of criticism " ; and that
they created a critical tradition which later generations have
been content to follow, and a critical method which their
successors have done no more than develop.

THE years 1801 to 1815, in contrast to the latter half of the
eighteenth century, are not marked by great names or great

G. TOWNS-
END
WARNER.
Industry
Trans-
formed.
inventions.   Inventions, indeed, were numerous enough, but they were small inventions, improvements on existing pro- cesses. Machinery was applied in all directions, adapted from one trade to another. It became increasingly complex in nature, but it was not novel in principle. The steam engine became familiar, and was used for many new purposes. The towns grew fast; mills sprang up; it was the day of the capitalist and the organiser of labour. The men who had money and business ability applied the inventions of the eighteenth century and made large fortunes. But the time called for alertness and enter- prise in business, and no manu- facturer was likely to succeed who closed his mind to the new ideas. Whatever the branch of industry the inventions of the past fifty years were being used more and more; the jenny, the water frame, the mule had be- come almost universal. Kelly had been trying to apply power to the mule, and, although he was not completely successful, he enabled one man to watch two machines. Puddling and rolling were widely used in the iron works, cylinder printing became general. The power-loom and the combing machine were coming into use, though somewhat slowly.

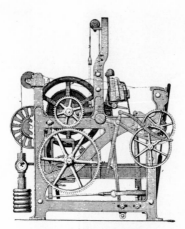

POWER LOOM (SIDE VIEW).
(See page 807.)

The power-loom was an unpopular machine with the men, but this is not the true reason of its tardy acceptance. As Cartwright made it, it embodied a magnificent idea, but was a very defective machine. It was clumsy, and it was slow, because it was necessary to stop it continually in order to dress the warp.

The credit of overcoming this difficulty must be divided between Johnson, a workman at Stockport, and William Radcliffe, his employer, who found the money for Johnson's experiments. Radcliffe was a public-spirited man, who ob- jected to seeing English cotton twist exported. He himself would not sell to a foreigner, and a great meeting of master spinners was held at Manchester in 1800 to consider what was to be done. The difficulty was to get the cotton yarn made up. From 1770 to 1788, says Radcliffe, "Cotton, cotton, cotton was become the almost universal material for employment"; the hand wheels were thrown into the lumber rooms; the new spinning machinery adopted in its stead. But even still the hand wheel lingered on. Radcliffe instances the

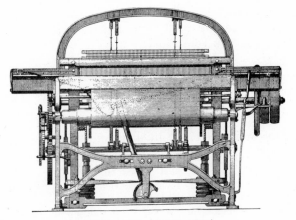

POWER LOOM (FRONT VIEW).
(*Baines, "History of the County Palatine of Lancashire," 1836.*)

Tomlinsons, four or five orphan sisters, the youngest upwards of forty; they had a complete spinnery, consisting of two pairs of cards and five hand wheels, by which they more than paid the rent of their farm. On this they kept three cows, one horse, and always ploughed a field, and were celebrated for butter and eggs. One of the sisters was still struggling on in 1822. Such establishments were, as a rule, speedily overcome by the competition of machine spinning. Weavers set up everywhere. Old barns, carthouses, outbuildings of every description, were repaired (windows being broken through the old blank walls) and fitted up for loom shops. New cottages sprang up. Every family brought home 40s., 60s., 80s., 100s., or even 120s. a week. The improvement in the standard of comfort was manifest. The men went to church in good clothes. Every cottage had a clock; plated tea services were common. This was the golden age of cotton. It was impossible to get enough weavers. "There was not a village within thirty miles of Manchester on the Cheshire and Derbyshire side in which some of us were not putting out cotton warps and taking in goods, employing all the weavers of linen and woollen goods who were declining these fabrics as the cotton trade increased." It was under this want of hands and looms that Radcliffe set about his improvements. Johnson was the son of a workman in his shop, who was "more ingenious about his loom than fond of close working." Radcliffe explained to this indolent and ingenious person what was required, and after many experiments the two completed

"a new system of warping, sizing, dressing, drying, winding on to the beam, drawing and twisting in, spinning on cops for the shuttle, inventing shuttles to receive them (all original), and to complete the whole a new loom half the size of the old ones, taking in its cloth by every motion of the lathe."

The process is described by Radcliffe thus:—

"The yarn is first wound from the cop upon bobbins by a winding machine, in which operation it is passed through water to increase its tenacity. The bobbins are then put upon the warping mill, and the web warped from them upon a beam belonging to the dressing frame. From this the warp is wound upon the weaving beam, but in its progress to it passes through a hot dressing of starch. It is then compressed between two rollers to free it from the moisture it had imbibed with the dressing, and drawn over a succession of tin cylinders heated by steam to dry it, during the whole of this last process being lightly brushed as it moves along, and fanned by rapidly revolving fanners."

Machinery and the Wool Trade. This process, which was patented, was much more elaborate than anything hitherto attempted. Further improvements in the power-loom were made by Horrocks, who had his looms made entirely of iron, smaller and more compact than the old ones. His pattern, being rapid and simple, came into general use. In 1813 there were 100 dressing machines, and 2,300 power-looms in use. Even this was only a beginning, for by 1820 there were 14,150, and in 1833 100,000.

The power-loom, although not popular, did not rouse the same violent feelings as did the combing machine. At first the power-loom was principally used for weaving cottons, whereas the combing machine affected wool. Cotton was a juvenile trade which had to fight its way against a good deal

of opposition. It had never been used to the indulgence of
Parliament. In fact, it had been treated at times with scant
favour. But the woollen industry had been the spoilt child of
English manufacture, and, as it were, had grown up cross.
In the past it had only to raise an outcry to have its wants
satisfied. It had been ancient and honourable, peculiarly profitable to the realm, the pet of centuries, fostered by kings
and statesmen, much considered by Parliament. As almost all
the great inventions in textile industry were first applied to
cottons, the woollen makers felt no immediate concern. But
the blow of Cartwright's combing machine was severe, for it
was not a machine modified from cotton to suit wool; it was
peculiarly adapted to wool, and did not affect cotton at all.
Hence the bitter antagonism to the machine. As almost all
the mechanical processes invented in cotton spinning were
capable of being applied, with a little modification, to the
woollen industries, it is somewhat remarkable to find the
application of them so tardy. By 1800, when the preparation
of cotton yarn by hand was almost extinct, the hand-spinning
of wool was still common. Hand-spinning went on side by
side with machine-spinning for some time, even in this
century. This gradual supersession of hand labour by
machinery in the wool trade, which contrasts markedly with
what happened with cotton, was due to the fact that the
woollen industry was scattered over the country instead of
being localised. When at the time of the Act of Union it
was proposed to allow the export of wool to Ireland, petitions
against any such permission came from a hundred and thirteen
firms in London, from Cornwall, Exeter, Totnes, Tiverton,
Welshpool, Frome, Bury St. Edmunds, Huddersfield, Tavistock,
Painswick, Rochdale, Huntingdon, Norwich, Somersetshire, Sud-
bury, Halifax, Gloucester, Bury, Preston, Market Harborough,
Witney, Wiveliscombe, Southwark, Bradford, Cirencester, Colne,
Burnley, Banbury, Shrewsbury, Leeds, Wakefield, Haworth,
Kendal, Addingham, Kidderminster, Keighley, Skipton, Salisbury.[1] Although many of these are from Yorkshire, yet the
variety is remarkable. Cotton was localised in Lancashire
and Cheshire, and thus knowledge of new machinery spread
fast; moreover, being a younger trade, it was more flexible

[1] Cunningham, "English Industry and Commerce," vol. ii. p. 459.

and less bound by tradition. The woollen industry was old
and comparatively rigid, and, being diffused as it was, imitation had less play.   Thus it is difficult to generalise upon the
introduction of machinery, for in some places it was received
amicably, while elsewhere it was the cause of rioting and
violence ; not only was the hostility local, but it was apparently
captious—some machines roused it, while others did not. The
dislike of the combing machine has been already mentioned.
But carding machines seem to have been fairly received, and
were in general use before the end of the century.   In 1793
Arthur Young speaks of machines for "unclothing and puffing
out wool."   In the West Riding hand-spinners took their wool
to the "slubbing engine to be scribbled, carded, and slubbed."
In 1790 mention is made of mills, "for grinding the wool
preparatory to carding, by means of which the master manufacturer has as much done for 1½d. as used to be performed
for 4½d."   The fact is, that there was plenty of employment in
spinning, even when the preparatory processes were done by
machinery.   But machinery did not stop at preparatory processes.   By 1791 machine-spinning by the jenny was performed
at Barnstaple, Ottery St. Mary, and Kendal.   The machines were
regarded with suspicion, but it was found that there was still
work for the hand-spinner.   The machine-spun yarn competed
with its rival, but did not at first oust it.   Hand-spinners
could no longer afford to be idle.   They had to work hard to
keep up, and their work was increased by the fact that the
machine-spun yarn was finer, and, consequently, spinners
being paid by the pound, more had to be done to earn the
same money.   About 1800 machine-spinning was becoming
general in the West Riding.   This was chiefly due to Benjamin
Gott, a great manufacturer, who took the lead in the application
of various new machines.   Hand-spinning was done at very low
rates.   In the Eastern counties spinners got 4d. a day, whereas in
1760 they had been earning 7d. and 8d. ; but trade was leaving
the Eastern counties and wages were naturally low there.   At
Halifax in 1791 spinners were getting 1s. 3d. ; but, as Radcliffe
shows, cotton was drawing off all the best spinners from the
woollen industries, so that it was often very difficult for
woollen manufacturers to get yarn spun at all.   The tendency
was for inferior spinners only to stick to the woollen and

worsted industries; the higher wage to be gained in cotton
spinning attracted everyone, and all the best hands had no
difficulty in getting employment. Although the pay which
the woollen employers gave their spinners was low comparatively with what was earned by cotton spinners, yet the
wool was not cheap considering its poor quality. In this way
Gott, and others following him, found it almost necessary to
adapt the spinning machinery to wool. Gott, however, was
not content with this, but went further and introduced
machinery for dressing and shearing. Both gig-mills and
shearing frames called forth bitter opposition. There seemed,
indeed, no province that machinery would not invade. The
pressure on hand work, at first slight, became severe, and
finally grew intolerable. It was under the cumulative effects
of one new machine after another that the artisans grew
desperate. From 1811 to 1815 there was a great deal of **Riots against Machinery**
disturbance in the West Riding, men being organised and
trained for the destruction of gig-mills. It only needed
twenty minutes for a body to assemble, wreck the mills, and
disperse. Foster's mill at Horbury was destroyed in this way.
A manufacturer named Horsfall was shot near his own house,
and three men were executed for the crime, as were fourteen
others for attacks on Cartwright's mill. Eight men were
hanged at Manchester for similar offences. Even this severity
did not put a stop to the spirit of violence which continued to
show itself here and there throughout the country. No
" Golden Age " in wool followed the introduction of machinery,
as had been the case in cotton. In the first place, the cotton
trade was capable of much greater expansion than the woollen.
Although the amount of cloth manufactured increased greatly,
the increase was not so great as in the case of cotton. And the
" Golden Age " of cotton was due to the fact that the new
machinery, not being at first worked by power, gave plenty of
employment—weavers, at any rate, were always busy—but when
the wool trade travelled over the same road of change and
progress, the case was altered. There was not only machinery
to reckon with ; there was power to work the machinery.
Steam power was ready to supply the place of hands ; the
power-loom supplanted the weaver, and could deal with the
great supply of yarn without calling for additional weavers.

And further, the country was feeling the pressure of a long war—a war which had, with the Berlin Decrees (p. 824), become industrial. Food was dear, commerce disorganised and fluctuating, and the lot of the working classes thus rendered doubly hard.

Stockings and Lace. Nottingham was the district where labour troubles were most severe. It was there that Arkwright's yarn had been first applied to the manufacture of stockings. He went into partnership with Jedediah Strutt, who had made a modification in the stocking-frame by which stockings could be knitted with a rib. Strutt's principle was modified and used for other purposes by Morris, Crane, and Else. Another Nottingham industry was lace, and lace machines of some sort were made by Frost, Crane, and Harvey. Dawson, in 1791, made further experiments in the same direction. In the meanwhile the distress in the district became marked. In 1783, stockingers working plain cotton or worsted hose got from 10s. to 12s. a week, but there was a steady drop in wages, and by 1800 wages were only 7s. In 1803 Joseph Heathcoat, then a young man of twenty, set about constructing a machine to make lace—a machine which would do the work of the pillow, the thread, and the multitude of pins. The task was a most difficult one, but Heathcoat persevered. He took out two patents in 1808 and 1809, and his machine, although extremely complicated, was a success. The first square yard of net made by it sold for £5; the cost of a similar piece now would not exceed 5d. Heathcoat set up a factory in Loughborough and had fifty-five frames in work.

The Luddite Riots. Just at this time, however, the labour disturbances came to a head in the Luddite riots of 1811. Frames had been extremely obnoxious for some time, and the chance freak of Ned Lud (p. 841), gave an impulse to what became very serious riots. Frames were broken throughout Nottingham, Derbyshire, and Leicestershire. The rioters worked at night, and the precaution of special constables and even soldiers was of little use. The streets of Nottingham were placarded with bills offering a reward for the delivery of the mayor dead or alive to the Luddites; the local militia were bribed, a manufacturer shot dead, arms seized, and oaths administered. Finally seven regiments had to be drafted into the district to keep order. In the midst of all this Heathcoat's frames were broken, and he in disgust left Loughborough and set up at Tiverton.

It is unnecessary to follow in detail the application of machinery to the silk and linen trades. Nor is it possible here to say anything of the later progress of the iron trade, which became more and more active as the demand for iron increased. The first iron bridge and the first iron vessel have been already noted (p. 420). The celebrated engineer, Rennie, had a great faith in the use of iron for bridges, but his plans were often too daring for the time. He proposed to construct cast-iron bridges to cross Conway Ferry and the Menai Straits, each in a single span. He began Southwark Bridge in 1815, making the arches of cast-iron, the centre arch of 240 feet span being the largest cast-iron arch that had then been erected. Rennie was also first in using iron gearing for machines. Very soon nothing but iron was used for not only the gear, but also the whole machine, and from this sprang a further development, the making of machines to make machinery. Complicated machinery is used now so commonly and with such confidence that we are apt to forget why it is so easy to use. All the machine is made to a set pattern, and if any piece breaks it can be replaced by another piece which is sure to fit because it is constructed with mechanical accuracy. This system of interchangeable parts has done more to spread the use of machinery than anything else. But in 1800 there was no general agreement over such a comparatively simple matter as the pitch of a screw. If a screw or a bolt broke, it was generally necessary to bore out a fresh thread in the nut to fit the new screw; that was simpler than trying to make a screw to fit the existing thread, and the same difficulty applied with even greater force to more complicated parts.

The task of establishing standard patterns and real accuracy of mechanical work was performed by a succession of remarkable mechanics, the first of whom was Bramah. His chief invention was the hydraulic press (1795), which first showed engineers in hydraulics how to make practical use of a number of small impulses to obtain practically unlimited pressures. His well-known locks were also of very delicate workmanship. One of Bramah's men was Henry Maudslay, whose dexterity as a workman was unrivalled. Maudslay soon left Bramah and set

[margin note: Iron.]

[margin note: Skilled Mechanics. Bramah and Maudslay.]

up for himself; his powers were the admiration of all who worked with him. "With an 18-inch file he was grand," was the opinion of one of his men. While with Bramah, Maudslay invented the leather collar of the hydraulic press—a simple device which, forced in by the pressure of the water, prevented any leakage alongside the piston-rod, and yet, when the pressure was taken off, allowed the piston-rod to move freely. He also invented (or re-invented [1]) the slide-rest, by which lathe tools could be held firmly. "Maudslay's go-cart" enabled lathe work to be done with great accuracy, and was of great use in screw-cutting. Indeed, Maudslay was thus the first to attempt to introduce uniformity in the pitch of screws—a work which was carried further by Clement and completed by Whitworth. He also made a series of forty-four intricate machines, to Marc Isambard Brunel's design, for making blocks. These were set up in Portsmouth Dockyard, and worked so well that ten men using them could do as much as 110 had done before. But Maudslay's influence in the direction of exact and systematic work was even more important than his inventions, and no better proof of this can be offered than that he trained such men as Clement, Murray, Whitworth, Roberts, Nasmyth, and Muir.

Steam-boats

Like many other good ideas, the idea of applying power in some form to drive boats was very old. In the sixteenth century Blasco de Garay had made experiments in Barcelona Harbour. Savery, Papin, and Jonathan Hulls have been already mentioned (pp. 425, 625). But at the end of the eighteenth century, with the completion of Watt's engine, the plan became practicable. It was worked at in America and in France before 1800, but in neither case was success attained. During the last years of the century, a Scotchman, Miller of Dalswinton, was experimenting with paddles turned by hand. Symington worked out for him the application of steam power, and built, in 1788, a small engine of two-horse power, which was fitted to a double boat having the paddles inside, and drove it at five miles an hour. A larger engine at a cost of £250, fitted to a vessel 90 feet long, was less successful. Miller then gave up the idea, but in 1801 Symington got another order from Lord Dundas, and

---

[1] A drawing of the slide-rest is to be found in the French Encyclopédie of 1772; but, according to Smiles, it is unlikely that Maudslay had seen it.

built the *Charlotte Dundas* on an improved principle. The boat was intended for use on the Forth and Clyde Canal, but though it worked well enough, the proprietors disliked the idea and refused to use the boat. The Duke of Bridgewater gave Symington an order for eight similar vessels, but, as he died immediately after, the order was cancelled and Symington

THE BRAMAH ORIGINAL HYDRAULIC PUMP AND PRESS.
(*Victoria and Albert Museum.*)

brought to a standstill. In the meanwhile, Fulton, who had seen the *Charlotte Dundas*, ordered a marine engine at Soho, and, taking it to America, fitted it to the *Clermont*, which ran successfully on the Hudson. In 1813 Henry Bell, of Glasgow, who had been meditating and experimenting off and on since 1786, built the *Comet* of three horse-power, which began to ply regularly on the Clyde. She was regarded with more alarm than admiration, and one skipper of a sailing craft, being over-

taken and jeered at by the crew of the *Comet*, cried out, " Get
oot of my sicht! I'm just gaun' as it pleases the breath o' the
Almichty, and I'll ne'er fash my thumb how fast ye gang wi'
your blasted deevil's reek!"

The period treated in this and the preceding two chapters is
usually called the Industrial Revolution. In 1740 industry, if

MODEL OF ONE OF MILLER'S PADDLESHIPS.

(*Victoria and Albert Museum.*)

**Features
of the
Industrial
Revolu-
tion:
1. Expan-
sion.**
not primitive, is at any rate somewhat old-world. In 1815 it is
modern. Substantially it is the industry of our own day. It is
convenient here to run over the main features of this " Industrial
Revolution," and see in what the revolution lay. In the first
place, there was an enormous increase in the volume of trade.
In 1740 there was no true cotton industry at all (that is to say,
all so-called " cottons " were made with a linen warp); the
import of cotton for fustians and candlewicks and various
purposes was 1,645,031 lbs.; in 1789 it had reached 32,576,023
lbs.; in 1815 it was close on one hundred millions. In 1775
yarn No. 80 cost 42s. the lb. to spin. In 1815 No. 100 (a finer

MODEL OF THE ORIGINAL MARINE STEAM ENGINE.
(*Victoria and Albert Museum.*)

yarn) cost 8d.   The sale price of No. 100 in 1786 was 38s. ; in
1807 it was 6s. 9d.   In the woollen industry the figures are not so
striking, but they are remarkable enough.   In 1771 the import
of wool was (in round numbers) 1,800,000 lbs.   In 1814 it was
15,700,000 lbs.   In 1742 there were milled in Yorkshire 45,000
pieces of broad width and 62,800 narrow.   In 1815 the numbers
were 330,000 pieces of broad width and 162,000 narrow ; and in
that time the average length of the piece had more than doubled.
The declared value of woollens exported in 1742 was £3,358,000 ;
in 1816 it was £9,387,000.   In 1740 there were 17,350 tons of
pig-iron made.   In 1806 there were 258,206 tons, and in 1825
581,367 tons.   In 1740 we exported hardly any iron and
imported a good deal.   In 1815 we exported 91,000 tons, while
between 1792 and 1812 the quantity imported had fallen from
51,000 tons to 24,000 tons.   The earthenware business had
grown enormously ; so also had the linen industry, and, in a less
degree, silk.   The value of exports rose from £8,197,788 in 1740
to £58,624,550 (official value) in 1815; of imports, from
£6,703,778 to £32,987,396 (p. 824).   The revenue rose from
£3,997,000 to £71,900,005 (net); the population from 6,064,000
to something over ten millions.

2. Machine Production.   But a change in volume, however great, need not justify the
term " revolution."   Revolution implies change in nature.   The
change in nature occurred also.   In 1740 industry was domestic.
Spinning and weaving were done at home in the cottages.   The
man worked the loom, working what hours he pleased : his wife
and children spent their spare time spinning yarn.   Spinning, in
fact, was a by-industry, practised as a subsidiary employment
when it was too dark to labour in the fields.   There were
practically no factories and no manufacturers in the modern
sense.   " In 1740 the Manchester merchants began to give out
warps " (*i.e.* linen) "and raw cotton to the weavers, receiving
them back in cloth and paying for the carding, rolling, spinning
and weaving."   In 1740, save for the fly shuttle (and Dyer in his
poem of " The Fleece," published in 1757, had not then heard of
it), the loom was as it had been since weaving had begun ;
spinning was equally medieval in its arts.   There were no
machines worked by power in use in the textile trades at all,
except that used by Lombe at Derby.   In 1815 how complete
is the contrast.   We have the master and the mill.   Men have

become "hands" working regular hours. Women and children
also have taken their places beside the machinery that is fast
superseding all the old methods. In 1740 the law of the land[1]
was that wages in each district should be assessed by Justices of
the Peace. In 1725 this was actually done; but so fast had the

THE ENGINE OF THE "COMET."
(*Victoria and Albert Museum.*)

practice fallen out of mind that in 1795 the Lancashire assessment of 1725 was published as a historical curiosity. It was,
further, the law that no one should be a weaver who had not
gone through his seven years' apprenticeship, and no weaver was
to have more than three apprentices unless he took a journeyman for each extra apprentice. In the course of the eighteenth
century these regulations broke down as completely as the

[1] Under the Act of Apprentices, 1563.

system of assessment.   Not that the use of apprenticeship disappeared.   On the contrary, it remained to become in some cases an engine of oppression.   But as weaving could be learnt in a year or so, the textile trades were full of "illegal" weavers, while masters employed any number of apprentices they could get, because after a year or so apprentice labour was exceedingly cheap.   As bad times came the artisans turned back to the Elizabethan legislation.   They petitioned Parliament to put in force the old clauses about wages and apprentices, and some of the Lancashire masters were not opposed to their plan.   But the majority of the House disliked the idea of what seemed to be retrograde; the assessment clauses were repealed in 1813; the apprenticeship clauses were swept away the year after, and with this all vestiges of medieval industry vanished.

3. Migration.   Industry, then, had changed in nature as well as in volume. It also changed in locality.   The migration of ironworks has been already mentioned.   But the migration in the textile trades was even more marked.   At first weavers were scattered over the country districts.   Then, as machine-spinning came into use, the spinners went into factories, and weavers gathered round them, working up the yarn which the master spinners gave out.   Then came the days of power; at first, water-power.   Mills clustered on riversides, and by degrees went further and further up the streams.   This meant the destruction of the woollen industry in the flat Eastern counties and wherever water-power could not be had.   Employment became scanty, and wages fell and fell, and, in spite of the fall, employment became even more scanty.   Those who were wise migrated to the North; those who were without enterprise stayed till the whole industry was killed by Northern competition.   The beckside masters, finding it difficult to get labour, used apprentices more and more.   They took children from the workhouses; an excellent plan for the masters, who got labour cheap, and for the parish authorities, who got rid of pauper children—excellent, in short, for everyone but the wretched apprentices set to work in low, unhealthy, ill-ventilated rooms, badly housed, either in the mill or in adjacent barns, underfed, overworked, often half-deformed by undue strain on immature frames, stifled with dust, bad air, and fumes of oil.   Apprenticeship is a hard system at any time; one safeguard is that parents are generally one party to the bond. But when Bumble took the place of the parent, then the apprentice was likely to find himself between the upper and nether millstone. It stands to the honour of a manufacturer, Sir Robert Peel, that he was the first to call in the law to the aid of the apprentice.

TRADESMEN'S TOKENS, ILLUSTRATING VARIOUS INDUSTRIES.

Under Peel's Act (1802) the hours were shortened to twelve (exclusive of meals), night-work was forbidden, some instruction was to be given, and inspectors were appointed to see that the law was kept. This was the first of the Factory Acts, and under it the evils of apprenticeship in a measure disappeared. But by 1802 steam-power was beginning to supersede water-power. Industry drew in again from the streams and settled into manufacturing towns, placed where coal was cheap and labour, especially child labour, likely to be fairly abundant.

Those who read history with a view to arraign the past

4. Results. will find much to blame in the Industrial Revolution. They will point to ill-built factories in smoky towns instead of domestic industries practised in the country. They will point to cruelly long hours, to low wages, to the new hostility between master and men. They will say that men found little or no work because the machinery put it into the hands of children, who, growing up without education or home influence, became in their turn hard and brutal. They will show that, if the workers benefited little, the inventors got almost less reward. Kay died abroad, neglected and poor; Hargreaves was driven from his home; Crompton was reduced to bitter misery; Cartwright's invention brought nothing of itself, for the Government gave him what reward he got; Cort died bankrupt; Radcliffe and Horrocks both failed; Wedgwood, Arkwright, Watt and Heathcoat alone reaped the fruits of their ingenuity. The men who profited were the masters who used the inventions that patents seemed powerless to protect. It is difficult to resist general condemnations of this kind, especially when there is enough truth in particular cases to give an air of verity to the whole. But in mitigation of judgment, it must be remembered that the trouble was aggravated by the long strain of the war, and that it was the very inventions themselves, the development of the new resources, that enabled England to bear the strain and come out victorious at the end. And it is further vain to mourn over what was inevitable. Periods of progress and change are often hard; but the temporary hardships should not be allowed to blind us to the real progress which accompanied them.

**J. E.
SYMES.
The Social
Economy.** THE Peace of Amiens naturally stimulated British trade. It removed many perils, and threw open to us the markets of those who had lately been our enemies. Our exports rose at once in value from 39·7 millions to 45·1 millions annually. They were paid for largely by the importation of foreign corn, which pushed down the price of food, to the great advantage of the English poor. Our merchants rushed to take advantage of the new conditions, and when the war was resumed in 1803 many of them were ruined. But this was the result of excessive borrowing and speculation rather than of

actual incidents of the war. There was soon a revival. Our **The War and Trade** complete naval supremacy enabled us to push our trade in all directions, and to monopolise more and more of the carrying trade of the world. Everyone seemed amazed at the progress of British commerce, and Napoleon soon saw that this was one of the most serious obstacles to his plans. He set himself to exclude British goods from Continental markets. But the scheme failed. To deprive the Continent of English

ARKWRIGHT'S MILL, CROMFORD, DERBYSHIRE.

manufactures would injure the Continent more than it would injure England.

Nevertheless, in the long run, the war could hardly fail to **The Reaction.** injure industrial progress. It diverted labour and capital alike to unproductive ends. From a patriotic point of view, it might be satisfactory that our enemies and rivals suffered more than we did. But from the point of view of commerce, the injury to foreign nations would react to our own hurt. Trade is ultimately the barter of goods for goods (or services). If foreign nations had no spare commodities to send us, they could not buy our productions.

Moreover, the renewal of the war revived the old disputes with neutrals (p. 650). As time went on the system of evasions

Disputes with Neutrals. was conducted with more and more skill and boldness. Our enemies, under the cover of neutral flags, were competing with us in all the neutral markets, and made our own commerce dangerous and expensive, in spite of our command of the sea. The neutral vessels had a great advantage over ours in their freedom from the risks of war, and the consequent need of extra insurance. At length, in 1806, we issued an Order-in-Council, declaring a blockade from the Elbe to Brest. There was in reality no effective blockade along much of this coast. Napoleon retorted by the Berlin Decrees (p. 812), in which he accused us of violating the laws of civilised nations. He declared that he would treat the whole British Isles as under blockade, and would seize all British subjects and goods under his jurisdiction. Both countries proceeded (1807) to more and more extreme measures, setting at naught the generally recognised principles of International Law, and treating neutrals who assisted the enemy by trade with extraordinary severity. A severe blow was thus struck at all trade by sea, and England suffered much. For orderly commerce there was substituted a general system of brute force and cunning. The new policy involved us in new quarrels with neutrals, and ultimately in a war with the United States (p. 713). In spite, however, of all checks, the general progress of our trade may be seen from the following figures :—

Year.	Imports in million £.			Exports.
1795 (Great Britain) [1] ...	20·1	...	...	22·2
1805 (United Kingdom)	28·5	...	...	28
1815 (do.)	32·9	...	...	51·6

Taxation. There was urgent need of such an increase in trade if the country was to bear the growing burden of taxation. After the Peace of Amiens the income-tax was repealed; but it was reimposed when hostilities were renewed. There had been much complaint of the "inquisitorial" character of the tax. It was, therefore, now decided to let the returns be split up into distinct schedules, and so avoid requiring a general declaration of total income. Incomes under £60 were to pay no income-tax, and an abatement was allowed for those between

---

[1] The figures for 1795 include trade between Great Britain and Ireland, but exclude Irish foreign trade. The difference is immaterial for our purpose.

£60 and £150. Heavy additional taxes were at the same time
(1803) laid on beer, wine, spirits, tea, sugar, and other commodities. In the following year there were more increases.
Great stress was laid on the temporary character of all these
taxes. Some were to cease with the war; others within six or
twelve months from a declaration of peace. As a matter of
fact, however, these pledges were not fulfilled. 1805 brought
fresh increases. The income-tax was raised to 6½ per cent.
Taxes were laid on auctions. The duties on bricks, glass, salt,
etc., were augmented. In 1806 the income-tax rose to 10 per
cent., and almost all the port duties were increased. The tax
on tea was now raised to 96 per cent. of its value. The years
1808 and 1809 saw further increases, as well as several fresh
taxes. Many of these proved almost unproductive. The
Chancellor of the Exchequer complained in 1811 : "There was
not an article of dress—boots, shoes, leather, breeches, etc.—not
an article in the house—locks, keys, bells, etc.—which had not
been recommended to him as objects of taxation." He pointed
out the miserable returns from the taxes on hats, gloves, and
mittens, and announced that these would be given up. Nevertheless, fresh taxes, almost as foolish as those then given up,
were imposed in 1812 and 1815. The latter included soap,
candles, glass, etc. In spite of all these efforts, there was not
a year from 1791 to 1817 in which the national revenue equalled
the expenditure. The debt steadily grew. The charge on it
grew still more rapidly. In 1790 it was 9·4 millions. In 1815
it was 30·4 millions a year.

But the growth of expenditure and debt was far less alarm- **Pauperism.**
ing than the growth of pauperism. The foundations of the old
Poor Law were laid by the Act of Elizabeth. It was modified
after the Restoration by the principles of parochial settlement, which led to the creation of close parishes, owned by
single landlords, who evicted the poor to prevent their becoming chargeable to the parish. In 1782 what is known as
Gilbert's Act (p 458) attempted to remedy this by grouping
parishes for purposes of poor relief. It further enacted that
able-bodied paupers were not to be sent to the workhouse.
They were to receive what we now call out-door relief. This
pernicious system received a great extension a few years later.
The magistrates sitting at Speenhamland, near Newbury, in

The Speen-hamland Plan. Berkshire, adopted the principle of granting allowances calculated as follows :—With wheat at a given price, they settled what was the minimum on which a man with a wife and one child could subsist, and how much each additional child would cost. Whenever the family earnings fell below the estimated minimum, the deficiency was to be made up from the rates. Other places soon followed the Berkshire example, and the "Allowance" system gradually spread over the whole country. Its results were what might have been anticipated. The path to pauperism was made so easy and agreeable that a large proportion of the labouring classes drifted along it. No unpleasant questions were asked, and it was natural that men should claim their share as a right. The system further acted as a direct encouragement to improvident marriage and reckless breeding of legitimate and illegitimate children. Finally it transferred a large part of what should have been paid as wages from the employers to other persons, and it lent itself to all sorts of administrative abuses. The poor rates naturally rose rapidly. In the three years 1848–50 the annual charge for pauperism had averaged less than £690,000. In the three years from 1783 to 1785 it averaged nearly two millions. In 1812 it had reached the gigantic figure of £6,656,105. The increase of population was also stimulated. The census of 1801 showed an increase of 11 per cent.; 1811 showed a further increase of 14 per cent.; 1821 a further increase of 21 per cent., being the largest increase for any decennium for which we have figures.

Currency and Crises. The state of the currency and of the par of exchange with foreign countries aggravated the troubles and difficulties of the later years of the war. We have seen that since 1797 England had had an inconvertible currency (p. 652). This tended to produce a rise in prices, an unfavourable foreign exchange, and a premium on gold. The extent of the evil would depend largely on the extent of the issues of paper, and amid the rapid fluctuations in prices and credit it was almost impossible to avoid over-issues. In 1811 the famous Report of the Bullion Committee of the House of Commons appeared, proving conclusively that there had been serious over-issues of bank-notes consequent on the restriction of cash payments. The Committee, therefore, urged that within the

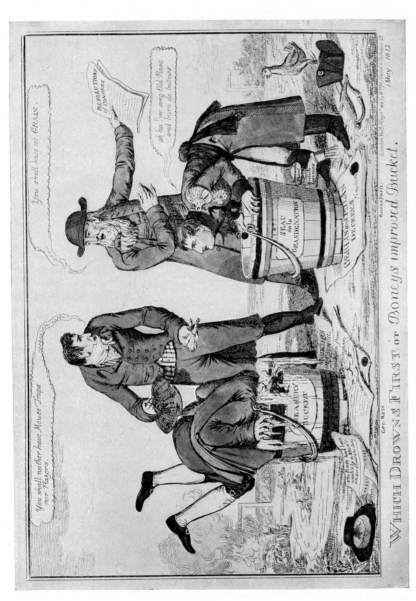

SATIRE ON THE BERLIN DECREES.

(From a satirical print of 1812.)

next two years cash payments should be resumed. But, after four nights' debate, the House not only rejected this proposal, but actually committed itself to the absurd doctrine that our paper money was not depreciated, though, as a matter of fact, the price of gold in terms of bank-notes had risen from £3 17s. 10½d. per oz. in 1800 to £4 10s. in 1810—a depreciation of over 13 per cent.

In the years following 1808 our foreign trade had become a sort of gambling. No one could guess what Napoleon's next step would be, nor how it would affect prices. When he occupied Spain the price of Spanish wool was increased

SILVER DOLLAR OF 1804, USED AS TOKEN MONEY.

by 250 per cent. Italian silk, American tobacco, and cotton, in fact, most kinds of imports, fluctuated similarly through the incidents or apprehensions of war. Thus, when the Spanish colonies in South America became practically independent, vast markets were suddenly thrown open to our traders. A speculative frenzy followed. The Bank of England's loans on discount rushed up to over fifteen millions in 1809, and over twenty millions in 1810, and in many cases the credit was given to persons who could offer no substantial security. Country banks multiplied, and lent still more freely. The number of such banks had been 270 in 1797. In 1810 it was 721, and the loans on discount of these banks were estimated at 30 millions. Then came the crash, and the contraction both of credit and of trade. Our imports in 1810 were valued at 39 millions. In 1811 they had fallen to 26 millions. Our exports similarly fell in a year from 48 to 32 millions. There were many bankruptcies, and the Government had to intervene, and authorise the Chancellor of the Exchequer to issue six millions in Exchequer Bills. But before the full effects of the crash had been felt there was a brisk revival. Napoleon had declared war on Russia, and soon the Russian and North German ports were thrown open to our trade.

"EXETER CHANGE" TOKEN.

Once more there were fortunes made, immense speculation and overtrading. Our exports jumped up to 41 millions in 1812, and the prices of the kind of goods that were being exported rose enormously in the home markets. On the other hand, the splendid harvest pushed down the price of wheat from 155s. per quarter in August, 1812, to 68s. in July, 1813. Then came the crash of 1814, and

LONDON TOKEN.

for three years there was a series of failures. Eighty-nine bankers were reduced to bankruptcy; and ruin and misery spread in all directions.

The doctrines of Adam Smith and Malthus continued to exercise a great influence on the more intelligent and thoughtful classes. But now the third of the great founders

LONDON TOKEN.

of the English school of Political Economy had come into the field. Ricardo was a Jew by blood, and had from his fifteenth

year been mixed up with Stock Exchange transactions. Born
in 1772, he was just entering manhood when the French
revolutionary Government made its audacious experiments in
inconvertible paper money.   Then followed the series of
financial crises from 1793 to 1814, the restriction of cash payments in England, the amazing fluctuations in the foreign
exchanges, the rise and fall, and rise again of the premium
cn gold, the fortunes made and lost on the Stock Exchange.
The acute intellect of Ricardo analysed all these movements

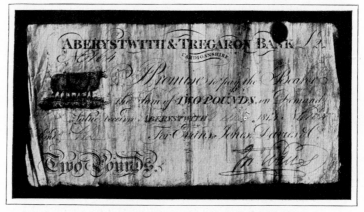

WELSH BANKNOTE OF 1814.
(The University College of Wales, Aberystwith.)

He made a fortune, but he was more interested in intellectual
than in financial speculation, and he had the advantage of being
able to test his theories, as he built them up, by a series of
observations.   For the whole world seemed to be turned into
a crucible for economic experiments.   The result was that he
obtained such a grasp of the principles that underlie many
questions of currency, foreign trade, and exchanges as no
previous writer had even approximately reached.   The masterly
report of the Bullion Committee was founded on Ricardo's
teaching, and especially on his pamphlet, "The High Price of
Bullion a Proof of the Depreciation of Bank Notes" (1809),
and his defence of that Report in 1811 was the soundest contribution made to the great controversy which grew out of its
publication.   Then he turned to other branches of economics,

in which he was equally original, but less successful. He had lived through the industrial revolution, and he now applied to the analysis of the new system of agriculture, manufacture, and commerce the same great powers which he had applied to the banking and Stock Exchange questions. But he did not sufficiently realise that men and women are

DAVID RICARDO, M.P.
(After Thomas Philips, R.A.)

not mere instruments of exchange. His theories of value, of wages, and of rent were brilliant deductions from the assumption of absolutely free competition, of a universal, enlightened, and unqualified desire to buy in the cheapest and sell in the dearest market. But the attempt to treat these theories as representing, or even approximating, to the facts of industrial life, led many later writers into absurdities and exaggerations, and greatly delayed the progress of sound economic theory. Individualists and Socialists were alike led astray.

Economic Summary.   In attempting to summarise the industrial history of England during the period dealt with in this chapter we are met by exceptional difficulties. The war (with all its variations of alliances and policies, of opened and closed markets), the rapid and constant changes of industrial processes in agriculture, manufacture, and commerce, the disturbing influences of the old Poor-law and the new paper currency, combine to conceal the general tendencies under temporary fluctuations. Some facts, however, stand out very conspicuously.

Population.   The first of these is the very rapid progress of population. The census of 1801 showed that Great Britain had then a population of 9·8 millions. In 1821 this had risen to 14·3 millions. There had been nothing like this increase in all our earlier history. In fact, during the five hundred years from 1300 to 1800 the total increase was far less than (probably not one-half of) the increase in these twenty years (1801–21). Equally remarkable was the change in the distribution of the population. In the same twenty years, while the gross population rose by about thirty per cent., London increased by about forty per cent. But if we take Liverpool, Manchester (with Salford), Glasgow, and Bradford we find an increase of nearly seventy-five per cent. This illustrates the fact that the population was growing far more rapidly in the towns than in the country districts, and that of the towns it was the manufacturing places of the North and the ports of the North-West which were increasing most rapidly. The growth of the big towns was not more remarkable than that of manufacturing and mining villages, of a character hitherto unknown in England.

Wealth.   The increase in the national wealth was probably somewhat less rapid than that in the population. The value of taxable income from lands, houses, etc., was estimated at forty-five million pounds in 1798, and at sixty millions in 1815. Now, considering that the war, the growth of population, and the improvements in manufacture and carriage all tended to augment rents, it seems not probable that other branches of the national income had increased quite so rapidly; and the very defective statistics and other evidence that are available seem to point to the same conclusion. Such increase as there was, was also far more heavily burdened. We have already seen how rapidly the charges for the relief of pauperism and for the interest on the National Debt were growing (p. 825). On the other side we have to put the increase of foreign trade (p. 824). The tonnage of shipping belonging to Great Britain and Ireland had risen from 1,453,000 tons in 1793 to 1,985,000 tons in 1803, and to 2,349,000 tons in 1813. This gives an increase of over sixty-two per cent. for twenty years, *i.e.* considerably more than the increase in the population.

Turning next to prices, we have already noticed the **Prices.** extraordinary fluctuations during the war period. In wheat, for instance, we find the average price (per imperial quarter) was £3 4s. in the years 1793 to 1799. It then rose to £5 16s. 8d. in the years 1800 and 1801. It fell to £3 13s. 8d. on an average in the years 1802 to 1808. It rose again to £5 7s. in the years 1809 to 1813, and fell to £3 12s. 9d. in the years 1814 to 1816. As for other prices, the fluctuations in forty typical commodities were combined by Jevons with the following results :—Taking 100 to represent their joint prices in 1783, they were at 98 in 1793, at 121 in 1796, down to 110 in 1797, up to 142 in 1800 ; then, after a series of very rapid fluctuations, they reached a maximum of 151 in 1809, and afterwards fell with moderate steadiness till 1816, when they stood at about 92.[1] It will, therefore, be seen that the statement that war raised prices has to be cautiously interpreted. Excluding wheat, it would be more accurate to say that, while the general level of prices was somewhat higher during the war than in the preceding years, there were extraordinary fluctuations of upward and downward tendencies, and that while the increase never exceeded fifty per cent. it was sometimes, as in 1797, not more than ten per cent.

It is impossible to get any satisfactory statistics of wages **Wages.** during this period. But it is probable that on the whole wages rose about as much as the average prices of all commodities, excepting wheat. This was, of course, a most important exception, and accounts for the intense distress at times when the harvest had been poor. It has also to be remembered that the very frequent financial panics were

---

[1] For details, *see* the " Journal of the Statistical Society," xxviii. 314.

followed by periods when employment was scarce. Many skilled labourers were displaced, or reduced to the level of the unskilled, by the constant inventions and the fresh applications of machinery and steam power. But, in the more prosperous years of the war, the mass of the people were probably somewhat better off than in the preceding years of peace.

MARY BATESON.
The State of Society.
The Peace.

THE enthusiasm for the peace was unbounded, for it meant provisions at normal prices. Every window in London was illuminated with a wooden triangle stuck with tallow candles or with coloured oil lamps on a black board arranged to spell a large " Peace." Boulton and Watt's premises at Birmingham were illuminated with gas (p. 631). The mail coaches started from the Post Office dressed with laurels and carrying large labels, " Peace with France." The rumour that peace was signed ran ahead of them, and crowds lined the London roads awaiting the arrival of the coach to have the news confirmed. There was a day of general thanksgiving and a grand royal procession through London. Only one disagreeable incident occurred. The French Minister's illumination was "G. R.," and "Concord." The crown over the G. R. was unfortunately missing, and the crowd, reading "Conquered" for "Concord," began a riot which was only stopped by the hasty addition of the crown and the substitution of "Amity" for the obnoxious word.[1]

The Last of Jacobin Sedition.

The old dread of an English revolution was not quite over, and the discovery of Colonel Despard's plot seemed to convince the anxious that their fears were well founded. He had established a Society for the Extension of Liberty and had plotted the death of the king and the seizure of public buildings. Lord Nelson was called as a witness to Despard's loyalty, but he was hanged with six accomplices out of forty-six who had been captured. Despard's last words were that the Ministers hanged him because he was a friend of liberty, and some of the crowd cheered.[2] But this was the last plot of the kind. It soon became evident that whatever form of republicanism had taken root in England, it was not French republicanism.

---

[1] *The Times*, April 29, 1802 ; reproduced April 29, 1902.
[2] *Ibid.*, February 21, 1803 ; reproduced on the corresponding day of 1903.

As soon as peace was declared the English, so long cut off **Foreign Travel** from foreign travel, crowded to Paris to see the art treasures which Napoleon had brought from Italy. So complete had been their isolation from Continental intercourse during the first period of the war that many writers express the sensation of complete estrangement which overcame them when they again visited France. Except through the refugees who had poured over at the time of the revolution, the English at

COLONEL DESPARD.
(*From an etching by Barlow*, 1803.)

home had had no opportunity for social intercourse with foreigners. Some, indeed, had formed close ties of friendship with the fugitives, some had married fugitives and were now anxious to visit the country of their adoption. In 1792 there were said to be 40,000 French emigrants in England, many of them distinguished members of the best French society. It was at Juniper Hall in Surrey that Fanny Burney met Madame de Staël, de Talleyrand, de Narbonne, and her future husband, General d'Arblay. General and Madame d'Arblay were among the first to leave.

But the peace had lasted only a year when war was again **War Renewed.** declared (p. 704), and this time there was no peace party to be found in England. A Patriotic Fund was started and £12,000 was subscribed at once. The merchants, underwriters, and subscribers at Lloyd's made a general subscription for the encouragement and relief of those who engaged in the defence of their country. Four hundred thousand men enrolled as volunteers, providing their own uniforms and receiving no pay. The English popular attitude towards France and towards the Government's war policy had undergone a marked change. In the first period of the war it was generally felt that England was fighting against an "armed doctrine," now she was fighting for her own existence. To the common people doctrine, whether republican or constitutional, was neither here nor there ; war for philosophical principles could not excite their enthusiasm when their own great want was bread. But when the war was against Napoleon, against a would-be invader, famine was made light of and not a voice was raised for peace. The wild alarm which had seized the best-informed, the upper and middle classes, lest revolutionary doctrine should take hold in England, was changed to an alarm which affected all classes, but was most strongly felt among the poorest and least well informed.

Threat to Invade England. In October, 1804, Napoleon was preparing to invade England, and huge patriotic handbills called upon all Englishmen to arm in defence of their country. In squibs and broadsides against Bonaparte everything was said that could excite popular feeling against him. He was a Mahometan who had poisoned his sick at Jaffa, he had incited his hell-hounds to execute his vengeance on England by promising to permit anything. " He promises to enrich his soldiers with our property, to glut their lust with our wives and daughters." The clergy preached on defence, the poets wrote patriotic ballads. Every county had meetings to organise defence. There were general fast-days solemnly kept, and used by the volunteers for drill. Every male housekeeper rated at £8 a year or over was to be sworn in as a constable, unless he were already a volunteer or physically disqualified. The job-masters offered their horses, Pickford's and other large firms offered their waggons for transport. Pitt, as Lord Warden, headed 3,000 volunteers and intended to take the field. Wilberforce writes, "his spirit will lead him to be foremost in the battle." On October 26th, 1803, George III. reviewed the Volunteer Corps of London, numbering 12,400

TO PARIS BY DILIGENCE, BY THOMAS ROWLANDSON.

men; seven of his sons rode on horseback at his side. Lord
Eldon calls it " the finest sight I ever beheld." The old king
meant to head the army, and arranged that the queen and
princesses should take refuge with the Bishop of Worcester;
a servant and furniture were to be sent with them that their
arrival might not inconvenience the bishop. The treasure
from the bank was to be removed to Worcester Cathedral in
thirty waggons escorted by volunteers, the artillery and stores
from Woolwich were to be moved to the Midlands by the Grand
Junction Canal. Elaborate arrangements were made for signal-
ling the approach of the enemy by beacons. The press was
to publish no accounts of the king's troops or of the enemy
except by authority of the Secretary of State, who twice a day
was to give an official report. The spy-craze raged; tourist
excursions were impossible. Arms and transports were very
deficient, and great dissatisfaction was felt with all Government
arrangements, but the prevailing feeling of intense discouragement and alarm made every individual certain that the fate
of the country depended on his personal exertions. Party
suspicions were almost forgotten, and Pittites were willing to
let Foxites arrange the removal of women and children to
places of safety provided that the more responsible duties of
actual defence were left in their own hands.

Arrest of British Subjects Abroad. At the end of 1805 the camp at Boulogne was broken up
and the scare was over. But the feeling of bitterness remained,
and was increased when, in 1806, by the Berlin decrees, all
British subjects wherever found were declared prisoners of
war. As an act of retaliation against the English seizure of
prizes before the open declaration of war, Napoleon had
placed under arrest all English travellers and residents in
France, between the ages of eighteen and sixty. This made
about 11,000 persons captive, and about 1,300 were taken in
Holland. Many were the strange domestic tragedies which
this proceeding caused, and the story of the lives of English
prisoners at Doullens, near Amiens, Lille and Valenciennes
has not yet been fully told. In England there were 25,000
French prisoners, kept chiefly at Plymouth, Portsmouth,
Norman Cross near Peterborough, Liverpool, and Chatham.
They were half starved and miserably provided for, and many
traditions have been handed down of their skill in making

THE ACCOMMODATION BARGE ON THE PADDINGTON CANAL.

(From an aquatint of 1801.)

42

baskets and toys out of odds and ends, by the sale of which they hoped to make a livelihood. They were set to no regular labour, and were allowed out till dark under parole, provided they did not wander more than a mile from the town where they were domiciled. For more than ten years it was only through these prisoners that French and English society came in contact.

No further doubts were felt as to the duty of the Govern-

MODEL MADE BY A FRENCH PRISONER OF WAR.
(Royal United Service Institution.)

ment to continue the war, but the popular sympathy with the war policy was not adequate to silence all political and trade agitations. The last were by far the most formidable. The trade unionists desired to see the Statute of Apprenticeship, 5 Eliz. c. 4 (Vol. III., p. 495), modernised, and extended to the new industries which had arisen since it was enacted, and thus escaped its rules. The masters opposed the Acts and sought their repeal, for the rule of seven years' apprenticeship prevented them from getting cheap mill hands to supply sudden demands, and made it possible for the employed to organise and bring strong pressure to bear on the employer. In

Trade Agitation.

obedience to the masters' demands the Government began
by suspending the Elizabethan statute, at first for one year,
then annually; in 1810 the code was repealed for the woollen
trade, and in 1814 for all trades.   The cloth-workers and
weavers, in defiance of the Acts of 1799 and 1800 against
combinations, formed "institutions" and spent between ten
and twelve thousand pounds on petitions against the suspension.   The manufacturers on their part formed similarly
illegal combinations against the "institutions."   The Act
against combinations was not very stringently enforced
against the unions of either masters or men, partly owing
to the inefficiency of the police and partly owing to the
ignorance on the part of the Government of the issues which
were at stake.

In 1805 an extensive association was formed by the
framework knitters of Nottinghamshire, Leicestershire, and
Derby to prosecute men who were following the business
without a legal apprenticeship.   They hoped to use their
powers as a chartered company to this end, but they lost
their case, and it was decided that in their right to choose
wardens, etc., and to regulate the internal government of
the company, the power to enforce apprenticeship was not
included.

The cotton trade and the calico printers were not affected
by the suspension of the statutes, for they had never come
under their influence, but the demands of the workers in
these trades were similar in character.   They desired apprenticeship rules to limit the number of workers, and a minimum
legal wage.   During the eighteenth century their wages had
been fixed approximately by the "statement list of prices," but
the practice of publishing these lists had been allowed to
lapse, and the workers now sought to recover them.   The silk
weavers had worked without disturbance since the Spitalfields
Acts had ordered the publication of price lists.

In 1802 Sheridan's Bill, framed on the report of a committee of the House of Commons, which advocated measures of
relief for calico printers, did not get a second reading, and the
calico printers' union revived.

As the unions wanted legislation they did not at first
attempt to gain their ends by strikes.   But it gradually

became clear that Parliament had accepted the theory then held
by the political economists that labour ought to obey the law of
supply and demand like other commodities. Then the unions
attempted to raise wages by means of strikes. A serious strike
was organised among the cotton-spinners of Lancashire in 1808.
In that year a Bill had been brought in proposing that a
minimum rate of wages should be fixed to relieve the extreme
sufferings of the operators. The masters declared that they
were suffering more than the men through the fluctuations
of the cotton trade during the war; the Bill was withdrawn,
and the "minimum rate" was declared impracticable and
false in principle. The spinners struck work, and 60,000
looms stopped. The men demanded a rise of 33⅓ per cent., the
masters offered a rise of 20 per cent. The men refused the offer.
At Rochdale the weavers forced the gaol and released the
prisoners, but the strike was futile, probably owing to insufficient
organisation.

The war went on, wages went on falling and prices rising.
The poor weavers of Hamilton, in Lanarkshire, refusing to eat
the bread of charity, would not take the money raised to relieve
their distress without earning it, and they set themselves to earn
it by making a footpath from Hamilton to Bothwell Bridge.
"They little knew," says Miss Martineau, "how they had thus
beautified that footpath to many that should come after them."

In 1811 many Nottingham hosiers had to dismiss workmen, **The**
for the newly invented frames worked so rapidly that the market **Luddites.**
was overstocked. The Luddite Riots began (p. 812). When
frames were broken it was said Ned Lud had been there.
Sutton, on the authority of Blackner, a leading Nottingham
democrat likely to possess authentic information, says that Ned
Ludlam was an ignorant youth, who, when ordered by his father,
a framework knitter, to square his needles, took a hammer and
beat them into a heap. Another version is that Ned Lud was
an imbecile boy who broke two stocking frames in a passion.
The Luddites not only smashed frames but attacked the millers
and corn dealers in their desire for bread. They were joined by
the lace makers, who smashed the new machines for making
lace. An Act of Parliament made it a capital offence to destroy
any kind of machinery used in manufactures, and in 1812
seventeen men were hanged together in York. By that time

624 stocking frames had been broken. The sympathy of the populace in the excited districts made it difficult to capture offenders. The spirit spread to the woollen trades and to the cotton trades. Mills were burned down; the militia depôts were stormed and the arms used by the mob. Then murders followed; churches and houses were stripped of lead to make bullets. The outrages recurred night after night; all owners of machinery lived in a state of siege.

In 1812, 40,000 cotton weavers went on strike, and the whole strike committee was arrested for the crime of combination. In 1813 there was a cessation of violent rioting, partly owing to a fall in prices; in 1814 it began again owing to the depression of trade, due to the disturbed state of credit. Lord Sidmouth, as Home Secretary, took in hand the suppression of riots, and from this time on he knew no peace.

Sir Francis
Burdett.

There were other popular stirs in the period, but as compared with the industrial agitation they appear somewhat frivolous. The democratic party gained in zeal if not in discretion when Cobbett began to fight in their cause in 1804. He was able to sow his ideas far and wide, and the seeds did not fall on stony ground. As yet, however, the reforming movements had made but little way. The most important agitation of the period was the ludicrous scene in which Sir Francis Burdett played a leading part (1810). The agitation began when it was proposed to close the Strangers' Gallery during the discussion of the Walcheren Expedition. The proposal was popularly considered an infringement of the liberty of the press. A debating society, called the British Forum, printed notices of a meeting in which a vote of censure on the Government was to be moved. The House of Commons summoned the printer and ordered his committal to Newgate for breach of parliamentary privilege. Sir F. Burdett questioned the proceeding in Parliament, but got only thirteen votes. He then wrote a letter to his constituents "denying the right of the House of Commons to imprison the people of England." Cobbett printed the letter in his *Political Register*. The House pronounced the letter libellous, declared the writer guilty of a breach of privilege, and the Speaker ordered the Sergeant-at-Arms to execute a warrant for Burdett's committal to the Tower. When the time came for the Sergeant to execute the warrant he found Burdett's house in Piccadilly

barricaded and guarded by the mob. The Sergeant repeatedly
knocked at the door and got no answer. The Speaker sought
legal opinions on the validity of his warrant before proceeding
to break doors open. Lord Eldon could give no advice. For
two days and nights the mob kept the streets, dispersing only
for a short time when the Riot Act was read. Troops were
summoned from all parts, and at length the Sergeant, under the
protection of the Lifeguards, forced the kitchen door in the area
and found Sir Francis appropriately reading Magna Charta to
his little boy. He was removed to the Tower, and the soldiers
were ordered to charge the mob and fire. The prisoner brought
actions against the Speaker and Sergeant, and after some
discussion it was decided that their position did not prevent
them from pleading in the Law Courts. There their action was
upheld, and Burdett was released on the prorogation of Parliament. To the indignation of the assembled crowd he did not
appear for the ovation which had been carefully prepared for
him, but left the Tower quietly by water. This act was ascribed
to cowardice, not modesty, and his popularity greatly diminished.
But though the affair ended in apparent fiasco, the House was
from that time less prompt to push its claim to repress free
public speech.

The power of the London mob to gain even frivolous ends The O. P. Riots.
was seen at the time of the O. P. Riots of 1809, when after
months of disturbance the old prices were restored at the new
Covent Garden Theatre. A trial was brought about by Mr.
Clifford, a barrister, who was charged with inciting to riot
because he appeared at the theatre with the letters O. P. in his
hat. In defiance of the judge's charge the jury acquitted him.
Kemble gave way in the face of this hostile verdict, and the
Londoners won.

Though there were many reasons why the period could not Public Works.
fail to be one of gloom, signs were not wanting that the energies
and resources of the country were nowise exhausted. Large
public works were made possible by the great development of
engineering. The lost art of road-making was recovered;
knowledge and invention made it possible to build aqueducts,
bridges, lighthouses, docks, and sea-walls, where former generations had found them impossible.

Thomas Telford of Eskdale, a stone-mason's apprentice,

Roads

whose father was a shepherd, had been steadily rising into fame. He had made the Ellesmere Canal to join the Mersey, Dee, and Severn, had built aqueducts, and used iron bridges as County Surveyor for Salop, and in 1802 he was instructed to begin a vast scheme of Scotch roads. In eighteen years he had opened 920 miles of good road with 1,200 bridges. Telford's roads required much labour and care in the making; the bottom course of freestone was set by hand and the spaces packed by hand, a drain was set across at every hundred yards, and on this course was set a top course of small broken whinstones, and a binding of one inch of gravel. Hitherto roads had been made as a rule of round flints and gravel, which the heavy waggons with their wide wheels were expected gradually to consolidate. But they failed to do this, and disturbed the loose substance of the road, making deep ruts. In 1815 Macadam ordered, instead of unbroken flints, angular granite fragments, and by this means and by careful attention during the process of consolidation he easily secured a good surface (p. 847).

London.

The eighteenth century had supplied London with two new bridges—Westminster, 1750, and Blackfriars, 1769. In 1810 Rennie began the Strand Bridge, now Waterloo Bridge, in 1815 he began Southwark Bridge. The Thames was ceasing to be the citizen's "silent way." Sir Francis Burdett elected to do an unusual thing when he left the Tower by water. The main streets were greatly improved for foot passengers; there were raised pavements along which streamed a continual line of passengers, those going and those coming keeping to the right. The roads were crossed by raised causeways of picked stones, very convenient for passengers, but bad for carriages. The side-streets paved with "kidney-stones" were unpleasant for those driving and walking. In 1810 gas-lighting (p. 834) first became general in the streets.

Manners.

Simond, a French American, visiting England in 1810–11, records that the pastrycook shops at the middle of the day are "full of decent persons of both sexes, but mostly men, taking a slight repast of buns, tarts, etc., and a glass of whey, the whole meal costing 6d. or 8d." Nobody is stirring in the streets, he says, before ten. The fashionable world gives signs of life at three or four, from six to eight dinner is going forward. The rout was already called an "At Home"; nobody sits, there is

no conversation, no cards, no music, only elbowing, turning and
winding from room to room, then escape to the hall door, and
the same proceeding at the next " At Home." More time is
spent waiting in the queue of carriages and on the threshold
waiting for the carriage than inside the house. Lectures at the
Royal Institution were the fashion; half the audience consisted

Photo: A. Brown & Son, Lanark.

CARTLAND CRAGS BRIDGE, LANARKSHIRE.

of ladies " timidly taking notes." Concerning a society so like
our own it would be out of place to moralise. Only in manners
at table it would appear that some slight change has taken place.
A dinner for ten or twelve persons consisted of two courses
and dessert. Mr. Simond's first course was soup, fish, roast and
boiled meat, and vegetables, spinach and bacon, all served together; the second course was a ragout, game, celery, macaroni,
cream and pastry. Dessert was served separately. This
menu was somewhat old-fashioned, dishes " were beginning
to be served hot and hot." The wines were Madeira, sherry,
claret, Burgundy, and champagne, small beer or sparkling ale

"in high-shaped glasses like champagne glasses." "Water acidulated by the carbonic acid gas" was being used, and a few drank wine and water mixed. One custom Simond found "not consistent with the delicacy the English pride themselves upon." Bowls of coloured glass are placed before each person at the end of dinner, and all, women as well as men, stoop over it, sucking up some of the water, rinsing the mouth, and swilling it out again. Smollett, sixty years before, says of the French, "they are utter strangers to what we call common decency," *but* each has his own cup, and all do not drink from one tankard, nor can any custom be more beastly than that of using "water-glasses." With the water-glass, the tankard and the two-pronged fork were still in general use in England.

JAMES COLVILLE. Scotland. Trade. GLASGOW was the pioneer in the oversea trade, but not till 1718 had she a ship crossing the Atlantic that was owned in the city. Her West Indian trade on a large scale dates from 1732, when merchants arranged to supply the planters' wants and sell their crops on commission. This was the foundation of the tobacco trade which, till the American war drove it into new channels, brought more than half the total import of the weed to Glasgow. By this time the city had correspondents in every port from Leghorn to Bremen. The outgoing cargoes were disposed of by youthful agents among the planters, thus fostering home industries, and diffusing Scottish intelligence and energy throughout the colonies. The effect on the prosperity of the city was very great. "Provost Cochrane," says Smollett in "Humphrey Clinker," "had ships on every sea." Glassford, during the Seven Years' War, owned twenty-five ships and traded for half a million. Their fortunes rivalled those of the manufacturers, one of whom died in 1819 worth £300,000, all made in the muslin trade. Brave efforts were made to find new business after the collapse of tobacco. In 1787 the first commission house was opened in London for Glasgow stuffs, and soon after a system of public sales there was inaugurated. Before this even Dundee sold her ducks through London factors, but the merchants had to lie two years out of their money. The Clyde, a fine salmon stream, but subject to violent floods and uncontrollable tides, could not long accommodate the growing

trade. Removing their medieval harbour from Dumbarton, the Naviga-
citizens converted the poor village of Newark on the opposite tion.
shore into the busy Port Glasgow, and here constructed one of
the earliest graving docks. But the citizens were still far from
their true harbour of the Broomielaw. Smeaton reported on the
river in 1755, about which time the whole Clyde shipping
numbered only sixty-seven vessels, but nothing was done till
Golbourn, of Chester, set to work. By jetties to aid the scour
of the stream and rude dredging, he got ships drawing six and
a half feet up to the city in 1775. To this only three feet were
added by 1816. In 1805 a ship of 150 tons discharged a cargo
from Lisbon in the heart of the city. Along with the deepening
of the river the national undertaking of the Forth and Clyde
Canal was begun in 1768 (p. 438), and completed from sea to
sea in 1790. The success of this and the contemporary English
schemes created quite a rage for canal projects, few of which
were ever heard of again. A far more notable step was the rise
of steam navigation (p. 817). The pioneers in it were Scotsmen
or of Scottish extraction. Fulton's father had emigrated from his
native Dumfriesshire. Their success developed a new spirit of
enterprise in navigation, and in 1816, when the East India trade
was thrown open, one of the first ships to engage in it was a
Glasgow venture. The voyage from Glasgow to London was
first accomplished by steamer in 1815.

Lord Cockburn, who had travelled *circuitously* for forty Roads.
years, tells us in his "Circuit Journeys" that "those born to
the railway, and even the stage, can scarce understand how we of
the previous age got along." Macadam, an Ayrshire road-maker
(b. 1756), has given his name to progress in travel as notable in
its way as that of George Stephenson (p. 844). He revolutionised
the old process of keeping up the bridle-tracks, made passable for
wheels by statute labour, that was almost as much hated and
neglected as the French *corvée*. Going south in 1758 Carlyle of
Inveresk found on the most frequented route no trace of a chaise
till he reached Durham, where turnpikes were just beginning.
For a portion of this route in East Lothian the first Toll Act was
obtained (1763). Progress north of Edinburgh had got so far by
1773 that Samuel Johnson found it pleasant to get along through
Fife comfortably without tolls. There had long been relays or
posts between the capitals, but nowhere else north of Edinburgh

Stages.   till 1776. In 1758 a regular four-horse coach from Glasgow to Edinburgh was started, and contrived to do the distance in the short period of twelve hours. After 1799 the time was reduced by one half. Meanwhile, on the western trunk line, road-making was going on. On the new road up Nithsdale, Burns could see, on his exciseman rounds, toll bars set up (1791), Plummer's coach (1788) doing the distance from Glasgow to London in sixty-five hours, and the Carlisle waggon leaving Dumfries weekly, drawn by six horses. The Forth was as yet crossed at

THE BROOMIELAW, GLASGOW, IN 1802.
(*R. Stuart, "Views and Notices of Glasgow in Former Times,"* 1848.)

three main points by the old ferries. Smeaton's fine bridge over the Tay at Perth superseded boats in 1771. Forsyth, an Elgin merchant, tells his experience in the Fly coach (1791). Through Forfar the four horses did thirteen miles in three and a half hours. Out of York he had done 150 miles in twenty-four hours, but north of Edinburgh only eighty-four in nineteen hours. Stage-coaches were tried between Perth and Inverness in 1806, but it was not till 1811 that regular mail-coaches were established between Aberdeen and Inverness. Post-runners followed the coast where there were no bridges over the large streams. The Spey had no bridge at Fochabers till 1801. North of the Dornoch Firth the country was almost in a state of nature

till the Marquis of Stafford began improving the Sutherland
estates (1807). Government gave some aid, but localities made
noble efforts, carrying main roads (1814) to Tongue and Wick
At the death of the Marquis he had made 450 miles of road
and 134 bridges over ten feet long. His worthy rival, Lord
Breadalbane, opened up the Central Highlands. Pennant, the
traveller, found (1770) his men busy road-making on Loch
Tayside and on by Tyndrum. Throughout the West Highlands,
however, travel for any distance had for long to be carried on by
sea, a state of matters still largely a necessity from the nature of
much of the country.

THE first meeting of the United Parliament of Great Britain and
Ireland was held in January, 1801, and the Irish Catholics
naturally looked for the fulfilment of the promise of Emancipation. But the matter was not so much as referred to in the
Speech from the Throne; which, it is understood, was due to
the king's obstinacy. Pitt resigned; a minister hostile to the
measure succeeded; and Emancipation apparently receded for
ever. *(margin: P. W. JOYCE. Ireland.)*

Meantime the United Irishmen, who now held their meetings
on the Continent, having been led to hope for help from
Napoleon, commissioned Robert Emmett, an ardent noble-minded
young man of twenty-four, to carry out their plans for a new
rebellion. He spent the winter of 1802 in Dublin making
arrangements and manufacturing pikes and other arms. An
accident precipitated matters; and in July, 1803, he issued
forth with about a hundred men, intending to make a dash on
Dublin Castle. But everything went wrong: the mob broke out
and began outrages; and Lord Chief Justice Kilwarden, a good
man and a most humane judge, who happened to be passing
through the streets at the time, was dragged from his carriage
and brutally murdered. Emmett, horror-stricken, fled from the
city; but he was soon after captured, tried, and hanged in
Dublin. *(margin: Emmett's Rising.)*

About this time the greatest of all the Irish popular leaders
began his career: Daniel O'Connell, or " The Liberator," as he is
familiarly called, who from that time forward was the chief
figure in Irish politics for nigh half a century. One of the first *(margin: Connell.)*

252

public questions in which he took a part was that of the Veto.
A small section of Catholics had expressed their willingness to
accept Emancipation with the condition attached of allowing the
king a veto in the appointment of Catholic bishops; but as
soon as the matter became public, the bishops, and the general
Catholic body led by O'Connell, repudiated any such arrangement; and, anyhow, Parliament rejected the petition for
Emancipation even with the condition (1808).

ROBERT EMMETT.
(*After James Petrie.*)

AUTHORITIES.—1802–1815.

GENERAL HISTORY.

Fyffe, *History of Modern Europe*, vol. i. ; Lanfrey, *Life of Napoleon ;* Alison, *History of Europe ;* Napier, *History of the Peninsular War ;* Mahan, *The Influence of Sea Power upon the Wars of the French Revolution ;* Cornewall Lewis, *Administration of Great Britain ;* Martineau, *History of England from 1800 ;* Erskine May, *Constitutional History ;* Stanhope, *Life of Pitt ;* Alison, *Life of Lord Castlereagh ; Life of Sir C. Stewart ;* Yonge, *Life of Lord Liverpool.* Some original authorities : The Cornwallis Correspondence, The Wellesley Despatches, Lady Clementina Davies, *Recollections of Society in France and England ;* Croker, *Correspondence,* and *Diaries,* vol. i. ; Castlereagh, *Correspondence.*

SPECIAL SUBJECTS.

Military History.—Oman, *History of the Peninsular War ;* Dupin, *History and Actual State of the Military Force of Great Britain ;* Clode, *Military Forces of the Crown ;* Bunbury, *Passages in the Great War with France ;* Marshall, *Military Miscellany ;* Holden, *Short History of the Green Packet,* in *United Service Magazine,* vol. iv., new series : *Diary of Lt. Swabey, R.H.A.,* in *Proceedings of Royal Artillery Institution,* xxii., 10 ; Holden, *History of the IIIrd and IVth Battalions of the Worcester Regiment ;* Curling, *Recollections of Rifleman Harris ;* Grey, *Walcheren Expedition ; Authentic Narrative of the Proceedings under Brigadier Craufurd* (Whitelocke's expedition to Monte Video) ; Craufurd, *Craufurd and his Light Division ;* Sir W. F. Butler, *Plea for the Peasant ;* Holden, *Vicissitudes of Regimental Colours (Journ. U. Service Inst.,* xxix., 204) ; *Diary* of Sir J. Moore, ed. Maurice.

Science and Philosophy.—Whewell, *History of the Inductive Sciences :* Biographical articles in the *Encyclopædia Britannica.* For the position of Thomas Brown in the history of Associationism, *see* Croom Robertson on "Association of Ideas" in the *Encyclopædia Britannica* and his *Philosophical Remains.*

Literature (1784–1815).—For the best account of the so-called Classical School of English Poetry, about to be displaced by the "Romantic-Naturalist" movement, *see* Professor Courthope's criticisms *passim* in Pope's Works, ed. *Elwin and Courthope,* with the poet's life by the latter author. For a general view of the literary history of the period, see Gosse's *Eighteenth Century Literature.* For precursors of the movement, the same author's "Gray," and Goldwin Smith's "Cowper" in *English Men of Letters* series ; also the paper on "Crabbe" in Saintsbury's *Essays in English Literature,* 1760–1860. But for a complete and correct comprehension of the "Romantic-Naturalist" revival, the nature of its aims and the sum of its achievements, the student, after a careful perusal of Wordsworth's preface to the *Lyrical Ballads* (2nd edition), should thoroughly master Coleridge's incomparable criticism of its theories in his *Biographia Literaria,* chapters xiv.–xx. For the prose of this period, *see* the critical studies prefixed to specimens of Burke, Gibbon, Robertson, Mackintosh, in Craik's *English Prose Selections,* vol. iv. ; also the monographs on the two first-mentioned writers in the *English Men of Letters* series. But this part of his subject is one on which "books about books" can help the student but little ; he will learn far more from a diligent study of the great models themselves.

Manufactures (1784–1815).—Textiles : E. Baines, *History of the Cotton Manufacture ;* A. J. Warden, *The Linen Trade ;* W. Felkin, *Hosiery and Lace ;* J. Burnley, *History of Wool and Woolcombing ;* A. Barlow, *History and Principles of Weaving ;* J. Bischoff, *A Comprehensive History of the Woollen and Worsted Manufactures ;* W. Radcliffe, *Origin of the Power Loom.* Iron and coal : H. Scrivener, *History of the Iron Trade ;* J. Percy,

Metallurgy; A Treatise upon Coal Mines, 1769; a few articles in the *Annual Register* and *The Philosophical Transactions*, and some information in the *Statistical Account of Scotland*. For the lives of the numerous inventors c nsult *Dictionary of National Biography*; F. Espinasse, *Lancashire Worthies;* S. Smiles, *Industrial Biography, Lives of the Engineers, Lives of Boulton and Watt;* Muirhead, *Life of Watt;* Bennet Woodcroft, *Brief Biographies of Inventors.* Ceramic Art: L. L. Jewitt, *History of Ceramic Art, Lives of the Wedgwoods;* Meteyard, *Life of Josiah Wedgwood;* Chaffers, *History of Pottery and Porcelain.* County histories give scattered information on various industrial subjects. A general sketch of the Industrial Revolution is given in Arnold Toynbee's *Industrial Revolution.* Dr. W. Cunningham's account of the same period in *English Industry and Commerce* is valuable, and the list of authorities at the end of the book elucidates the social effect of the inventions. *See* generally Arthur Young's *Tours;* and C. Knight's *Popular History,* for a general summary.

    The Navy.—Capt. A. T. Mahan, *Life of Nelson;* Fitchett, *How England Saved Europe*, 1793–1815; and other works as in chap. xix. *The Church, Art, Economic History,* and *Scottish History* as in c. xix. *Social Life* as in c. xviii. *Ireland* as in c. xix.

A RELIC OF THE LONG WAR.
(Royal United Service Institution.)

INDEX.

R CLAY AND SONS, LTD., BREAD ST. HILL, E.C., AND BUNGAY, SUFFOLK.